RESOURCES *for* EXTRAORDINARY HEALING

SCHIZOPHRENIA, BIPOLAR AND OTHER SERIOUS MENTAL ILLNESSES

EMMA BRAGDON, PHD

ISBN-10: 1466340835
ISBN-13: 9781466340831
E-book ISBN: 978-0-9620960-0-6

Website: www.ResourcesforExtraordinaryHealing.com

Previous Books by Emma Bragdon, PhD

A Sourcebook for Helping People with Spiritual Problems

The Call of Spiritual Emergency:
From Personal Crisis to Personal Transformation

Spiritual Alliances:
Discovering the Roots of Health at the Casa de Dom Inacio

Kardec's Spiritism:
A Home for Healing and Spiritual Evolution

Spiritism and Mental Health:
Practices from Spiritist Centers and Spiritist Psychiatric Hospitals in Brazil

---

Disclaimer

The ideas and information contained in this book are for your education only and are not intended as a basis for diagnosis or treatment or a substitute for careful medical evaluation and treatment by a competent, licensed personal healthcare professional. The authors cited in this book do not recommend changing any current medications or adding any new therapies without personally consulting a fully qualified physician. The authors specifically disclaim any liability arising directly or indirectly from information contained herein.

Neither the publisher, editor, authors, nor suppliers make any claim that the information they provided in this book will cure or heal disease. No responsibility is assumed by the publisher, editor, authors or suppliers for any injury and or damage to person or property from any use of any methods, products, instruction or ideas referenced in the materials herein. Any unfinished course of treatment as well as any use of a referral and/or subsequent treatment regimen sought or as a result of buying or reading this book is the sole responsibility of the reader.

Note

The information is current at the time of publication, and is distributed as a courtesy to the public. We intend to make future editions available as new resources become known and information needs to be updated. Although we prefer to use the term "extreme states" instead of "mental illnesses," which we associate with stigma, we have used the latter term so that the information we publish will be easier to find.

ADVANCE PRAISE

"*Resources for Extraordinary Healing* provides a unique, ground-breaking contribution to the treatment of severe psychiatric disorders.

We are undoubtedly in urgent need of an alternative strategy, as the conventional approach sentences patients with serious mental illness to lives unbearably compromised by the treatment of their illnesses. The centerpiece of mainstream psychiatric treatment in 2011 is psychoactive medication that only palliates symptoms. It is often accompanied by such untoward and severe side-effects that patients feel chronically physically ill. With courage and clarity, Emma Bragdon introduces the reader to effective modalities of treatment that are very foreign to the conventional, western, rational "scientific" mind. She sensitively anticipates how the Spiritist philosophy and methodology will strike the ear of a mainstream reader, as the modalities she introduces posit a complete paradigm shift in our thinking about the cause of psychiatric disorder. Dr. Bragdon makes this unfamiliar perspective accessible with simple, clear explanations and moving case histories."

—*Judy Tsafrir, MD, on Faculty at Harvard Medical School,*
Adult and Child Psychiatrist and Psychoanalyst, Newton, MA. USA

"Through dramatic stories Emma Bragdon reveals the wisdom, grace and authentic power in deep spiritual healing and advocates that it needs to be an integral and vital component of recovery from mental illness. The most impressive results come with a compassionate, inclusive and collaborative approach to healing mental illness that is closely integrated with medical and therapeutic practices. This powerful book is a reference and guide for anyone wanting to fully heal from profound emotional disturbances, as well as their families and health providers."

—*Jill Leigh, Founder and Director, Energy Healing Institute, Boston, MA*

"Western bio-psychiatry has tried to disprove the existence of Spirit, but yet it refuses to go away. The reductionist focus on pure biochemistry and drugs has had devastating effects, producing some of the worst outcomes in the world for mental distress. With this book, Emma Bragdon is pointing us in another direction. When we allow those suffering from mental distress to engage with spiritual realms, in whatever form that takes, then they are able to access their most potent source of healing. Other cultures have figured this out. It's time that we did as well. This is an excellent overview of integrative--and successful--ways of discovering and recovering mental wellness without resorting to brain-altering drugs that may be harmful and numb the soul."

—*Mark Foster, DO, family physician and author of the forthcoming book A Ghost in the Machine: Essays from the Front Lines of a Mental Health Revolution*

"*Resources for Extraordinary Healing* is a valuable compendium on integrative approaches for healing from serious mental illnesses, useful for both mental health practitioners as well as those suffering from mental illness. Instead of merely masking symptoms with potent and potentially harmful medications, practitioners and patients who read this book will be encouraged to explore the underlying spiritual imbalances that are often at the root of mental breakdown. The book offers the reader guidance as well as many resources for embarking on a spiritual approach to healing from mental illness. The author, Emma Bragdon, PhD, writes in a style that is concise, yet full of wisdom and compassion. Her depth of knowledge about her subject is apparent throughout the book."

—*Erica Elliott, MD is in private practice in Santa Fe, New Mexico. She has consulted with John of God twice for her personal healing, and she encourages her patients to incorporate some of the methods described in this book to further their healing.*

"Bragdon has done an admirable job of pulling together a diverse chorus of voices and resources, all pointing to the shortcomings of the bio-medical model and the need to re-integrate spirituality into treatment and recovery. I highly recommend this book to anyone who wishes to learn more about the practical application of spirituality to healing from addictions and emotional distress."

—*Leah Harris, MA, Communications and Development Coordinator*
The National Empowerment Center

"Having been involved over the past half-century with young students in the USA and abroad, I have seen the huge rise in the use of standardized testing and "therapeutic" drugs to combat so-called learning "disabilities," ADHD, poor social skills, uninspired teaching and basic boredom. Far too often a child and family face various labels and prescribed medicines as the only acceptable option to combat continued failure, confusion, and frustration. This book is the result of well over a decade of international research, scholarship and personal anecdotes regarding other kinds of evaluations and methods to facilitate emotional balance. It lends deep insight into the effectiveness of approaches and treatments well known to most of the older cultures of the world and is a handy resource book for a vast array of available social service agencies. This book can save lives. It has much to offer our modern world of education."

—*Kent Ferguson, Co-Founder and Headmaster, Santa Barbara Middle School;*
Co-Founder and Headmaster, The School Down Under (New Zealand);
Trustee; consultant; advisor to various public and independent alternative,
progressive, Waldorf, Montessori, and therapeutic schools.

DEDICATION

This book is dedicated to helping all those who suffer with mental illness and yearn for mental health.

ACKNOWLEDGEMENTS

Grateful acknowledgement to the authors and publishers who allowed us to quote from their published works and the photographer Karen Leffler, who contributed photos:

Karen Leffler Photography, www.johnofgodphotos.com

Singing Dragon Press, for excerpts from *Spiritism and Mental Health*, ed. by Emma Bragdon, 2012.

NIMH, for excerpts from the "Final National Institute of Mental Health Report: Grants Number R12MH 20123 and R124H 25570," prepared by L. Mosher, R. Valone, and A. Menn.

Author: Richard A. Kunin, MD for excerpts from "Principles That Identify Orthomolecular Medicine: A Unique Medical Specialty."

Author: Andrew Feldmar, PhD for excerpt of "Minute Particulars," previously published in the newsletter "In a Nutshell."

Author: Susan Musante for excerpts from "Business Plan for Start Up and Sustainability Submitted to the Alaska Mental Health Trust for FY 2008 and FY 2009: Soteria-Alaska: An Alternative to Hospitalization for People Diagnosed with Serious Mental Illness."

Peter Lehmann Publishing for excerpt of Judy Chamberlain's "Preface" to *Coming Off Psychiatric Drugs* (2004).

The authors who have contributed to this book are extraordinary people who are pioneers in the arena of integrative health. I feel blessed to know them and collaborate with them, and am happy to provide a vehicle through which their work can become more well-known.

Deep gratitude to those who contributed stories of serious mental illness and the loved ones and practitioners who are part of their stories. Through your experiences, I trust others will be helped. May you all have everything you need to find balance in this life.

The great choreographer has led me to meet people from all continents of the world, to help me rise above the cultural constraints of my birthplace, North America, and broaden my perspectives. I am very grateful to all the people I have met who have contributed their viewpoints, skill and knowledge. I am especially grateful to the people I have enjoyed in Brazil who continue to help me explore the resources of Spiritism, and those in the USA who encourage me to bring back to my homeland what I have learned abroad. Special thanks in that regard go to Leah Harris at the National Empowerment Center, Mark Foster, DO, Toni Merrick, Gina Starr, Logan Roth, Kent Ferguson, and Laura Delano. My copyeditor, Leonard Rosenbaum, is an angel.

TABLE OF CONTENTS

About the photo on the cover:

We've come a long way since Herman Melville published Moby Dick in 1851, romanticizing the fierce hunt for whales, to dominate and butcher the beasts and render their oil as a source of energy and light. One hundred and fifty years ago, whales were the enemy, feared because of their size and their physical potential to wreck whole ships, sending crew and captain to their deaths.

Today, we recognize the gentleness of whales, and we can sometimes make benign and quite extraordinary connections with them. The photo on the cover of Marco Queral snapped by an unidentified fellow diver came to me in an email with the story of a 50-ton humpback whale that had been caught up in nylon crab trap lines that immobilized her at the entrance of San Francisco's Bay in 2005. Divers went out to carefully cut her free, swimming close to her in the water, often touching her. Afterwards, the whale swam to each diver and made contact, seemingly to express her gratitude, before she swam away to her freedom. The diver who cut her head free, James Moskito, said, "the whale had her eye on me the whole time, watching, as if grateful. I will never be the same."

Not long ago, we also held spirituality at arm's length, as well. We wanted to make use of the power of the Spirit, and we supplicated so that our prayers would be answered. We were taught to fear the power of the Spirit. We were taught about the judgmental nature of God and about God's capacity to punish us for our sins. Priests were given the authority to mediate between us and Spirit--as if Spirit was too vast and powerful to connect with personally. Fearing the power of Spirit, we even treated those who said they personally talked to God as crazy. Their reports of contact were at least "blasphemy," as most believed no one could talk to God but Christ or, possibly, one of his apostles. Earlier in our history, during the Inquisition, as the Christian Church was positioning itself to be dominant in legal and spiritual affairs, millions who claimed they had a personal relationship to the Spirit were killed in public--burned at the stake or drowned. This reinforced the idea that only those endorsed by the Holy

Mother Church Fathers could have the privilege of a personal relationship with God.

Currently, research scientists have shown that those who can personally move into and sustain transcendent consciousness--feeling the presence of God, angels and higher beings—are the ones most likely to experience extraordinary healing, also called "spontaneous remission." This is how to disrupt the hold of illness, recall our innate intelligence, and recover balance.

We start by developing a personal relationship with the spiritual realms, whatever that means to each one of us. Prayer, yoga, meditation are all avenues. The attitudinal steps are to nurture forgiveness, gratitude, compassion, and appreciation for life. They help us recover both meaning and purpose.

Notice in the photo—that love and a desire for kindly connection have replaced fear.

INTRODUCTION

"The boisterous sea of liberty is never without a wave."
—Thomas Jefferson (1743-1826)

Those having extreme states of emotional turbulence (also known as mental illness), and their loved ones seeking care for them have few resources to turn to for help outside of conventional care. Psychiatrists and hospital psychiatric wards usually base their treatment on psychiatric medications but there are other ways of treating extreme states that can be more effective than psychiatric drugs. This resource book is for people touched by serious mental illness in themselves or their loved ones and the health providers wanting to know more about resources for *integrative* models of effective care. "Integrative" implies that treatment programs are woven together from the most effective treatments available, including psychological, and spiritual—not just biochemical. You will find information in these pages in a language that is straightforward and accessible.

Readers interested in studying the history, philosophy and the practical applications of the spiritual side of mental health--please refer to *Spiritism and Mental Health* (2012). This groundbreaking book, a collaboration of health professionals in Brazil, the United States, and Britain, describes the way in which Brazilian Spiritists view the origin and treatment of mental health issues, as well as the way Spiritist treatments are used outside Brazil. The book you are now reading is a companion book—offering practical resources to a general audience.

Why is the phrase *"extraordinary healing"* in the title? The most typical or "ordinary" treatment for mental disturbance in the USA today is psychiatric medication. The resources for healing that we describe here are *out-of-the-ordinary treatments*, primarily involving psychosocial and spiritual protocols, as well as nutritional supplementation and bioenergy work (e.g., acupuncture, Reiki). These are considered complementary to what conventional medicine offers, and they fit well into an integrative medical treatment plan. These treatments can help lead to complete remission of all symptoms of serious mental illness (aka recovery), and even an *extraordinary* life of being a healer or peer counselor for others. In contrast, psychiatric medication is often considered part of a life-long maintenance program that manages symptoms, that may be debilitating in the long run because of negative side effects, and that cannot heal mental illness.

An attractive, young woman, whom I'll call "Gerry," illustrates the need for this book. In her late 20s, when she was in graduate school, she became overly stressed out. She was working with teenagers at risk, and, as she wrote me, "I was taking on a lot of their stuff energetically." She also had a knee injury that happened while she was in training for a marathon, and she was breaking up with a man whom she had been living with who was a heavy smoker of marijuana. (Gerry was consistently in rooms where he was smoking, but she did not smoke and drank alcohol only moderately.) The stresses in Gerry's life threw her into an extreme state, in which she lost not only her inhibitions but her rational thinking. One night she walked alone in her pajamas through a city park in the middle of the night, interacting with people she found there. The police found her, and took her to a psychiatric ward. She was diagnosed as "psychotic," given antipsychotic medication, and kept in the hospital for observation.

Gerry's parents, terribly upset by the situation, tried to come to terms with Gerry's condition. They were asking themselves: "Does she need hospitalization? Does she deserve the diagnostic label she was getting? Is she truly "psychotic," "manic," or "bipolar" as the psychiatrists led them to believe? What do those labels mean? Would she be this way for the rest of her life? What does she need? Will she be living with us for the rest of our lives, completely dependent on us, or need to be institutionalized?" These questions beset most parents in their situation.

As a consequence of her hospitalization and the psychiatric assessment, Gerry moved back home to live with her parents and began consulting a psychiatrist once a week. He advised her regarding the psychiatric drugs he thought she needed to take. He also noticed that she was having unusual experiences of a psychic nature. At times, he questioned if she needed antipsychotics all the time, or periodically. Gerry did not like the side effects of the drugs: weight gain, fatigue, lack of clear thinking, and lack of motivation. She was frightened to think about what she had done, and how she had upset her parents. Her self-confidence had plummeted around her hospitalization and the stigma of being "mentally ill," but Gerry still expressed a desire to be pro-active and explore alternatives to treat her condition. Her parents also felt Gerry was not doing well on the antipsychotics, and they were open to other forms of treatment.

In 2007, I was called by Gerry's parents to advise them. As a result, I was able to be with Gerry and participate in the healing she experienced in Brazil with Spiritist treatments and able to stay in touch with the work she received through an acupuncturist and an orthomolecular psychiatrist closer to her home in the USA after she returned from Brazil. Gerry had the courage to confront the depths of her illness, practice meditation and prayer, and make life style choices that would keep her out of harm's way and support a more balanced life. She is now (mid-2011) managing life on her own in her own apartment, planning her wedding with her fiancé, and is on her way back to graduate school without the need of using any psychiatric medications. Gerry's story in particular made me aware of the challenges patients and their families are now facing when given labels of serious mental illness and prognoses that are unduly negative.

In Gerry's case, what made her ill were poor life-style choices, and a hyper-sensitivity to alcohol and recreational drugs—not unusual for people in their teens and twenties. Psychiatric drugs were not healing in the long term, but were helpful in the short term, when Gerry was especially disoriented and confused and needed rest. Her recovery was facilitated by empathy, encouragement, a caring family that took time with her to be supportive, health professionals who spent time with her (in addition to their techniques and assessments), a kind employer who allowed her time off for rehabilitation and teachers who helped educate her about lifestyle choices. What Gerry needed from herself was a steady motivation to change, discipline with food intake, adequate rest, and choosing friends who could be positive influences in her life.

More details of Gerry's story are woven throughout this book.

Mythologies and Cultural Biases

A problem that must be faced in a mental health crisis is our lack of understanding about the origin of mental illness. Ideas about the causes vary from culture to culture (Watters, 2010), but the American Psychiatric Association's *Diagnostic and Statistical Manual* (DSM) is gaining more influence throughout the world and is overriding the perspectives of other cultures—even when those other cultures have been more successful in treating serious mental disorders than we have been. The DSM tends to perceive serious mental illness as mainly a medical issue, with psychiatric drugs as the central treatment. This is regarded as superior to theories that mental illness has other roots—such as spiritual problems or previous trauma—and thus needs a different kind of treatment.

A 1992 report by the World Health Organization (WHO) notes that schizophrenic people in third-world countries who receive only modest amounts of psychiatric medications fare better than those with serious mental illness in developed countries treated primarily with psychiatric medications. Thoughtful people still wonder: are medications really helping us? And, what is the universal cause of serious mental illnesses that transcends cultural biases? We still don't know for certain, as is readily admitted by top authorities in psychiatry. In his 1999 Mental Health Report, US Surgeon General Satcher wrote, *"The precise causes [etiology] of mental disorders are not known."*

Yes, it is easy to understand that many emotional crises (i.e., not longer lasting imbalances) are set off by particular circumstances related to loss of a loved one, loss of health, a financial mishap, a break-up of a close relationship or trauma. This psychosocial understanding is true across all cultures. Most, if not all, people understand that what helps most in getting through these "high seas" is time to rest, re-evaluate, and re-map our plans for navigating life within a supportive network of close friends or family, and possibly a psychotherapist. In time, the high wave passes, the seas grow calmer, and navigation is less stressful. Short-term use of medication (for a few days), to ease sleeping or allay anxiety, can be especially useful during these situations.

But what about serious mental illnesses that have a longer course than emotional crises? North Americans treat these imbalances with very specific cultural biases: we think about schizophrenia, bipolar disorder, and psychosis as having a genetic basis, and/or coming from a chemical imbalance (aka "broken brain"). Unresolved emotional traumas, clearly one of the most significant factors contributing to mental illnesses, are often overlooked, as our psychiatrists are trained to follow a drug-based treatment paradigm. Consumers might assume that psychiatry is the branch of medicine that *should* be best suited to address emotional wounding; unfortunately, it's uncommon to find a recently-trained psychiatrist who is well-versed in tools for healing other than prescribing drugs that mask symptoms.

These biases are beginning to break down now, as more people are becoming aware of the long-term detrimental effects of psychiatric drugs and the possibility of recovering from emotional imbalances--referred to previously as "mental illness" and considered a diagnosis to be assumed for life.

Recovery is, by definition, not a quick fix. It is a journey that takes time, needs attention, and benefits from social-support structures such as peer counseling, supportive groups, complementary healthcare protocols such as acupuncture, and, if necessary, an extended stay in a "safe home" (see chapter devoted to "Safe Homes"). Recovery requires the willingness to cope with the resolution of previous emotional trauma as well as make positive life-style choices. (This does not always necessitate long-term psychotherapy, as there are effective and relatively quick methods for dealing with some traumas and other emotional problems, as described in Chapter One.) Full recovery does necessitate getting adequate sleep, exercise, time in nature, and appropriate nourishment. Finding an expression for one's spirituality may be the single most valuable component of recovery, as it directly addresses the lack of meaning and purpose in a person's life, which contributed to the emotional imbalance in the first place.

Let's look more closely at the cultural, genetic and chemical points of view regarding serious mental illness:

Cultural: When we "medicalize" mental illness, we tend to interpret unusual perceptions, strong moods, upsetting emotional outbursts, and acting in unconventional ways as evidence of a problem in brain function. We live in a culture that feels safest in a steady, upbeat, light, happy mood. What lies outside of that harbor of safety can be seen as not ok, and off limits. That is our cultural bias at work. Psychiatric medications are often used to dissipate strong emotional experiences, and dissolve unusual visionary and auditory experiences, so we can indulge a desire to do away with what seems to be unacceptable feelings and perceptions through medication. They throw a blanket over the feelings and sensations—much like pain relievers make it possible for us not to feel physical pain.

Genetic: It has previously been thought that mental imbalance in a family is passed on through "bad genes," that mental illness is genetically transferred through generations. It has not been adequately proven that this is a significant factor. Certainly, we can be *predisposed* to mental illness after growing up with a family member, or someone in our extended family, who models behaviors that are self-destructive or lack compassion for others, but that does not necessarily mean that all mental illness is "genetic."

Chemical imbalance: For decades, consumers have been told that mental imbalances come from chemical imbalances in the brain. Mental illness is not categorically a chemical issue: it does not come solely from a "broken brain". There are no accurate physical markers that can be measured through blood or other body fluid tests or brain-imaging that establish accurate, exact diagnosis for mental illnesses. Diagnosis is then subjective and depends on the insight and training of the healthcare provider who is in charge. Research shows that psychiatric medications that supposedly supplement brain chemistry actually *cause* brain imbalances when taken for extended periods. Some people respond to psychiatric drugs by becoming increasingly more agitated, suicidal or even homicidal but mistake their deepening emotional problems as more evidence of the disease, rather than a side effect of the medication.

It is true that many people can be helped by short-term use of psychiatric medications, eg. when they need to sleep after not sleeping for a long period of time, or when they need to calm down after an extremely emotional experience. This does not mean that 'more is better', in other words, if it helps in the short run, it will be even better long term. Judicious and moderate use when necessary is a safer course. Psychiatric medications are extremely powerful.

The Role of Spirituality in Health

In the USA, spirituality is often defined as the umbrella that encloses those thoughts, feelings and attitudes connected to ultimate meaning and purpose in life. It is formally recognized as an important component in health. The Association of American Medical Colleges (AAMC) Medical School Objectives Report III from 1999 made this definition:

> *"Spirituality is recognized as a factor that contributes to health in many persons. The concept of spirituality is found in all cultures and societies. It is expressed in an individual's search for ultimate meaning through participation in religion and/or belief in God, family, naturalism, rationalism, humanism and the arts. All these factors can influence how patients and health care professionals perceive health and illness and how they interact with one another."*

The way spirituality manifests in a hospital setting is changing: it is required that patients be asked about their spiritual and religious orientation. Their answers are a possible lead to understand the dynamics at play in the complex web of their diseases. However, there is little agreement about what a treatment plan that is "spiritual" might be. In fact, hospital staff are generally not allowed to perform procedures that might be considered spiritual or religious unless the patient has asked the staff member to pray with him; hospital staff usually rely on visiting religious chaplains, or spiritually-based healers authorized by the patient and his or her family to attend the spiritual needs of each patient. This perpetuates a strong sense of separation between medical treatment and the healing that is available through spirituality, and it capitalizes on the hospital being geared to biochemical treatment and treating all health issues as having a physical basis.

One of the strongest healing aspects of spirituality may be that it helps us shift attention away from self-absorption to the beneficial qualities personified in highly spiritual beings who transmit love, compassion, truth, and joy. When human beings are mentally imbalanced they easily become self-absorbed, locked in the narrow scope of their perceived problems, their negative thinking, helplessness, and despair, unable to think about what they might do for others. Learning how to shift attention to a benevolent force, to invoke one's higher power, inner divinity, or spirit guide can be liberating and empowering and a significant part of an overall treatment plan. Being encouraged to participate in helping others is helpful in rising out of negativity.

A Perspective from Brazil

> *"Biologists suggest that within the dense and vital biodiversity of the rain forest are chemical compounds that may someday cure modern plagues. Similarly, within the diversity of different cultural understandings of mental health and illness may exist knowledge that we cannot afford to lose. We erase this diversity at our own peril."*
>
> —E. Watters, 2010, p. 7

Spiritism is a branch of Spiritualism that grew out of the writings of Allan Kardec, a French academic. In the late 19th century, Spiritists started a social movement in Brazil that has spawned community centers and psychiatric hospitals, which have proven to be highly effective in a program of integrative care, treating the needs of the public side-by-side conventional medical practitioners. Some of the Spiritist physicians are excellent both as MDs as well as spiritual healers.

The Spiritist Community Centers are valuable as centers for spiritual growth, as they offer classes to address the most important questions in life without proselytizing a specific religion. Answering such questions as "Why am I alive?" "What happens at death?" "Do spirits interact with those in body?" "What or who is God?" helps one establish one's own sense of meaning and purpose. People come to their own answers within a supportive classroom setting, inspired by the writings of various authors, as well as their classmates, and all continue as members of whatever religion or philosophy they choose. Classes are also offered for those who want to learn how to perform laying–on of hands, a therapy that is healing for both receiver and giver. These centers also perform charity for those in need of food, shelter and free medical advice. Participation in these centers can strengthen mental health and wellbeing. As such, we can view the Spiritist Centers as preventing mental imbalances, or lending support to those in emotional crisis so that the crisis does not turn into an imbalance. When patients dealing with emotional imbalances leave Spiritist Psychiatric Hospitals, they are encouraged to participate at Spiritist Centers to further strengthen their stability.

Let's consider, as Spiritists do, that the origin of most mental disturbances—when they are not obviously connected to a transient life circumstance, or an organic disease—lie in our own spirit and its history over lifetimes. The Spiritist point of view is that our spirit is eternal and never dies; it is the more powerful part of who we are. Our bodies and our psychology are only a reflection of our Spirit. According to Henry (2005), reincarnation is a belief held by most of the religions of the earth except Christianity and Islam, and 20-30 percent of Christians in Western countries who may report they are Christian also believe in reincarnation.

Life in a body presents an ocean of possibilities. Each of us has free will and can choose how we are going to respond to our circumstances.

Spiritists believe that we are here to grow in wisdom and compassion—to learn to fully accept ourselves with compassion and treat others with empathy, respect, and care. The way we choose to treat others will come back to us: when we are kind to others, we will more likely be treated with kindness. When we are mean, we will more likely be treated unkindly. This bundle of cause and effect (karmic) consequences goes with us from lifetime to lifetime. Challenges in this lifetime may relate to mean-spirited experiences we had in prior lifetimes.

According to Spiritists, optimal wellbeing is ours when we are (1) doing the mission that we agreed to do before coming into this life and (2) treating ourselves and others with compassion consistently. If we lose our way and cannot steer ourselves to the goal of why we were born, then we may become despondent and need time out to get back on course. Our spiritual guardians (always represented by positive, life-affirming messages) are ever with us to help us remember why we are here. They are part of our inner circle, the "still, small voice within" that helps guide us whenever we quiet enough to enter the silence and listen humbly to their advice.

Emotional extremes can arise when we meet one or more experiences on the high seas of life that are traumatic or highly challenging. Emotional extremes can also arise out of a passion for one's life purpose—an absolute need to write, compose music, do research, figure something out, etc. Either or both of these can influence us in the direction of not eating, sleeping, getting adequate exercise, or enjoying the nurturing that comes from being in nature.

A Spiritist considers that pervasive and long-lasting mental imbalance that threatens life may come because a person is rebalancing themselves after a life experience that was not compassionate or may come from having lost his/her purpose in life. What needs to happen? The "unbalanced" person needs to find out what was done in the past without love and compassion, balance the books, and/or discover the life purpose that must be fulfilled and get about doing it.

Laurence Kirmayer is director of the Division of Social and Transcultural Psychiatry at McGill University in Montreal, Canada. He is also Editor-in-Chief of the *Transcultural Psychiatry Journal.* He believes:

"Americans are unique both in being willing to openly express distressful emotions and feelings to strangers and in our penchant for viewing psychological suffering as a health care issue...[Whereas people] in other cultures find social and moral meaning in such internal distress, they often seek relief exclusively from family members or community elders or local spiritual leaders."
—Laurence Kirmayer, MD (in Watters, 2010, p. 196)

How does a Spiritist proceed? If it is possible:, meditation and prayer may provide the needed insight and energy to right what needs righting, or recommit to the mission to be achieved. If that quiet work is out of reach:, highly-trained (clairvoyant) sensitives (also called *mediums* in Brazil) may be consulted to apprehend the origin of the problems and ways to rectify imbalances. In either case, those firmly grounded in Spiritism can help with prayers, blessed water, and energy work to clear the individual's physical and subtle-energy pathways of unwanted debris. This clears the mind and balances emotions.

Doing this clearing in a positive energy field of a Spiritist group at a Spiritist Community Center maximizes the positive effects in the same way a fuel additive can make regular gasoline burn more cleanly and effectively.

In addition, group and individual psychotherapy may also be used. (Psychiatric medications are used as needed, but typically not used on an ongoing basis as readily as we do in the USA.)

To continue with the analogy of navigating the ocean: the rebalancing helps clear the decks that have been swamped by large waves, awakens the navigator, and rights the ship. We might call this *extraordinary healing* because some it is done through nonphysical agents: guardian spirits, clairvoyant sensitives who can see into our past lives, and the inner knowing of the deep resources of our own heart. These are beyond the reach of the physical sciences, which may treat through medication and electroshock, and analysis of genetic factors. The rebalancing may also bring individuals into states of consciousness that are *extraordinary*, where they awaken deeper resources of love, vision, and connection to God, as well as their own healing abilities.

Safety Rings for Those Needing Help

If you are currently feeling adrift, out to sea, and/or amidst waves that seem too big for your skill or craft, and you are tired and in need of extra support:

In Brazil, there are more than 12,000 Spiritist Community Centers available that offer free help to those with modest psychological issues. There are also 50 Spiritist Psychiatric Hospitals offering an integrated approach to serious mental disturbances that includes psychiatric drugs, psychotherapy and Spiritist treatments by mediums and healers.

Two of the best groups to assist you in the USA if you do not have financial resources are The Icarus Project (www.theicarusproject.net) and the Freedom Center (www.freedom-center.org). Two of the Freedom's Center's goals are to support effective alternatives, such as nutrition, exercise, holistic healthcare, nature, and animals and to provide voluntary, non-paternalistic social supports such as peer-run programs, housing, a modest amount of spending money, and individual and family therapy.

Some supportive groups in the USA are listed in the back of this book under "Supportive Organizations." The book *Alternatives Beyond Psychiatry* (2007) lists resources for support groups and individual counselors. In the United Kingdom a good resource is MIND, (http://www.mind.org.uk).

To explore what Spiritism has to offer, look into the US Spiritist Council for a list of Spiritist Centers in the United States: http://www.spiritist.us/spiritist-centers/. Those outside the US can visit the International Spiritist Council: http://www.intercei.com.

What This Book Offers

We endeavor to consider mental imbalance as a wake-up call to rebalance the system: recognize we are off course, right the course, and reorient; thus it is a psychological crisis rooted in the life of the spirit. The healing process may include righting our values and addressing meaning and purpose. However, we do not yet have many resources in the US that can address mental disturbance as a spiritual issue with spiritual treatments.

This book, and coming new editions, will attempt to stay abreast of what we can do as "consumers" looking for that kind of assistance.

The first section, "Who Needs It?" gives context, starting with the prevalence of people diagnosed with mental illness in the USA. We begin by telling stories about people who are living through extreme states and stories of people who are looking after family members in extreme states. These stories help us reflect on the varieties of treatments, the outcomes people experience, and the paths to recovery. We further define *integrative medicine* to assist us in making steps towards working with the best treatments there are for the physical, psychosocial and spiritual problems we face. Selene Almeida, a Brazilian medical doctor and clairvoyant, shares spiritual guidance she received about the nature of mental illness and mental health. She represents a growing number of doctors in Brazil who are also spiritual healers.

The second section, "Spiritism in Brazil," reveals how Spiritists work in Brazil. The components of spiritual treatment at a Spiritist Psychiatric Hospital are defined so that the reader can envision an integrative model that draws from conventional biochemically-based medicine and spiritual diagnostics and treatment, including prayer, meditation, peer support, classes, blessed water, and consultations with sensitives (clairvoyant mediums). The Spiritual Hospital of the Casa de Dom Inácio provides a different model that centers on the work of mediums, psychic surgery and longer meditation sessions. Selene Almeida, MD writes about her use of flower and mineral essences. Many private practitioners in Brazil, like Dr. Almeida, are grounded in Spiritist philosophy, and they also use spiritual therapies stemming from Europe and the Far East, as well as their own research. Practitioners at a Spiritist day treatment program for those struggling with addiction, in a Spiritist Psychiatric Hospital in Curitiba, Brazil, detail how patient motivation to change can be assessed and encouraged. This hospital also invites paraprofessionals into the hospital to assist patients in their healing.

The third section, "Resources in the USA," addresses what we have in the USA that is in harmony with the Spiritist approach but is not Spiritist in name. These resources allow the person coming to treatment to continue their allegiance to their religious preferences; like Spiritists, the practitioners are ecumenical and welcoming. As in the best of medicine, the practitioners are knowledgeable about the needs of the physical body and may prefer to use natural supplements. We survey options: residential care, private practitioners, clinics, collaborative arrangements between private practitioners, and the use of mediums and medical intuitives. Linda Haltinner's reflections on Brazil and her USA clinic, Sojourns, illustrate integrative care that gives weight to the spiritual nature of healing.

We pay particular attention to the efforts that are being made in the USA to establish sanctuaries, or safe "healing" homes, for those in crisis. These function more like homes than hospitals in that people live together in extended family, taking on responsibilities for household management and engaging in caring relationships. These have a more egalitarian structure, unlike the more authoritarian structures of most hospitals. This enables participants, when they are ready, to responsibly take on the full power of who they are. Peer support is included as a vital aspect of healing, as well as supporting those choosing to withdraw from some or all of their psychiatric medications.

"The Road Ahead," the final chapter, gives a summary of the book's message.

Appendix A gives guidelines for those who are looking for and those who may want to set up a safe home for those in crisis. It covers what to look for, and encourage, in the paraprofessionals who assist those in crisis. These guidelines were taken from a 1992 booklet prepared by Loren R. Mosher, MD, and associates to explore alternative approaches for helping those diagnosed as schizophrenic. Soteria, the original facility and the focus of this report, lasted twelve years (1971-1983).

Appendices B-E offer readers resources for supportive organizations, covering the themes that are described in a more narrative form in the first thirteen chapters of the book. Appendix B provides contact information including websites of supportive organizations. Appendix C profiles Models for Peer Support in Massachusetts with contact information. Appendix D provides ways to find safe homes/therapeutic communities in the USA and Europe. Appendix E lists resources for safely getting off psychiatric drugs and treating children without psychiatric drugs. Appendix F offers more perspective on what orthomolecular psychiatry has to offer.

Final Note

When the tsunami is over, the ocean waves are back to normal height, and people are assessing their situation and what needs to be done, we would diminish them by calling them "sick" for having survived the experience. Nature unleashed herself, and these people were there—managing the changes as best they could. Period.

In a similar vein, we need not stigmatize a person for having an emotional or spiritual tsunami in his or her own life, either. Instead, we can offer each one a safe house, food, water, warmth, some tools to build a new life, and sustaining friendship for stability over time, just as we would for someone who had literally been overpowered by a tidal wave and was lost at sea for some time. To do this, we must often step out of our own culturally-biased comfort zone--become bigger than our ego identity and become a large, benevolent force that empowers and shares with compassion, as equals.

Since the late 1960s, we have come to understand whales as basically benevolent beings—not the fear-inspiring Moby Dicks that symbolized the menacing forces we projected on Mother Nature. Whales maintain communications with each other by sending subtle vibrations (sound waves) over long distances. They do not attack unless provoked or threatened. Like us, they are mammals, and social creatures who are loyal to their young, taking care of them consistently until they are ready to go solo. Unlike us, they are adapted to life in the water. They know how to be safe in the midst of ocean storms and approaching tsunamis by staying under the most turbulent waves. Thus they are a good model for those of us learning how to weather the turbulence that our emotional lives can bring to us. Like whales, it behooves us to learn to recognize the vibrations of change in the sea's waters so we can keep ourselves out of harm's way, and stay in close contact with our loved ones in that ocean of consciousness referred to as "the Field."

At our most elemental, we are not a chemical reaction, but an energetic charge. Human beings and all living beings are a coalescence of energy in a field of energy connected to every other thing in the world. This pulsating energy field is the central engine of our being and our consciousness, the alpha and the omega of our existence. There is no "me" and "not-me" duality to our bodies in relation to the universe, but one underlying energy field. This field is responsible for our mind's highest functions, the information source guiding the growth of our bodies.

—Lynne McTaggart, *The Field,* p. xiv

Art by Daniel B. Holeman, www.AwakenVisions.com

SECTION I
WHO NEEDS IT?

CHAPTER ONE
WHAT'S THE PROBLEM?

Bi-Polar kills tens of thousand of people, mostly young people, every year. Statistically, one out of every five people diagnosed with the disease eventually commits suicide. But, I wasn't convinced, to say the least, that gulping down a handful of pills every day would make me sane.
—Sascha A. Dubrui, in "The Bipolar World"

The following two stories involve families that are well-to-do. They have the means to go to the best clinics, hospitals and private practitioners available in the world. Most people do not have these privileges due to lack of financial means; therefore, there is little is available to them for assistance except what is offered for free by governments' welfare systems: psychiatric medication only.

I. Caught in the System: Low Functioning

(Names in this story are fictitious in order to protect the privacy of the people involved, but the story is an exact retelling of real circumstances.)

Sylvia is the youngest of 7 children, and although the family was not well to do in the early years of her life, Sylvia's demands were always considered first. She generally got what she wanted as a child. When Sylvia was 18, she was diagnosed as schizophrenic and later as bipolar. She is now 56 years old. For 30 years, she has been taking a phenothiazine called "fluphenazine", or Prolixin. This is used to reduce psychotic symptoms in schizophrenia, as well as to reduce the acute manic phases of bipolar disorder.

Sylvia is under the care of her sister, Ann, a highly successful, wealthy businesswoman, aged 58, who worked closely with the mentally ill for two years before going into business. Ann chose to place Sylvia in a low-income apartment building close to Ann's home, where Sylvia can walk to her psychiatrist and group therapy, as well as the bank and market. However, Sylvia is not able to follow the simple rules of the house, and her habits of being half-dressed in public places, and being abrasive and belligerent to others in the building may lead to her being evicted soon.

Sylvia says she stopped drinking alcohol 15 years ago, but Ann believes she continues to drink vodka regularly, and it's her mixing alcohol with psychiatric medications that cause the hallucinations. "She knows how to take herself right to the edge, and she does it every day," Anne told me, exasperated with how consistently Sylvia seems to take pleasure in disempowering herself, not taking any responsibility for herself, and manipulating others to care for her without regard to how that caring impacts their lives.

Thinking that it might be the drugs that kept Sylvia in this state, Anne asked the doctor, "What would happen if you weaned her off the drugs?" The doctor ushered her into a room to view a patient with severe tics and tremors to illustrate what Sylvia would be left with as the effects of taking the drug for 30 years and then stopping. Ann was horrified.

According to Ann, the conventional treatments of our mental health-care system only mask the symptoms of schizophrenia. Everyone with psychotic symptoms is given the same treatment, and the mental healthcare system seems incapable of treating each person as an individual, let alone addressing the spiritual nature of their situation.

> In a way this supports the patients not taking responsibility for themselves. They continue to be self-indulgent and self-absorbed, unable to relate to the needs of others or to the way their emotions or behaviors are impacting others.
> My sister likes to be medicated. All she can do then is sit with an open mouth, drooling. She doesn't have to face the world. She doesn't have to function.

In group therapy Sylvia doesn't tell the truth. She is constantly manipulating the system, manipulating others to get what she wants. It's all about her and she's very smart at using her intelligence to get what she wants.

The only way to get her to do something is when she understands the consequences that her actions or non-actions will have and understands that people will not always bail her out. But, our system continues to give her what she says she wants: medication to help her escape and remain self-indulgent.

Sylvia doesn't appear to want to take care of herself, or help herself. She seems to want to ruin her own life. She also seems to have a crisis whenever I am about to celebrate something big: a wedding, a grandchild being born, etc. If she lived with me and my family--our life would be in chaos. But, it's really hard for me to institutionalize her in a state hospital. Our family is used to taking care of each other...but, I wonder always how I may be enabling her illness by making things easy for her.

I know if Sylvia was alone, our system would institutionalize her in a locked ward, or leave her on the streets with minimal care. As it is, her life will likely be cut short by a drug overdose and/or her unhealthy habits, like smoking, eating poorly, and never exercising. It's just a horrible situation.

Ideally, she would be treated as an individual and would be encouraged to be responsible for her actions and their consequences. Instead she is treated as a passive victim, and she continues to not take responsibility for herself or her actions, and to be insensitive to others and their needs.

I've come to believe that the common denominator in the seriously mentally ill is that there is nothing else in their worlds but themselves. They need to be put in a situation they can manage where they are sometimes attending to others: dogs, kids, someone else. They need to perceive that there is something greater than themselves, including what we call God or Spirit. Indulging them by helping them escape the world into themselves, into being passive, is not helping them to heal and it creates more dependency on the governmental welfare system, too.

I feel sure there is a better way than this. We have to get to the roots of what caused the self-destructive behavior in the first place. This means really treating each person as an individual. Next, we have to encourage self-responsibility and actions to assist others.

2. Creating a Better System: High Functioning

Sascha Altman DuBrul (his real name) wrote his personal story of "The Bipolar World," published in the *San Francisco Bay Guardian* in September 2002. It was published again in 2004 in *Navigating the Space Between Brilliance and Madness: A Reader and Roadmap of Bipolar Worlds,* edited by The Icarus Project. I met Sascha in 2008 and was impressed by how articulate he was, as well as his willingness to take a position of leadership in creating supportive community for those diagnosed with mental illness.

Sascha's family considered him a highly sensitive youngster, maybe even too sensitive for his own good. Like Sylvia, he was first diagnosed with mental illness at age 18. He had not slept for months and had delusions and hallucinations. The symptoms of this manic state were first caused by an allergic reaction to penicillin that was supposed to be relieved by another prescription for prednisone, a steroid that he dutifully took on the advice of his physician.

Watching his struggle with the mania, his mother took Sascha to a hospital where, after observation, the attending psychiatrist diagnosed him with bipolar disorder. He was given another drug, Depakote, to stabilize his moods, and they were told Sascha would be managing this mental illness for the rest of his life.

Six years later, in 1999, he ended up returning to the same program, being diagnosed with schizoaffective disorder. This time he was given an antidepressant called Celexa (citalopram) and an antipsychotic called Zyprexa (olanzapine). Within a few weeks he began working at an organic farm, and eventually moved there—sowing seeds and taking care of plants. The drugs worked and afforded him some stability, but he didn't like being dependent on them for his sense of wellbeing. He moved again after a few months.

In 2001, he was again put in a psychiatric unit as a result of destructive behavior in the streets of Los Angeles. He said, "I was convinced that the world had ended, and I was the center of the universe before they picked me up...[After I was apprehended] I spent the next month locked up in the LA County Jail." This time he was again diagnosed with "bipolar disorder" and given medication. After being released, he spent a couple of weeks in a Kaiser psychiatric ward, followed by four months in a half-way house. Eventually he returned to live with friends in a collective house in North Oakland, California. By that time he was on lithium for mood-stabilization and the antidepressant Wellbutrin (bupropion).

Stabilized with the help of medications, at age 27 he began to study books about his condition. He studied psychopharmacology to understand the chemistry of the illness. He wrote, "*I started coming to terms with the paradox that, however much contempt I feel toward the pharmaceutical industry for making a profit from manic-depressive people's misery and however much I aspire to be living outside the system, the drugs help keep me alive, and in the end I'm so thankful for them.*"

Sascha also studied books that helped patients and their families with creating lives that work. He was especially inspired to read about the connection between creative genius and bipolar disorder. Authors such as Virginia Woolf, T.S. Eliot, Hermann Hesse, and painters like Vincent van Gogh and Jackson Pollock all experienced serious mental imbalances and channeled their eccentricities into creative expressions that have offered profound sources of inspiration to many exposed to them.

Sascha wondered how to help teenagers find inspiration and support—especially those not exposed to the study and perspectives he had gained. He then went on to co-coordinate "The Icarus Project (www. TheIcarusProject.com)," a place for people like himself to connect, tell stories, and create a shared language that reflects both "the complexity and the brilliance that we hold inside."

Although Sascha has found a way to positively contribute to society, he has to monitor himself and make sure he lives a life with a balanced diet and enough sleep, exercise, and time in nature, as well as the right balance of psychiatric medications. He has developed the self-discipline to monitor his lifestyle choices and make himself do what he needs to do for himself. He lives knowing that if he fails to provide for himself in these ways, he might again slip into an episode that is destructive to him and others.

How Much Mental Illness Do We Have and What are We Doing About It?

According to the National Institute of Mental Health's "National Survey on Drug Use and Health" of 2008, serious mental illness (SMI) cripples almost 5% of the population. They defined SMI as *"a mental, behavioral or emotional disorder resulting in serious functional impairment that substantially interferes with or limits one or more major life activities and was diagnosable within the last year."* Five percent of the population of 311,500,000 today (mid-2011), is more than 15.5 million people in the USA now experiencing serious mental health issues.

A 2004 study revealed the outcome of first-episode psychosis in USA, treated in the usual way primarily with drugs: Only 13.7% of subjects met full recovery criteria for two years or longer (Robinson et al., 2004).

Robert Whitaker, author of *Anatomy of an Epidemic* (2010), which made him the winner of a 2011 national award for investigative journalism, reported it this way: In 1955, when psychiatric medications were not yet used, there were 355,000 people [in the USA] with a psychiatric diagnosis primarily cared for in state and county mental hospitals. Four million American adults under 65 years of age are on Supplementary Security Income (SSI) today because they are disabled by mental illness. One in every fifteen young adults (18-26 years old) is "functionally impaired" by mental illness. Some 250 children and adolescents are added to the SSI rolls daily because of mental illness.

Psychiatric drugs are now being given more frequently to children. Dr. Mercola wrote a special report on Ritalin on June 30, 2011 (available through Mercola.com). He reported:

> *Consider the drug Ritalin (used for Attention Deficit Hyperactivity Disorder). U.S. pharmacists distribute five times more Ritalin than the rest of the world combined, according to Dr. Samuel Epstein's Cancer Prevention Coalition (CPC). In all, 60 to 90 percent of U.S. kids with attention deficit disorders are prescribed this powerful drug, which amounts to 3 percent to 5 percent of U.S. children and teens on Ritalin.*

By definition, Ritalin stimulates your central nervous system, leading to side effects such as: increased blood pressure, increased heart rate, increased body temperature, increased alertness, and suppressed appetite. Research has also linked Ritalin with more severe health problems such as cancer as well as an increased probability of suicidal thoughts and behavior. Ritalin has the same pharmacological profile as cocaine, yet its effects are even more potent. Using brain imaging, scientists have found that, in pill form, Ritalin occupies more of the neural transporters responsible for the "high" experienced by addicts than smoked or injected cocaine.

Unfortunately, diagnosing ADHD really comes down to a matter of opinion, as there is no physical test, like a brain scan, that can pinpoint the condition. There's only subjective evaluation, so it's easy for kids to be misdiagnosed.

As for antidepressants, they have been shown to cause both suicidal and homicidal thoughts and behaviors. For example, seven of the last 12 school shootings in the USA were done by children who were either on antidepressants or going through withdrawal from using them.

Whitaker reports that the increase in use of psychiatric medications has led to a rise in disability and clearly a fattening of the bank accounts of pharmaceutical companies. Whitaker wrote, "In 1985, outpatient sales of antidepressants and antipsychotics in the US amounted to $503 million. Twenty-three years later, US sales of antidepressants and antipsychotics reached $24.2 billion, nearly a fiftyfold increase. Total sales of all psychotropic drugs in 2008 topped $40 billion" (p. 320).

The following is reprinted from a section of the introduction in *Spiritism and Mental Health* (Bragdon, 2012):

We are currently facing a sharp increase in the cost of health care, as well as an exponential increase in people on disability because of mental health issues. In the USA, our conventional medical establishments have the resources to administer excellent emergency medical care, but, according to the World Health Organization (2000) our overall health system performance ranks 37th, and Americans rank 72nd in overall level of health compared to 191 countries—even though we have the most expensive health care system in the world. We can extrapolate that our knowledge and practices regarding the healing of mental illness and chronic degenerative physical disease is not exemplary.

This obviously signals a need to look outside our borders for ideas about how to improve our health care systems, to prevent disease and maintain wellness. Possibly we can also learn more about the causes of illness.

Whitaker (2010)...reflects that our top medical authorities still do not know the real cause of mental illness. While many benefit from conventional psychotropic drugs the majority of individuals who use these powerful medications do not experience significant or sustained improvement or are unable to tolerate their long-term use because of associated toxicity and serious adverse effects including weight gain, loss of libido, gastro-intestinal distress, and in some cases, worsening of the mental health problem for which they are being treated. Whitaker suggests that conventional psychiatry relies too heavily on psycho-tropics and too little on viable non-pharmacologic alternatives:

The drugs may alleviate symptoms over the short term, and there are some people who may stabilize well over the long term on them, and so clearly there is a place for the drugs in psychiatry's toolbox...However, (given the long-term outcome research) psychiatry would have to admit that the drugs, rather than fix chemical imbalances in the brain, perturb the normal functioning of neurotransmitter pathways...[Psychiatry has to figure out] how to use the medications judiciously and wisely, and everyone in our society would understand the need for alternative therapies that don't rely on the medications or at least minimize their use. (Whitaker 2010, p. 333)

Recent systematic reviews of quality placebo-controlled trials bear out Whitaker's observations and provide confirmation that available pharmacologic treatments do not adequately address common mental health problems including major depressive disorder (Kirsch 2008; Thase 2008; Fournier, DeRubeis, Hollon, Dimidjian, Amsterdam, Shelton, and Fawcett 2010) bipolar disorder (Fountoulakis 2008), schizophrenia and other psychotic disorders (Dixon, Dickerson, Bellack, Bennett, Dickinson, Goldberg, Lehman, Tenhula, Calmes, Pasillas, Peer, and Kreyenbuhl 2009; Tajima, Fernandez, Lopez-Ibor, Carrasco and Diaz-Marsa 2009), dementia (Birks 2006; Lam, Kennedy, Grigoriadis, McIntyre, Milev, Ramasubbu, Parikh, Patten, and Ravindran 2009), obsessive-compulsive disorder (Schoenfelt and Weston 2007), post-traumatic stress disorder (Berger, Mendlowicz, Marques-Portella, Kinrys, Fontenelle, Marmar and Figueira 2008), and generalized anxiety disorder (Katzman 2009). In spite of compelling evidence to the contrary, we continue to treat symptoms as if they are caused by a 'broken brain' in which deficiencies or "imbalances" of serotonin and other neuro-transmitters are regarded by modern psychiatry as sufficient explanations of mental illness.

In 2009, one out of eight adults in the USA was taking psychiatric medication, most believing that medications are necessary for bolstering brain function in the way that insulin is essential for the diabetic. The results to society have not been positive. In 2007 the disability rate due to mental illness was 1 in every 76 Americans. That's more than double the rate in 1987 [a year before Prozac was introduced], and six times the rate in 1955 [before psycho-tropics were being used] (Whitaker 2010, p. 10). The tremendous increase in the number of people claiming disability for mental illness is an indictment of contemporary biomedical psychiatry and points to serious unresolved problems of efficacy and safety with available psychotropic medications.

In other words, when psychiatric medications are used as the sole sources of healing and do not address the root cause of illness, they may be ineffective or result in worsening, to the point where patients turn to more potent synthetic medications sometimes resulting in debilitating adverse effects that interfere with their ability to function socially and at work. Research on the long-term effects of psychiatric medications reported by the Director of the National Institute of Mental Health in 1996 reveal that they compromise brain function rather than enhance it (Hyman 1996, pp.151-61).

We have hunted for big simple neuro-chemical explanations for psychiatric disorders and have not found them. (Lacasse 2005, pp.1211-1216 in Psychological Medicine, 2005)

Cultures and healing traditions outside our borders that offer effective therapies other than psychotropic drugs can add to our toolbox for improving mental health and promoting wellness. In order to transform mental healthcare into a more effective, more humane model it is incumbent on physicians to remain rigorously open minded about the range of alternative therapies and integrate those that work and are safe into the current model of biomedical psychiatry. Only in this way can the general population achieve a higher level of wellness.

Techniques for Releasing Trauma

Are there simpler and safer techniques to release the energy trapped in emotional imbalances and dysfunctional patterns related to trauma? If severe mental imbalances originate in trauma, wouldn't it be more direct to simply resolve those traumas, rather than try to mask the results of trauma that have become the symptoms of mental imbalance?

In the not so distant past, long-term psychotherapy and psychoanalysis attempted to resolve deep-seated trauma through offering individuals a healing relationship with the therapist, entailing months or years of one-hour sessions, often more than once a week. Through the 1980s, some long-term therapy could be billed to insurance, which made it more affordable for the general public, but that has changed. The popular book *I Never Promised You a Rose Garden* chronicled the healing of a woman diagnosed with schizophrenia who came to be a successful and prolific author. She attributed her healing to her psychotherapist. The filmmaker Daniel Mackler interviewed the author, Joanne Greenberg, on camera, for his documentary *Take These Broken Wings*. She said her own story was reflected in the book and, "I never would have healed in today's world if I had been given drugs and not had years of psychotherapy [to heal from the trauma she experienced as a child]."

Today, long-term therapy is categorized as "actualization" and cannot be billed to insurance as it does not relate to a disease category in the DSM. Instead, brief therapy of 2-3 sessions is billable and considered sufficient to deal with emotional illness.

There are excellent therapies for post-traumatic stress disorder (PTSD). These therapies include EMDR, EFT, and WHEE. They are especially effective for eliminating the effects of past traumas, as well as lingering negative emotional states, such as anxiety, depression, fear, frustration, sadness, and anger. They have been effective in treating panic disorder, chronic pain, and addictive cravings. Following is a brief description of these therapies. Please keep in mind we do not feel these replace long-term therapy and a healing relationship with a therapist; we do believe that these therapies can be a helpful component in treating a serious mental imbalance in some cases, and that they may be more ideally suited to those with less serious mental illnesses.

Eye Movement Desensitization and Reprocessing (EMDR) is currently recommended by the American Psychiatric Association as a treatment of choice for PTSD and is considered as effective as cognitive-behavioral therapy. EMDR has an extensive research base to confirm its efficacy in treating PTSD and requires therapists to facilitate it, as it is complex and may catalyze extreme catharsis. It is based on unlocking specific sites where emotional pain is buried. It does not appear to have a "spiritual" basis.

Emotional Freedom Technique (EFT): Psychologist Roger Callahan and Stanford engineer Gary Craig developed EFT. The technique is gentle and quick. In a session, the client is instructed to recollect thoughts, feelings, or images of a painful situation (emotional or physical) of which he or she wants to be free (e.g., an irrational fear) while the practitioner guides him or her to gently tap specific points of the face, neck or chest. The tapping on specific points on meridians of the body neutralizes disruptions in the body's electrical system, which stops the chemical chain reaction causing the unwanted response pattern and thus frees the client from the associated emotional and physical discomforts. As the client gently taps on a point, the neural receptors under the skin convert the pressure to an electrical impulse that is transmitted to the brain--similar to using a remote control or tapping a key on a keyboard to send an electrical signal to the computer generating the output, balancing the right and left hemispheres of the brain.

WHEE is a wholistic hybrid of EMDR and emotional freedom technique (EFT) created by psychiatrist Daniel Benor. WHEE can be easily done without a therapist. Benor writes,

> It invites the body to participate in releasing anxieties and stresses. It is a way to reduce the intensity of negative feelings and to reprogram negativity in general... simply alternate tapping on the right and left side of your body while reciting an affirmation, and the negativity melts away. You can then use the same process to install positive feelings, beliefs and awareness--to replace the negativity you have

13

released. This is not about doing away with issues so that we can forget, ignore or run away from them, but transforming the energy that has been locked up in trauma" (see http://www.wholistichealingresearch.com).

To repeat, although techniques for releasing trauma are available and psychotherapy is sometimes used, mainstream medicine and managed care focus on the biochemical roots of illness. After all, managed care visits with health professionals have been reduced to 15-20 minutes—time to review medications but not much else.

Spiritual Practices

As we abbreviate the human, empathic dialogues and treatments that take more than 15-20 minutes, do we add to a spiritual imbalance? Is this rushed way of life aggravating the very mental illnesses more people are seeking help for? What can people do to assist in their healing?

Spiritual practices such as mindfulness meditation (an offshoot of Buddhist practices) and varieties of Christian contemplative practices have also been helpful for those motivated to learn how to cope with pervasive symptoms of serious mental imbalances that are not easily released. These can often be learned and then practiced in groups associated with spiritual organizations or churches, as well as in weekend or weeklong retreats. One can find teachers who will teach the techniques for free.

Shealy and Church's research review (2008, p. 25) found that spiritual practice and spiritual and religious beliefs have a marked positive influence on longevity and health. They have been found to:

- *Improve the survival rate of patients after operations*
- *Ameliorate pain*
- *Raise levels of pleasure-inducing hormones in the brain*
- *Improve mental acuity*
- *Reduce depression*
- *Boost immune system function*
- *Reduce the time it takes wounds to heal*

- *Reduce the frequency and length of hospital stays*
- *Increase marital happiness in men*
- *Reduce alcohol consumption and cigarette smoking*
- *Reduce the incidence of cancer and heart disease*
- *Improve the health of older adults*
- *Add years to the average life-span*

Spirituality involves each person in the quest for ultimate meaning and purpose in life. It supports connection to and relationship with the sacred dimensions of life and, with each other. A life directed by one's spiritual intention is more likely, then, to move a person towards wellness.

Perhaps we have invested our financial resources into researching and treating serious mental illnesses primarily with drugs or our culture-specific modes of psychotherapy because we have let go of spiritual belief systems that previously gave meaning and context to our suffering, or we do not respect the resources available from other cultures because we are so wrapped up in material science. Watters (2010, p. 255) wrote:

What is certain is that in other places in the world, cultural conceptions of the mind remain more intertwined with a variety of religious and cultural beliefs as well as the ecological and social world.

CHAPTER TWO
APPROACHING THE SPIRITUAL SIDE
OF MENTAL ILLNESS

From Dysfunction to Extraordinary Functioning:
One Man's Path from Mental Illness to Mediumship

This is reprinted from *Kardec's Spiritism* (Bragdon 2004, pp. 60-63). It is one of the clearest cases of a patient being assisted by the Spiritist integrative approach to helping someone diagnosed with schizophrenia.

Marcel Teles Marcondes came to Palmelo, Brazil in the Spring of 2002. Although he had enjoyed a normal life (with no significant early trauma) with satisfying work as a travel agent, and many friends, he began to experience emotional problems when he was in his late 20s (in 1996). His father, Arnoldo Marcondes Filho, a bank manager for the Bank of San Paulo State, Banesba, was able to afford excellent medical care for his son, and took Marcel to the best psychiatrists in Sao Paulo.

Marcel was first diagnosed with depression, then schizophrenia. Anti-psychotics were prescribed as well as sleep medication. The prognosis: Marcel would have to manage his symptoms with these strong medications for the rest of his life.

But Marcel never felt well when taking the medications. When he was committed to a psychiatric clinic for twenty days, the hospital environment only added to his stress. His parents then tried touring Brazil with Marcel for eight months in a motor home, to help him relax. Marcel continued to experience bizarre delusions: seeing and feeling crabs and spiders crawling all over him, grabbing at him. He could turn unpredictably aggressive and hostile for periods of time. Sometimes, he would hear two to three voices in his head talking to him, simultaneously.

Although the family was Catholic and had been advised by their physicians not to trust the services of Spiritist healers, they took a chance and drove Marcel to Palmelo. He was committed to Euripedes Barsanulfo Hospital, a Spiritist psychiatric facility in Palmelo, and stayed there as an inpatient for one hundred days.

As an in-patient, Marcel continued on anti-psychotic medication, under the care of a licensed psychiatrist. Marcel also participated in the mainstream modes of therapy offered at the hospital: physical activity (playing soccer or gardening), occupational therapy, and attending group therapy three times a week. He also participated in the Spiritist activities, including private "laying-on of hands" performed by trained healer/mediums once a week, who transmitted healing energy to Marcel, without touching him. He would also have private sessions of medical intuition once a month.

"Disobsession" was performed by mediums three times a week in a group format to rid Marcel and other patients, individually, of negatively motivated disincarnates who had attached themselves to the energy field of the patients. This was not an exorcism as we know it, as there were no special rituals or incantations performed by a priest.

All of the Spiritist work was either supervised or done directly by Bartholo Damo, the spiritual head of the hospital. Soon after his arrival, Marcel was told by some of the hospital's mediums that he was being troubled by spirits who had known him in past lives. Although initially disconcerting, this perspective proved to be very helpful, pointing him in the direction of very specific work he had to do to forgive himself and others, make amends, and thus find a way to regain his stability.

After several weeks of medical intuitive reading and disobsession, Marcel's periods of violent aggression stopped, as did his delusions. He then began studying Kardec's philosophy in the first books, "The Spirits' Book" and "The Mediums' Book." Damo was continually monitoring Marcel's emotional stability, also his understanding of Kardecist philosophy. Damo could see, by indicators in Marcel's subtle energy field (aura), that Marcel was a medium with healing abilities. This became more evident as disincarnate entities causing his obsessing were liberated. Marcel needed more study and supervision to gain conceptual understanding of spiritual realms and the practice of mediumship. Marcel also needed to come to terms with how his prior lifetimes had contributed to the internal stresses of the present lifetime.

I met Marcel twice in 2003, after he had done a considerable amount of study and skill building as a medium, under the direct supervision of Damo. Marcel was then functioning as a member of a team of healing mediums performing disobsession through laying-on of hands, and was still taking a minimal dose of psychiatric medications.

Johann Grobler, a psychiatrist from South Africa traveling with me, asked Marcel:

"Why does a person get possessed by a disincarnate entity?"

Marcel answered, "When the etheric body (a subtle energy field around the physical body) is weakened by stress or depression, spirits driven by negative emotions, like anger, greed, lust, addiction, fear and vengeance, can take possession of him or her. The weakened person is unable to over-ride the willfulness of the negative disincarnates in this case and he or she is driven to irrational behavior. The undeveloped spirits may come to hurt the person or his family in response to hurt they felt in other lifetimes at the hand of that same individual. These entities get trapped in obsessing and part of releasing them is to help them be free to go on to their next step in their own development."

Marcel's current inner balance and peacefulness is obvious and clear testimony to his having successfully confronted his "demons." His healing depended on "inner transformation," called "reforma intima" in Portuguese, that necessitated his making amends for prior wrong-doing (acting in a way that is not compassionate to oneself or others) in this and other lifetimes. His dedication to be of service to others through healing is a significant way he is making his amends.

The negative patterns of the mind brought about by obsession take time to heal. Marcel has been asked by Damo to stay for two years in Palmelo, to study Kardec and other Spiritist teachers, and continue his service work, receiving spiritual healing, and living a life in which stress is minimized. According to Damo, "This will completely restore his balance."

I had the opportunity to visit Marcel at the home he shares with his mother and father. The love that flowed among them all was palpable, and obviously contributed to Marcel's healing. The three reported that they had been through a lot of soul-searching together, including sharing the events from past-lives, where

19

various difficulties had arisen among them, causing conflict that had continued into this lifetime. Marcel's reforma intima had involved all three of them resolving these issues and making a deeper commitment to treat each other with compassion, in brotherhood, that transcends the roles of this lifetime: as mother, father and son. I feel sure the simple diet, with plenty of Acerola juice (high in Vitamin C) also contributed to Marcel's healing.

When I first met Marcel he was ushering visitors as they prepared to have a personal session with Vania Damo, the wife of Bartolo Damo. She is gifted in channeling spirits through automatic writing. ("Dona Vania" is one of the most well respected teachers in the community, as well as the main person who performs the service of automatic writing, to assist those who want to communicate with loved ones who have died.) I had also watched Marcel giving "laying-on of hands" during disobsessions at the hospital. At his present level of development he is learning to deliberately 'incorporate,' that is, allow a highly evolved discarnate to use his body for a specific period of time, to transmit helpful information or do psychic healing.

Arnoldo, Marcel's father, has come to believe that the majority of cases of schizophrenia are caused by disincarnates possessing a person, or causing an individual to obsess. As he and his wife witnessed their son improving dramatically, they felt they had to accept the principles of Spiritism. Arnoldo told me, "I got back my son. I thought he might be gone forever."

Even as Catholics, the family began believing in reincarnation and the necessity of making amends for mistakes in previous lifetimes. Like Marcel, they learned to strengthen their focus on peace and love, and control the images and thoughts in their minds, to deliberately be more positive. Kardec's Spiritism considers this discipline is essential to healing. It helps individuals separate from the negative influence of undeveloped discarnates—and paves the way for those entities to be "educated," learning that they too are free to develop.

I asked Marcel, his mother and father, what they would want others to know about Marcel's healing, if they could address the world. His mother said, "What makes healing possible is our faith in God's goodness, and our ability to see life from new perspectives, getting over our prejudice against Spiritism." Both parents agreed, "The patient must actively participate in his healing through study and other activities of a Spiritist center, like Palmelo." Marcel said, "My story is concrete evidence that medication in combination with Spiritism work. You need both."

Spiritist Treatment: Perspective from a Brazilian Social Movement

It takes a willful blindness to believe that other cultures lack a meaningful framework for understanding the human response to trauma...We (often) take their cultural narratives away from them and impose ours. It's a terrible example of dehumanizing people.

—Watters, p. 107

A Spiritist medical doctor once told me that Spiritists believe that those with bipolar symptoms were mediums or healers in past lives who did not have a full understanding of the responsibilities that accompany those gifts and thus hurt others. They had a well-developed sixth sense as clairvoyants, and their sources of inner knowing that are invisible to the five senses were far greater than normal. They now need to harness their abilities as "sensitives" and creative people in order to be more consistently in service to others and so as not to manipulate others to serve their personal needs. A psychotic break is a time when the memories and intuitions locked up in the subconscious mind break through and demand to be dealt with.

It's an interesting way of looking at what the origins of these mental illnesses are, isn't it?

If this perspective is accurate, it means that those who are labeled bipolar or psychotic need to rebalance themselves by harnessing their sensitivities in a disciplined way, *under supervision of well-trained mediums* who know the territory. Study and discussion of the purpose of life and the nature of being a medium and relating to spirits can be part of that rebalancing. As we have recognized in psychology and practice in psychotherapy, the mentally ill also need to make amends for prior wrongdoing and to weave more compassion and love into their relationships. This is known to be essential in twelve-step programs aimed at recovery. Judicious use of psychiatric medication may also hold an important place. From this point of view, Spiritism can take a significant role in bio-psycho-social and spiritual healing.

The role of spirituality may be even more important with some of the mentally unbalanced than with those with physical disorders seeking healing.

That becomes apparent in the course of each individual's journey in healing. With everyone having emotional issues, there is a need to develop the skills to sort out relationships; learn more positive, accepting and forgiving ways of relating to oneself and others; and to manage anxiety without acting out that causes needless suffering. This is the work of personal transformation. It is a path of taking more responsibility for oneself, one's physical health, and creating a positive role in one's community.

There are many spiritual paths—East and West, North and South—that can assist in this endeavor. What is essential to all of them is accepting and relating to the existence of a Higher Power, be it God or a less-defined but still greater intelligence.

Integrative Medicine

I admire the way Brazil's Spiritist Psychiatric Hospitals and their Spiritist Community Centers view spiritual therapies as just one part of an integrative approach to health and healing. We might be physically healthy but depressed. We might have many friends but feel spiritually empty because we are not connecting deeply with ourselves or with anyone else. If we reach a higher state of consciousness but can't relate to our loved ones in a consistent, compassionate, and real way, we are out of balance. We might be great at giving to others yet depleted and sick because we are not capable of taking good care of ourselves. In other words, if we find ourselves out of balance, we need to attend to all aspect of health: the spiritual, the physical, the emotional, and community relationships.

Those who represent an integrated approach, now called the bio-psycho-social-spiritual," assert that to experience wellbeing, we must be mindful of all areas of our lives. This means take in good food, get plenty of rest, have an outlet for our spirituality that invites spiritual growth and inspiration, exercise, relate to nature, maintain deep connections with loved ones, and participate meaningfully in our communities. When one thing is forgotten, we become out of balance.

The Center for Integrative Medicine at the University of Arizona defines *integrative medicine* (IM) as "healing-oriented medicine that takes account of the whole person (body, mind, and spirit), including all aspects of lifestyle. It emphasizes the therapeutic relationship and makes use of all appropriate therapies, both conventional and alternative."

They define the principles of integrative medicine as:

- *Patient and practitioner are partners in the healing process.*

- *All factors that influence health, wellness, and disease are taken into consideration, including mind, spirit, and community, as well as the body.*

- *Appropriate use of both conventional and alternative methods facilitates the body's innate healing response.*

- *Effective interventions that are natural and less invasive should be used whenever possible.*

- *Integrative medicine neither rejects conventional medicine nor accepts alternative therapies uncritically.*

- *Good medicine is based in good science. It is inquiry-driven and open to new paradigms.*

- *Alongside the concept of treatment, the broader concepts of health promotion and the prevention of illness are paramount.*

- *Practitioners of integrative medicine should exemplify its principles and commit themselves to self-exploration and self-development.*

But, when we approach the spiritual side of health, do we know what we are trying to accomplish?

> *When someone does not know what harbor he is making for, no wind is the right wind.*
>
> —Seneca

Today there are many many options open as far as where to pursue spirituality--maybe too many. Do we go to church? Attend spiritual retreats? Be in nature or our garden as our place of communion with the sacred? Attend a twelve-step program? Meditate and pray by ourselves?

Get a Reiki treatment from a practitioner who can channel the energy of the Divine to us for healing and balancing? Seek a spiritual healer? Visit a psychic who can help us contact loved ones who have died? Drink in *Chicken Soup for the Soul*? Do we get overwhelmed and just forget it because we don't easily recognize our path? Is our path not yet created? Questions, questions, questions.

Gerry (from the Introduction) came to me after her parents asked if I could help their daughter with what appeared to be a "spiritual emergency." Although her psychiatrists labeled her "psychotic," there was room to believe Gerry was highly sensitive and in need of one or more teachers to harness her abilities as a healer. Gerry immediately was drawn to an acupuncturist, who modeled how to be a healer and maintain balance within. Gerry learned from her when she received acupuncture. Gerry also took part in training seminars with other teachers.

It is up to each person to sort through the options and find their own path, but find it one must. We each are a spirit and hold a spark of Divine light within us; and we must attend to this side of ourselves or suffer the consequences. These usually turn up as a lack of meaning in life, or lack of an anchor point when the seas become turbulent or a tsunami approaches.

That said, this book you hold in your hands is not meant to indoctrinate you into the path or the destination that is right for you. My intention is only to introduce you to some ideas you may not have been aware of--new viewpoints that may facilitate you finding your own way.

I like to keep in mind a dear friend, Gerald Magnan, whom I met when traveling in Brazil. He is a Frenchman who lives in Brazil. He has been the supervisor of more than 100 healers who work in the community of Porto Alegre, Brazil. In that role, he paid attention to and gave advice about the ways the healers maintained a state of balance in order to help others. He always made it clear that our meditation and prayer life, as well as practicing healing for others, must be balanced with eating well, getting enough rest, enjoying our family, and having time in nature. He would, at times, send the healers to the beach to make sure they got enough direct sunshine, exercise, and communion with nature.

Recovering Mental Health

Selene Almeida, a pediatrician who is also a medium and healer in Brazil, was inspired by her spiritual guidance to define mental health and the way we achieve it. It is deeply spiritual but should not be confused with the accepted philosophy of Spiritism, as written in Spiritist books. What follows below in italics is a transcribed quote from Dr. Almeida—the rest is paraphrased (as the original is quite long):

There are spiritual guides to give us direction if we just listen to them in prayer and meditation. With their guidance we become inspired to become more knowledgeable, aware, and loving.

On this journey, we must learn to confront and overcome our shadows. Our current preoccupation with science and technology also provides countless mental and emotional challenges to our spiritual evolution.

Spiritual evolution is accelerated as more people become aware of the information that lies in subtle energies. The individual practitioner of energy medicine needs to maintain inner harmony. This state of balance is ideal for encountering the Real Self and being connected to the Divine. Without this encounter with the Real Self, we do not truly find mental health. When we have mental health, we feel reverence for life, and we can perceive beauty in all things at all times. Immaturity is reflected in those who do not have this kind of connection.

The more expanded our consciousness is, the more mature we are. The more we mature, the more we realize we eternally continue to grow, and our growth is enhanced if we are deliberate in focusing on spiritual matters. Spirit is everywhere, all the time, as the Source of all Creation.

What we focus on and think about becomes more real to us. When our minds are clear and connected to the Divine, we are the most powerful. This power stems from aligning with Love. We are given many opportunities in many lives to get to know ourselves better and become one with all of life. We may get caught in our shadow side at times, but the more awakened we become, the easier it is to return to clarity and love.

Mental disease is like a parallel reality built upon the foundations of pain, guilt, sadness, anger and fear. Thus, this state indicates a profound alienation with oneself, causing lack of belief in life and in the beauty that is present inside oneself. It is a mental construct separate from beauty and harmony. Each painful thought or emotion is like a brick that blocks us from our true Self. Each brick represents illusion, but the truth that feeds our dreams and nascent hope remains stored in the memory impregnated in its structure.

When we are able to drop the illusions perpetuated by pain, pride, anger and doubt, we see again and can feel our innocence. From that vantage point, we recognize each one of us is like a child of God, with a direct relationship to the Divine. This is the turning point in which true healing begins to occur.

Once one is in touch with the Divine self within, healing then progresses, inspiring images become more accessible, and one can feel again the purity of happiness one first experienced as a child. From this point, firmly connected to the Divine, one truly knows what he or she is born to do, and can set about accomplishing his or her mission.

As we go through the stages of life guided by unawareness, we are like vessels at sea, wandering without a compass to direct us, sometimes getting stuck at the edge of the waters, hindered by branches that were generated in us in the past.

When we take over the situation, and humbly decide to change, accepting our condition, strengthening our personality under the command of the Light that dwells within us, we find that we are bearers of skills hitherto unknown. Thus, we can take control of our boat without guilt, fear, inadequacy, doubt or pain.

Knowing the multidimensional nature of life and maintaining connection with the Divine both within and outside of us leads to wellbeing. Separation from the Divine and a sense of isolation occur whenever we get wrapped up in anger, fear, and/or guilt.

We limit ourselves when we engage in habits of negative thinking. We not only lose our connection with Spirit and the Real Self but we create splits between the essence of our being, the Divine and our personality. In

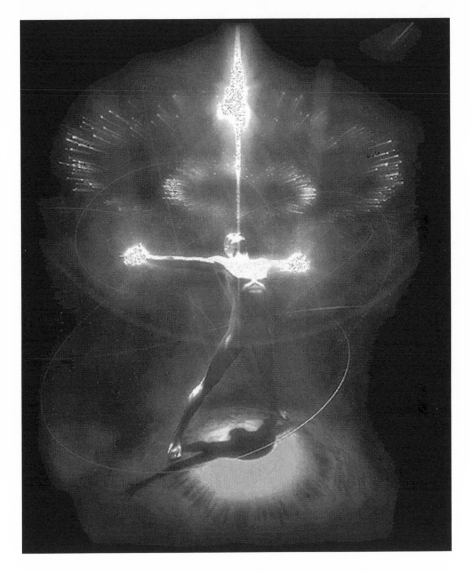

that situation, it is hard to feel connected to our conscience, and we may then act unethically.

If a religion knows how to reconnect a person with the Divine self within, it can help an individual regain his lost sense of unity.

When someone regains the direct knowing of the Divine self within, he or she opens to accept all the blessings of life. Guilt and ego-driven fears dissolve. A positive sense of life and the future is rekindled. One feels connected to and protected by the Divine again.

Care and acceptance of oneself and one's community enhances one's inner experience of spiritual connection. To summarize, the development of one's own consciousness is essential to spiritual, emotional, mental and physical healing.

SECTION 2
SPIRITISM IN BRAZIL

Editor's Note: Before launching into more specifics about how spirituality is included in the integrative practices of Spiritist Psychiatric Hospitals and some MDs in Brazil—a word about some things that you may find at first strange, unusual, even off-putting or crazy. Please be patient enough to read the next nine pages before you react too quickly from preconceived notions.

Spiritists believe that we are spirits having a physical experience in our lives on earth, and as spirits we alternate between life in a spiritual domain and life in a body as we progress in our spiritual evolution. In the process of evolution, we become less centered in our ego (small self) and more identified with thinking and acting in a charitable way toward others with compassion and wisdom.

Meaningful interaction can occur between in-body and out-of-body spirits. Well-trained mediums who can facilitate this conversation are usually essential for human beings to contact those that have passed on. However, many people report having some interaction with loved ones who have "died" even without qualified mediums.

According to Spiritists, it is also possible for spirits to be trapped, lost, or fixated in a dimension between physical life and purely spiritual life. These spirits have not yet let go of self-destructive or angry intentions that they associate with life in a body. In that in-between dimension, they can interact with human beings in physical bodies, causing them harm (e.g., physical illness, negative thinking patterns). Could this be true? Do we have any reference points in our culture for this?

If we refer to the Christian Bible (and many other ancient religious texts), we read that Jesus Christ (and other religious leaders) interacted with spirits and angels and was able to drive out demons from people who presented themselves to him for healing. Therefore, the recognition of spirits who are either positively or negatively motivated is contained in the Judeo-Christian tradition—in fact, it is held in high regard. However, it is rare for people today to give voice to anything like interactions with a being akin to a spirit (real or imagined) for fear of being called *crazy*.

Alan Sanderson, MD, a psychiatrist from England, believes it is not important for a patient to believe in the existence of spirits, because negative patterns of thinking can be perceived as "an entity" without subscribing to any metaphysical notions. Giving negative thinking a form allows one to more easily work with it. Sanderson perceives his job as helping the patient to separate from the negative pattern of thinking and to replace it with positive patterns of thinking. In this way, "to believe or not believe in spirits" is unimportant; the goal of establishing positive thinking is all that is needed. As you read this section on Brazilian Spiritism, you too may feel more comfortable replacing the word "spirit" with the idea of a negative pattern of thinking; thus you may think of "spirit" metaphorically.

Brazilian Spiritists have retained and built upon the Christian belief in the domain of spirits. The author of the Spiritist's primary books defined the life of spirits and the way spirits (like humans) are also on a path of evolution. An important notion that must be remembered is this: there are spirits of positive intent, who help humans (e.g., guardian spirits), and spirits of negative intent, who obstruct humans. Spiritists encourage people to strengthen their bonds with spirits of positive intent, just as conventional Christians encourage their members to strengthen their relationship to Jesus (who is also a spirit not in body). Spiritists encourage people to be discerning and not invoke the presence of entities that might be ignorant, immature, or negatively motivated. You would never find a Spiritist playing with a ouija board, which leaves the door wide open to any spirit's communications. You would more likely find a Spiritist in communion or prayer, evoking the spirit of a highly evolved spirit who can be a source of spiritual guidance.

My Study of Spiritism

When I first came to Spiritism in 2001, I had already studied indigenous healing for twenty years under the guidance of two indigenous healers from the Lakota and Yurok traditions in the USA. I was thus more accepting of the notion of out-of-body spirits than most people are. I espoused the notion that each of us is a spirit having an experience of being in a body. Of course, like every child, I had been fascinated by ghost stories and haunted houses. Christened in the Episcopal Church as an infant, I also felt a deep connection to the mysteries of Christ's life, especially his abilities as a healer who communed with God and angels and drove out demons. The full landscape of the realm of spirits had become more understandable for me with my study of shamanism from 1969 to 1989.

I was first introduced to Spiritism when I was invited to teach a course in personal development in Brazil in March 2001. After I had completed my week of teaching in a nearby town, I came to visit the sanctuary of John of God in Abadiânia. I was so impressed and moved by the healing I saw that I accepted the invitation to bring groups wanting healing to his center, and I extended those trips to Brazil to do personal research on other Spiritist Centers and Spiritist Psychiatric Hospitals. From 2001 to 2011, I have spent 3-6 months of every year in Brazil on these trips, often being inspired during my meditations to write or create films so that others could learn from the knowledge I had acquired and my experiences.

Since 2001, more than 48 groups of individuals from the USA, Israel, China, Europe, and Africa have come with me to visit Brazil. All are amazed at the resources the Spiritist centers and hospitals provide and wonder how we might create something similar to benefit others in our own homes, as nothing outside Brazil seems to match these resources. It seems obvious to us that the Spiritist Centers and hospitals are giving us a model of integrative health maintenance for physical and mental health.

Words cannot describe how deeply excited I became by what I discovered. This was not the domain of "faith healers" that I had seen on TV in which people seem to passively await a magic touch and then are healed by a dramatic TV personality. Instead, what I observed was individuals seeking healing and doing their own work via meditation and prayer, with the added benefit of a supportive community of people and benevolent spirits. Each of them had to leave home and make a long journey in order to be present. Their sacrifices and faith usually resulted in valuable spiritual experiences. They then had to make lifestyle changes to integrate what they received.

The following is a story of one man's recent experience at John of God's Sanctuary, which calls itself a "spiritual hospital," and "the most powerful center for disobsession (removing negative thought patterns) in all of

Latin America." What is unique to this man is how his healing manifested. What is not unusual is the spiritual transformation he experienced at the Sanctuary that is ongoing.

41 years of anxiety and depression–replaced by peace!!

My name is Eddie–I live in a large city in Florida–USA–below is my personal experience. 30 days after returning from Abadiânia—this story is absolutely true—and ongoing—I am healing physically and mentally every day—anxiety and depression/have been replaced by peace!

Brief history of why I went to John of God

I had a drinking problem in my early teens—by the time I was 16, I was totally hooked—I had no idea who I was—and felt very uncomfortable socializing with anyone unless I was drinking—I started seeing a great psychiatrist when I was 17 years old—he was really concerned about me and over the years he suggested— that I try the new psychiatric drugs that were coming out—but it was ultimately my decision—when I did try them—they made things worse—they just did not work for me–at age 19, I had an upper neck injury—and combined with the anxiety and depression—I had a nervous breakdown–treatment at that time was electroshock treatments, of which I had eight. When I walked out of the hospital–I felt like every nerve in my body had been pulled out and put back in wrong–I was dealing with a nervous system that was totally foreign to me–if I thought my life was bad before the breakdown–it was now infinitely worse–the only comfort I got was from drinking and street drugs like cocaine–over the years–the anxiety and depression was a constant in my life–I never had any peace–I was not comfortable around people–I always felt terrible–and felt so alienated from this world–I've been in and out of AA and NA the last 29 years–it helped–it helped a lot–but there was still never any real lasting peace–God was so elusive–I'm 61 years old now–and all I wanted now was peace–life had become a 50-50 proposition for me–I didn't really care if I lived or died–but the thought of living another 20 years in this neurological and mental hell was overwhelming. Absolutely nothing in 41 years had ever worked for me–it was a nightmare.

Nancy, a very good friend of mine, told me there was a show on "Oprah Winfrey" that I might be interested in–I called her after watching the show on John of God and asked her "when are we going?"—I did believe that there were people out there who were able to tap into the power of the healing force of God—but I thought they were one in a billion—after watching the Oprah show—I thought John of God was one of those—but honestly I really didn't think it would work for me—but I was desperate and had to give it a try—here is my experience with him in Brazil:

I had two [psychic] surgeries with John of God*—the first one was very different than the second one.*

In the first one a group of us sat in a meditative position and John of God came into the three different rooms and said something in Portuguese [but did not touch us]—I believe it was a prayer—that was Wednesday afternoon—I did not notice anything much different until Friday a.m.—I went to the Casa—and was meditating for about 30 minutes—and then I felt this wonderful peace—and a physical and mental letting go—this stayed pretty constant until the following week, on Thursday—when I had my second surgery—this was completely different from the first.

That day I was scheduled for two o'clock [psychic] surgery with a group of others—[in the surgery room] we were instructed to place our hand over our heart— but they also said you could place your hand on where you wanted the surgery—I sat with my hand over my heart for about 30 minutes—I was not feeling anything but quietness—then I decided to put my hand over the parts of my body that I felt I needed surgery on—I first put my hand—over my right eye and then my face—Why I did that I don't know—and all over the base of my skull—upper left shoulder—and lower back—I was not in a meditative state—just quiet—almost immediately after touching, where I thought I might need surgery—I noticed a small twitch in my upper left cheek—and then it spread throughout my whole face—and almost instantly my whole face became contorted—every part of my face was in violent spasm—my lips—my nose. My entire face was in violent contortion—and when I use the word violent I absolutely do not mean that in a bad way—and there was absolutely no pain—I instinctively knew it was a good thing—and then my right arm and left arm started to jerk up and down violently—like somebody having a grand mal seizure—I was totally calm inside—and overwhelmed that something that I had absolutely no understanding of was happening—this lasted for about 10 or 15 minutes—I did not hear the room monitor say it was time to leave—I opened my eyes—my arms were still shaking violently—the facial contortions had stopped—when I went to get up—I fell back down—I was so very weak—I finally got up. My left hand had stopped shaking to some degree—but my right arm was still shaking badly—I stepped outside and I slipped again—a lady caught me—and she helped me up the step to where post-surgery instructions were given—my right arm was still shaking like before as the instructions were given—this lasted about another 10 minutes more—everyone had left except the interpreter—he asked me if I was okay—I said "yes, that nothing like this had ever happened before"—he got me a glass of water—and he asked me again. If I was sure I was okay—I knew I was okay—I was too weak to get my prescription filled. So I walked directly to the cab and was driven to my Inn—

When I got back to my Inn I laid down in absolute amazement of what just happened—I fell in and out of sleep for the next 23 hours——but mostly awake (you're supposed to stay in bed 24 hours with your eyes closed)—I was feeling so weak—and still in wonderment of what was going on—but as time passed I was getting disappointed because I was not feeling anything except weakness—but then in the 23rd hour—I started feeling this stillness and openness at the base of my skull where my spine connects—like some sort of—all I can say is it was very still and very peaceful—and the feeling of healing—

—Gratitude started to well up in me—and started to feel so peaceful inside and then that thought spread to everyone and—then the feeling of God came in—as of this writing it has been 30 days since my surgery—things have gotten better daily—

—-Now, physically my body is letting go every minute—also mentally I feel so happy and so full of joy—my heart is filled with love—my fear of people is vanishing daily—this is absolutely a true miracle!!—I know God's hand has truly worked a miracle in my life through John of God.

To anyone who may read this—if you have a physical or mental problem—please come see this wonderful man—it does not matter if you believe or not—he is legitimate—and he is for real—I wish everyone all the love and peace that I'm finding—Eddie, June 18, 2011.

—Over the years of going to NA and AA—the discussion of should I take the drugs my psychiatrist prescribed for me?—usually the conclusion was to do what your doctor says—personally I am opposed to any drugs—especially the psychotropics—Prozac—Effexor—Zoloft—etc.—they alter your state of reality—and really it's just trading one drug for another—it's just another form of escape—if it was not for the pain that I suffered—I would have never had the motivation to try alternative forms

of healing—or to go see John of God—pain is a great motivator—and I believe it is
God's way of saying—you're not doing something right—if I could make a suggestion
to anyone on drugs of any type —and especially psychotropic drugs—and you've been
on them for a while— and you're still not happy—you might want to try coming
off all of them gradually—and if your psychiatrist does not want to work with
you—change your doctor—reality is tough—but that's when you grow and change—I
personally do not take any drugs except for an occasional Valium—and I believe it
is one of the best decisions I've ever made in my life—I feel blessed—and especially
blessed.

Did John of God take care of a chemical imbalance?—to me it felt like I had a
blockage of energy—and he was able to free that—

In 2001, as I was beginning to hear more stories like Eddie's, I
wondered, "Why hadn't I learned about John of God, his spiritual hospital,
or Spiritism in graduate school?" With further study of the field, I noticed
the dearth of documentation on this fascinating topic and felt I was
prepared to be the reporter for whom I was looking. I could be the bridge
from the unusual world of Spiritism to the conventional world of Western
medicine. I was primed for it academically; I was a published author, and I
was passionate about the subject. I have also developed my intuitive abilities
and am recognized in Brazil as "a well-trained medium"; therefore I can
understand much of what goes on with the work of mediums in Brazil
"from the inside." John of God asked me to be near him when he works,
and, with his authorization, I work as a medium in the room where psychic
surgery is done at his sanctuary. Other Spiritist groups in Brazil's Spiritist
psychiatric hospitals have also invited me to participate as a medium in
their healing groups.

A question I had for the Spiritists: *"Why haven't you displayed your success*
to the world outside of Brazil?" Their answer: *"When God wants this to happen,*
the right circumstances will come about. We need not try to push to prove something to
anyone."

Mysteriously—but in very real terms, I have been the recipient of
good fortune and have been able to publish books and produce films to
get the word out.

With the help of a steady stream of grants from generous individuals and organizations, I wrote a book about the work of John of God's sanctuary, *Spiritual Alliances* (2002), and subsequently produced a 30-minute documentary, *I Do Not Heal, God Is the One Who Heals* (2006). I also wrote a book documenting Spiritism titled *Kardec's Spiritism* (2004), followed by another 30-minute documentary, *Spiritism: Bridging Spirituality and Health* (2008). All these top-rated, internationally acclaimed books and films can be purchased through Amazon.com. These documentary films can be viewed on Amazon.com's Video-on-Demand for a modest fee.

Others followed my excitement about John of God, and he has become the center of many television specials. On November 17, 2010, Oprah Winfrey dedicated her internationally acclaimed afternoon talk show to stories about John of God, opening the door for more people to learn about his work. CNN aired a report on John of God in December 2010. BBC, ABC, and Discovery Health produced hour-long reports on him in previous years, after my film was produced.

Clearly, TV network attention is pointing in the direction of the extraordinary phenomena of Brazil's spiritual healing resources, but rarely has the limelight extended to include anything about Spiritist Centers and hospitals. I was pleased to be invited to report on these to health professionals in medical journals (Bragdon, 2005, 2011) and a medical school textbook (Bragdon, 2010), and recently I edited *Spiritism and Mental Health* (2012) for the audience of health professionals, but this book you are reading is one of the few books that describe the Spiritist Centers and Hospitals for a general audience.

Results of Spiritist Therapy

Since the late 1960s, with the increased hope that biochemistry would find a cure for all mental disease, researchers were not funded to study Spiritist therapies, and thus the successes of Spiritist Psychiatric Hospitals have gone largely unnoticed. However, Spiritist mediums and healers have reportedly been effective in helping people heal from mental illness in these hospitals. Dr. Ferreira (1993) wrote about his successes in a Spiritist Psychiatric Hospital in Uberaba, Brazil, in the 1930s and 1940s (Moreira-

Almeida and Moreira, 2008). He reported that 30 percent of the patients were healed and then discharged after Spiritist treatments.

Ivan Herve, MD (2003, 2006), reported about 181 cases of treatment at a Spiritist Center in Porto Alegre that he tracked over a 20-year period, giving a description of their disorders and the results:

- *20 schizophrenics: all improved significantly, with 6 returning to work or to school*
- *18 with autism: 17 improved significantly, learning to communicate and show affect*
- *21 mentally retarded: all improved, with 8 showing exceptional improvement*
- *13 children with panic attacks: all symptoms disappeared*
- *14 with epileptic convulsions: all stopped having convulsions*
- *10 with Down syndrome: all showed significant improvement*
- *5 with West syndrome: 3 improved greatly; 2 abandoned treatment*
- *4 with auto-obsession, 5 with bipolar disorder, 4 drug abusers: treatment was difficult to assess, as it involved consistent psychotherapy as well as Spiritist therapies*
- *60 classified as "special": all improved modestly to exceptionally.*

Anecdotal reports, the fact that patients continue to ask for Spiritist treatments in hospitals and Spiritist Centers and the enthusiasm evident in the increased numbers of Spiritists are additional testimony to the effectiveness of Spiritist therapies. (See *Spiritism and Mental Health* for more details on Spiritism, Spiritist Hospitals and Spiritist Centers.)

In Chapter Three, you will read a more formal presentation of the Spiritist Psychiatric Hospitals in Brazil. Chapter Four will give you insight into the concept of a spiritual hospital, which helps accelerate spiritual evolution and healing. John of God prefers to call his center a spiritual hospital as it is an unconventional Spiritist Center.

CHAPTER THREE
SPIRITIST PSYCHIATRIC HOSPITALS IN BRAZIL

(An article with this name was first published in the May 2011 issue of *The International Journal of Healing and Caring*. More detailed descriptions of these hospitals are in *Spiritism and Mental Health: Practices from Spiritist Centers and Spiritist Psychiatric Hospitals in Brazil* [2012]. Below are excerpts from the article.)

Background

Brazil's census (IBGE, 2000) reports that more than 2 million Brazilians call themselves Spiritists. However, 20 to 40 million Brazilians make use of the resources of the more than 12,000 Spiritist centers in Brazil. Why? Spiritism is not a religion. It is a social movement, serving the spiritual needs of people of all religions and cultural backgrounds as a free service, including coordinating charitable pursuits to serve all people in need. According to the 2000 IBGE census, the number of those attending the Spiritist Centers is growing, with the majority of new people coming from among the most well-educated and wealthy in Brazil. There are also more than 160 Spiritist centers in 34 countries outside of Brazil. More than 70 of these are in 18 states in the USA (USSC, 2011). They are all supported by private donations and function independently of any formal religion, political entity or governmental agency.

Spiritists also run fifty Spiritist Psychiatric Hospitals in Brazil where patients can elect to have Spiritist treatments in addition to conventional psychiatric care (including psycho-tropics, psychotherapy, art therapy, music therapy, occupational therapy, physical education, etc.). The specific Spiritist Centers and hospitals I am referring to all draw their original inspiration from books by the French academic, Léon Dénizarth Hippolyte Rivail (1804-1869), aka Kardec (2000a, b), as well as several more recent books by Brazilians. They are not following the protocols of other spiritualist groups that have developed out of Afro-Brazilian or indigenous Brazilian belief systems.

What Spiritism Offers

> *If the spirit is not acknowledged as existing and real, psychiatrists will only pay attention to effect. They will be impeded from divining the root causes and will never cure effectively...New theories—with solid experimental foundation—point at illuminating and unveiling the spirit. But, we need courage, not only to acknowledge these theories, but also to examine them.*
>
> J. L. Azevedo, MD (1997, p.66)

The statistics currently available in Brazil report unusual success in healing at these Spiritist centers, even though contemporary studies are few. In April 2004, the president of the Federation for Spiritism in San Paulo (FEESP), Avildo Fioravanti, remarked in an interview with me that FEESP has more than a 90% success rate in helping addicts and the suicidally depressed recover normal functioning, without dependence on drug therapy. Another Center in San Paulo, Grupo Noel, was profiled by social psychologist Cleide Martins Canadas (2001), who reported that 70% of the community experience great improvement and a definite cure of their problems, including all manner of physical and mental illnesses.

Bear in mind, in the USA, in 2002 an estimated 22 million people suffered from substance dependence or abuse (US Dept. HHS, 2003). The US Department of Health and Human Services' Office of Applied Studies (2011) reports that 6.8 percent of the population in the USA are considered "heavy" drinkers, that is, "five or more drinks on the same occasion on each of 5 or more days in the past 30 days" and that 18.6% had alcohol dependence or abuse issues as of 2000-2001. A 2003 report by Fuller and Hiller-Sturmhofel notes that the best success rate (outpatient care) for alcoholics after only one year is 35%. More typical is a success rate lower than 30%.

Some researchers in the USA (Maisto et al., 2002; Maisto, Clifford, and Tonigan, 2010) indicate that 10 years after formal treatment, *total* abstainers report significantly higher rates of a perceived purpose in life and a higher quality of life. We might speculate then that finding one's purpose in life is essential in increasing the likelihood of making healthful lifestyle choices. Perhaps Spiritism has been so successful in its treatments because it facilitates individuals' clarifying their life purpose and aligning with that purpose.

The Origin of Mental Illness

From the Spiritist point of view, more than 60% of mental illness, including addiction, originates through interaction with negatively motivated spirits who attach themselves to a weakened individual (Kardec, 1986). These spirits influence a person's thoughts and diminish his or her willpower by insistently repeating specific negative thoughts that the person assumes belong to him or her. The negatively motivated spirits are perceived by Spiritists as confused, often not knowing they are dead, and still attached to the pleasures of material life (e.g., drinking alcohol). Others are seeking retribution for harm caused to them in previous lifetimes, such as having been murdered by the person to whom they are now attached.

When a medium perceives that it is the attached spirit that motivates a patient to perform a negative behavior, Spiritists consider the person to be "obsessed." This is not to say "The spirit made me do it!" Rather, to recognize that negatively motivated spirits can attach to a person through his or her weak points, aggravating and adding strength to the weakness, and thus increasing that individual's motivation toward negative thinking and behavior. When a person has no ability to exercise will over the negative influence that manifests as habitual negative thinking and negative behaviors, that patient is considered to be "possessed."

The Spiritist way to mental health is to learn one's life purpose, align with that purpose, understand universal principles such as the law of karma (cause and effect as it applies to human relationships), and align with those principles so as to become wiser and more compassionate. Spiritist therapies facilitate this process. They also suggest steps to release the relationships with negatively motivated spirits and replace these with direct connections with highly evolved guardian spirits, including Jesus Christ and other elevated spiritual beings.

Treatments Using Spiritist Healing in the Hospitals

A few of the key practices used for all patients who elect to have Spiritist treatments are laying-on of hands, blessed water, prayer, fraternal assistance, and listening to inspired speech. Some patients, especially those who have more severe problems and/or are not responding to conventional treatment, have sessions with a medical intuitive and may be the focus of a group of mediums practicing *disobsession*. Each practitioner donates his/her time at no charge. This may range from a few hours to more than 40 hours per week, depending on how much time each has outside of other family and work responsibilities. (Keep in mind there are no rituals, religious symbols, priesthood, special clothing, hypnotic activities, or mind-altering drugs involved.)

Laying-on of hands ("passé" in Portuguese)

The Spiritist-trained mediums/healers enter into a ward of patients at an arranged time. Those patients who choose to participate are asked to sit in rows on chairs or in a circle previously set up by the ward staff. The healers are volunteers who have been trained onsite or at other Spiritist Centers so they know the healing protocol as well as the proper way to interact with patients in the hospital. They have minimal verbal communication and physical contact with patients so that their interaction is focused on the healing work. Although typically regimented to circumscribed gestures where the healer passes his or her hands 3-6 inches above the body of the patient, individual styles are permitted.

Treatments last only a few minutes per person, during which time each patient remains seated, with eyes closed, if possible. One at a time, the healers stand in back or in front of the patient. The healer will be focusing on transmitting a perceived Divine energy (e.g., the Holy Spirit, God, or Christ) to the patient. First the healer becomes focused, which usually involves shifting to an altered state of consciousness (Hageman et al., 2010). Healing takes place through a continuum of transmission of energy, first from the Divine source to the spirit of the incarnate healer and then from the healer to the patient's spiritual body (*perispirit*).

Kardec (2004a, p. 190) described the *perispirit* as "a subtle, ethereal, nearly massless covering...a kind of energy body that serves as a blueprint for the human form." This etheric body permeates the physical body in every detail, creating an exact duplicate of every organ and limb. Its main function is to transmit energy to the physical body. Congestion of energy in the perispirit or a weakening caused by stress, negative thinking, being overly judgmental, lack of forgiveness of self or others, or depression, can link to a particular organ or system in the body. These can cause a physical or mental manifestation of illness. Intervention through focusing a high vibration (associated with pure love) in the "pass" of the hands changes the blueprint in and around the physical body and lays the foundation for the healing of the physical body as well as the mind and psyche. Spiritual healing is also practiced as preventive care to preclude the development of disease states by maintaining an appropriate flow of energy in the perispirit and, in turn, the body.

> *The soul...forms a single unity with the perispirit, and integrates with the entire body, which constitutes a complex human being...We can imagine two bodies similar in form, one interpenetrating another, combined during life and separated at death, which destroys one while the other continues to exist. During life, the soul acts through the vehicles of thought and emotion. It is simultaneously internal and external—that is, it radiates outwardly, being able to separate itself from the body, to transport itself considerable distances, and there to manifest its presence." (Kardec, 2004b, pp. 154-155)*

Inspired Speech/Prayer

Before each healing session, a supervisor of the mediums offers a prayer and inspiring words about the nature of health and healing. Rarely is anything said of a negative nature, although it is believed that patients may be mentally ill as a karmic consequence of prior negative behaviors, such as behaving in a way that hurts others. The inspired speech directs the patients to focus on the value of compassion and love, helping them recollect loving relationships they may have had or may long for, assisting them toward greater self-acceptance, compassion and tolerance.

Blessed Water

At the end of the healing session, small cups of water are passed to each individual who has had a healing. These paper cups contain 4 ounces of water that has also been given a "pass" and thus holds the vibrational frequencies of divinity and the intentions of the one doing the "pass." Biophysicist Beverly Rubik, PhD (2012) suggests that water can absorb and hold frequencies that contain information, such as high vibration, so these practices are not just placebo effects. Some patients bring plastic water containers filled with water to be blessed during the healing session. The patients then take that water back to their bedrooms and drink it as they wish between healing sessions.

The healers then leave the ward, often waving to the patients with friendly words. Nurses on the wards report that patients are noticeably more calm and peaceful for two or three days following these healing interactions.

Fraternal Assistance

Volunteers who are Spiritists and trained to interact appropriately with patients sometimes come into the wards and speak individually with patients and their families on request. Volunteers offer patients explanations of Spiritist therapeutics and philosophy. The volunteers are responsible for listening to the patients and their inner conflicts, as well as providing guidance about ways patients can take advantage of the spiritual assistance they can receive at the hospital and in Spiritist Centers in their communities.

The Most Serious Cases

In the event that a patient is not responding to conventional care plus the treatments above (offered generally twice a week on the wards), then the staff may suggest more intense interaction with Spiritist mediums for case review and other treatments. In the André Luiz Spiritist Psychiatric Hospital in Belo Horizonte (de Souza and Paulo, 2012), a meeting is held once a week with about seventeen members, including twelve who are full mediums. Five are clairvoyant (able to see intuitively into the contents of the subtle body of the patient); five offer support by giving energy to the more active practicing mediums, when necessary; and two perform healing through laying-on of hands. The clairvoyants can sense the drama in patients' present and past lives and their current psychological and spiritual condition. The healing mediums can observe each patient's spiritual body and assess the type of issues that affect the spiritual body through the patient's spiritual associates who are present (patient's disincarnate friends and enemies). Three doctors, an event coordinator, and an assistant (who is usually an expert in the area of spiritual assistance) complete the team. The doctors involved in the meeting assess the medical records of each patient and then share all the relevant details they are allowed to divulge to other team members, respecting privacy and ethics.

When it is a patient's turn, he or she walks into the room where the twelve mediums are located, sits in a chair and is invited to remain silent, if possible. Two team members responsible for laying-on of hands apply this therapy to the patient. Meanwhile, the other team members maintain their concentration and perform their work; some only observe; some mediums take notes about the patient; others hold their concentration in order to provide the spiritual-energetic foundation needed for the work to be performed.

After patients have been seen, they are taken back to the ward. At that time, additional notes are appended to each medical chart when the mediums report what they have observed or written. The review team then suggests guidelines that assist the multidisciplinary team in reassessing their work with each patient.

In each meeting, one of the hospital team members also goes through the same process that the patients receive. This way the team member not only benefits from the work itself but also is reminded of the magnitude of the work he or she is performing.

All serious cases are reassessed weekly so that the work of the multidisciplinary team can be readjusted according to changes that are noted in the patient for as long as the patient is in the hospital. In cases with imminent suicide risk, violence or treatment sabotage, the team decides how to report to medical staff or others who need the information.

A final assessment of each patient is performed at the time of discharge. At that time, patients receive a formal series of recommendations for continued spiritual assistance. This follow-up can take place in Spiritist Centers (independent of the hospital) in which patients can continue to receive laying-on of hands, as well as participating in prayer and discussion groups to support their living a balanced life and continuing personal growth.

Post-hospital Care

The educational classes offered at Spiritist Centers discuss life principles and thus awaken the mind and the will through sharing many points of view, including those derived from modern science. The activities do not depend on blind faith but rather are founded on everyone's natural desire to progress. They are given without charge.

A basic class is a prerequisite for all participants who wish to use the services of the center. This class emphasizes the concept that every action has a consequence—the law of karma. Under the guidance of a teacher, students discuss the most essential life questions, such as

- *Why are we alive?*
- *Is there a God?*
- *What happens at death?*
- *Does life go on for our loved ones who have passed on?*
- *Which human beings represent a model of an enlightened way of living life consistent with what the evolved spirits recommend?*

The books of Allan Kardec (pen name of LDH Rivail) and other current Spiritists are read to stimulate discussion, alongside news from contemporary media. Chico Xavier (1910-2002), who wrote more than 400 books, is the most popular author in the lineage of spiritualism I am describing.

Belief that our purpose in life is continued progression and that we are influenced by cause and effect, helps the individual to take charge of her or his life. This orientation leads to a positive outlook and mental equanimity. The practicing of positive thinking, as well as feeling joy and gratitude for life, grow with the practice of prayer and meditation within the supportive community. There are also deliberate exercises to attune to the divine aspects of the self. This attunement generally opens each person to inspiration and guidance. Being positive strengthens the immune system and enhances physical functioning as well as emotional and spiritual wellbeing.

Disobsession

Most Spiritist Psychiatric Hospitals also offer a form of disobsession in which a team of highly-trained mediums work together to liberate the patient from one or more obsessions (in which one or more disembodied spirits have exacerbated habits of negative thinking and destructive behaviors) (Bragdon, 2004, 2008; Hageman et al, 2010; Moreira-Almeida, 2012). This work is done remotely with only the mediums and their supervisor present, although all patients or their families have authorized the intervention. Patients remain in the wards for the most part; they are not even aware that the work is being done to benefit them at the time it is being done.

During the session, one or more mediums may channel and then incorporate the spirit(s) who is causing the obsessive behavior. The supervisor verbally counsels the obsessor to help the spirit release the patient and proceed onto its next level of growth. In this way, both obsessor and obsessed are freed from the negative relationship they have with each other in which one has been the dominator and the other the victim.

Conclusion

You recognize a true Spiritist by their moral transformation and the effort they make to dominate their negative tendencies.

—*Allan Kardec*

Spiritism, in its essence, is a path of inner transformation, whereby we become more rational, compassionate, and wise and we align our actions with our true purpose in life. In this way, mentally ill patients learn how to reorient their lives, release congested energy from the subtle body, and participate in a supportive community. Spiritists believe we must also study books related to Spiritism to deepen our understanding of life and death, why we are each here on earth, and what gives life meaning. This is a path of healing and also a way to accelerate spiritual growth. Without study and cognitive understanding, people do not comprehend the steps of spiritual evolution and have less commitment to be responsible for their own growth and healing.

At this time, there are next to no controlled studies on the healing practices of Spiritist Centers in randomized double blind controlled trials (RCT). However, we must also recognize that this standard method of research may not do justice to the subject matter of Spiritist protocols. Spiritual healers work with each individual as a unique entity, attending to all aspects of body, mind and soul—not just a disease state. A consideration of all the variables within spiritual healing cannot be contained within the typical parameters of RCTs. Several organizations, including The

International Medical-Spiritist Association in Brazil (AME) and the Foundation for Energy Therapies, are creating ways to increase dialogue and encourage further scientific research about spiritual healing protocols in Brazil.

The treatments clearly have considerable success, considering the numbers of people attending Spiritist centers, their expanding popularity, and the fact that some centers have been developing their protocols for more than 130 years. The Federation of Spiritists of San Paulo (FEESP) serves 7,000 people *each day* in one building. Most of these people are coming to attend classes and/or receive spiritual healing—as well as to become more balanced individuals capable of successfully meeting the challenges of daily life.

The techniques employed as a free service by healers at Spiritist Centers and Hospitals may be a partial answer to the skyrocketing costs of our current healthcare system and our need to rework current standards of care for the mentally ill and to renew the education of the public about how to create mental health and a deep feeling of wellbeing.

Disclosure: The Marion Foundation, Rudolf Steiner Foundation, Lloyd Symington Foundation, Foundation for Energy Therapies, Laurance Rockefeller, and several other generous individual philanthropists funded the original field study for this article and other works produced by Emma Bragdon from 2001 to 2011.

CHAPTER FOUR
WHAT IS A SPIRITUAL HOSPITAL?

I was sitting in the Blessing Room at John of God's sanctuary, the Casa de Dom Inácio, preparing for the day's "work" of meditation and prayer. The Brazilian man sharing my bench was intensely concentrating, reading the "Prayer of Compassion" in Portuguese. He kindly offered me a copy of the folder he was reading. It was titled *"Hospital Espiritual do Mundo"* (Spiritual Hospital of the World), with the subtitle *"Casa de Dom Inácio de Loyola"* (House of Saint Ignatius of Loyola), under which was written *"Medium: João de Deus"* (Medium: John of God).

As far as I know, there are no "spiritual hospitals" elsewhere in the world.

We have ear, nose and throat hospitals for people with problems in these areas. We have cancer hospitals for people who want to get rid of cancer, and psychiatric hospitals for people who want to resolve psychological problems. What is a spiritual hospital?

Is a spiritual hospital designed to help a person heal a problem in his or her spirit? Do we come here because our spirits are sick and our spirits need medication, bandaging, therapy or surgery? No. Our spirits are eternal and they never become ill. It is our small self, ego, soul (after its excursions in and out of the body through lifetimes), and emotional reaction to life that become burdened and out of balance, leading to confusion, fragmentation and unhappiness. The small self loses sight of and disconnects from the essence of spirit–infinite love and wisdom.

At a spiritual hospital, we come to heal from such disconnection and connect fully with our own spirit (aka higher self). We also come to connect with the transcendent, that which is much larger than ourselves, whom some call God or the great choreographer. We come to refresh ourselves in the river of Infinite Love that is the source of all religions and thus experience the oneness that goes beyond religious and cultural differences.

In a medical conference in 2008, physicist Amrit Goswami revealed that when a person reconnects with the transcendent and becomes absorbed in that spiritual experience, an immediate extraordinary healing may result. Spontaneous remission of cancer is just one an example of this. The key factor is *surrendering fully to the experience of the transcendent.*

Many visitors to the Casa de Dom Inácio have spontaneous physical healing—probably because they connect with the transcendent so fully in the "Current." In the Current rooms dedicated to prayer and meditation, we are asked to close our eyes and not cross arms or legs so that the stream of good feelings stimulated by prayer can flow through us, joining each of us in an unbroken chain of positive intention and energy. We sit for 2,3,4 even -5 hours at a stretch. Those who sit in the Current rooms often report having contact with Jesus, Mary, angels, saints, and other supra-conscious beings with pure souls who live in the realm of spirit and do not have physical bodies.

Surrendering to the transcendent is an essential step. It opens up a portal for Grace and more resources to come through. It definitely can shift one's attention from more egoic identification to a vaster sense of God as who one is. However, it seems that the karma and the momentum of habits in one's life continue to demand attention and healing, which may involve the need to change one's behavior and/ or way of thinking. That can often take a long time, so complete healing is not instantaneous.

The Current has been an incredible way not only to experience this Great Vast Love but also for that Love to penetrate any areas where there is still that sense of separation and the emotional pain and trauma within that sense of separation. That to me is where healing happens. I also think healing happens as a result of direct intervention from the non-physical assistance that is very specific and works on different levels.— a member of the Casa community

The chain of connection in the Current certainly explains why most visitors report feeling happy there and often come to believe "The Casa is my spiritual home." It is set up to bring us back to our innermost selves, our true home where we sense our connection to our extended spiritual family, which includes ascended masters.

On a practical level, guided meditations given in the first current room in English and Portuguese facilitate the special work of inner transformation. Current room leaders remind us to forgive, make amends to those we have hurt, remember to appreciate life, treat others in a charitable way, and not only recall our mission for this life but re-new our commitment to it. This guidance helps us to let go and let the energy we call "God" move through us, unobstructed.

John of God (as the Casa medium, medical intuitive, and psychic surgeon) facilitates contact with Spirit in other ways. When we stand in front of him for a consultation, John is incorporating a being with an evolved level of consciousness and compassion. As this "entity," his eyes see through us— body, mind, and soul–and then he prescribes specific treatments. He consults, free of charge, with all visitors who want to see him three days a week, and he stays until the last person is seen. He sometimes does physical interventions on those who request it; more often his treatments involve "invisible psychic surgery," in which benevolent spirits perform interventions that positively effect healing on the physical as well as and on the subtle bodies. This often includes helping disincarnate entities who come to the Casa for help as well. The Casa is uniquely prepared to assist both disincarnates and incarnate beings who are ready to evolve spiritually.

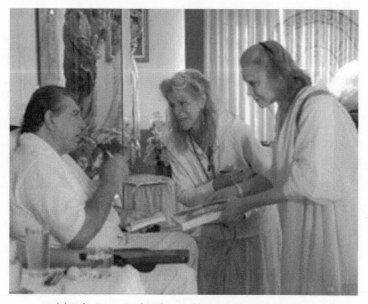

(*Photo by Karen Leffler Photography, www.johnofgodphotos.com*)

One day, unexpectedly, I had a stroke. The left side of my body became paralyzed and I couldn't speak. My husband and I prayed to John of God and the Entities of the Casa to help. That night, I sensed an invisible being doing acupuncture up and down my left arm. I felt needles going in and out of my body—but no physical person was there. As this happened, the sensations of the left side of my body began to return. By the morning, I was a bit weak, and needed rest, but I was no longer paralyzed, and my ability to think and talk had returned. —a hotel manager in the Casa community

No matter how phenomenal the healing, John of God *always* says, "I do not heal, God is the one who heals." His lifelong dedication to be of service to others healing through mediating with Higher Forces is a model of humility, compassion and generosity.

Thus, the Casa, as a spiritual hospital, restores us to our eternal spirit, higher self, and reconnects us to our guardian spirits. We are given the opportunity for deeper connection with spirituality and the discarnate beings who can help humankind. We are freed of negative thought forms and entities that have interfered with our ability to connect with the purest aspects of our spiritual nature. We are allowed to identify more intensely with the spiritual self that we are, and that may have been dormant throughout lifetimes. We remember that at our core, we are Love and we have access to profound Truth and wisdom through the guidance of benevolent Spirits who are with us in order to help us.

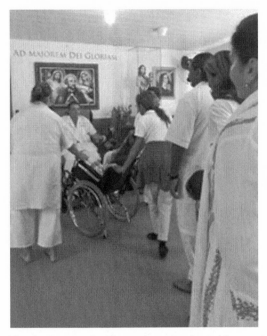

(Photo by Karen Leffler Photography, www.johnofgodphotos.com)

My intuition said I must come here for two months, so I came. Every day I sit in the current I feel new sensations in my heart. Actually it pulsates and many times it feels like it is on fire. Always, there is tremendous movement of energy. I often feel overwhelmed. Friday tears were streaming down my face all morning. But I know this is important because my heart is opening. I am feeling my real feelings, and letting go of what other people told me I should feel and think. I am also sensing what my true direction in life is—what will give me real joy to do. I am so glad I came. —a 30-year-old man visiting the Casa

Along with the Current, the presence of higher beings, and John of God, the Casa community welcomes visitors with good food, blessed water and soup, a sacred waterfall for purification, sunshine, and laughter with the town comedienne, Grainne McEntee. Visitors relax in simple, clean hotels that function as recovery wards for those resting after surgery. Ramble through town and you enjoy exotic birds' singing, extraordinary flowers, gentle horses that walk freely in the street, and more than one ice cream shop. A way to say good-bye after a chat is "Fica com Deus" ("Be with God"). These elements of life, although not absolutely necessary, certainly support the work of the spiritual hospital.

(Grainne McEntee, the town comedienne, practicing "Ascension."
Photo Credit: Emma Bragdon)

Given the success of the Casa de Dom Inácio in Brazil—that participants are healing from cancer and all manner of physical and mental diseases—we could consider the Casa as a model to use elsewhere. After all, it is called "Spiritual Hospital of the World." That doesn't mean it has to be the only one. We can bring components of the Casa back home and see what fits the needs of our own communities. We can't find a John of God anywhere else, but we can find good medical intuitives and energy workers capable of assisting others in recovering health.

God knows, our fractured world needs the healing and positive transformation that occurs in "spiritual hospitals." Although most US hospitals have dedicated health professionals who care about their patients, these hospitals are usually managing disease for profit. That system is prohibitively expensive and may exclude those who can't afford it. The Casa de Dom Inácio is teaching us how to have wellness for free for everyone, and the healthcare comes with liberal doses of spiritually enlightening experiences.

Certainly, one aspect of John of God's mission is to demonstrate how a good spiritual hospital functions in Brazil. It is up to us to seek contact with the inspired beings of Light who can help us seed such hospitals where they will be welcomed in other parts of the world. Both the light-beings of the spiritual realm and the light-workers of the physical realm will be working together to create and maintain this new kind of hospital.

CHAPTER FIVE
A PRIVATE PRACTITIONER–
SELENE ALMEIDA, MD

Editor's Note: One of the most interesting medical doctors I met in Brazil, Selene Almeida, is a medium, medical intuitive (able to accurately diagnose through intuitive knowing without reference to any physically-based diagnostics) and healer, as well as a homeopath and pediatrician who creates flower essences that have helped some of her patients heal from mental imbalances. At the end of chapter two, I paraphrased and at times quoted how she has been inspired to look at mental illness and the goal of mental health. Dr. Almeida has been able to use flower essences in her clinical work in a large hospital in Brasilia.

I met Selene Almeida when she was spending a day at the sanctuary where John of God works in Brazil, about a two-hour drive from where she works. Subsequently she invited me to visit her at her farm in the *serrado* (a naturally dry area at high elevation), where the flowers grow from which she makes the essences. Dr. Almeida is a joy to be with, and her children clearly enjoyed all their time with her. (One is a medical school student, and the other is in graduate school to become a physicist.) Imagine a combination of earth mother, spiritual warrior, healer, and elf, and you get a sense of what it feels like to be with Selene.

When I asked Selene to write for this book, she reflected on her work with researching the impact of flower essences to help those with serious mental disturbance. Although she does not think of herself as a member of the formal groups of Spiritists, she is a private practitioner familiar with Spiritist beliefs who is bringing spirituality into healthcare with good results. In her case, she includes the spirits of the plant and rock kingdoms.

Flower and Mineral Essences, Homeopathy and Herbs
by Selene Almeida, MD

Two Cases: Healing with Flower Essences:

I. In 2003, a seven-year-old girl we can call, "Teresa," was brought to my office in the hospital in Brasilia at which I work. She had a small degree of cognitive impairment with other complications in processing information as a result of perinatal anoxia (too little oxygen to her brain at birth). She was unable to sleep well and could not read or write. She had been given a lot of conventional medications prescribed by her physicians with no effect, and her present physician suggested stopping these medications.

The hospital's neurologist had sent Teresa to me because he hoped my therapy could help. I gave her Millefolia Essence and essences to recover from birth trauma and emotional trauma during pregnancy: Quaresmeira do Serrado Essence and Evolvulus to help with sleeping. When Teresa started this flower essence therapy, she was no longer using any other medications.

About one month after treatment with the flower essences, Teresa was sleeping well. Six months after treatment, she had recovered from her cognitive impairment, and her abilities in processing information had improved. She was counting, reading and writing.

2. In 2003, an eleven-year-old boy, "Hermann," was brought to me for treatment. He had a high level of hyperactivity (ADHD). The family could not take him to restaurants, nor could they enjoy sitting and watching TV quietly together. Hermann was unable to stop to focus on anything. Even going to sleep and sustaining a good night's rest was difficult. He was not relating to anyone, and sometimes he showed aggressive behavior.

Hermann was under my care for one-and-a-half years. I gave him the following formulas: Formula for Autism and Canela de Ema, which helps organize all energies; Sucupira Preta to help develop personal responsibility; Jasmine Manga to balance the heart chakra; and formulas for the emotional and mental bodies.

It took 6 months for Hermann's behavior to radically change. By that time he was also better able to sleep. He became more serene; he was watching TV at home, and he could go to a restaurant with his family without causing disruption. His teacher at school was amazed at his new behavior. He was learning how to read and write for the first time. Hermann even began to speak to the bus driver of the school bus—something he had never done before. In my office during consultation he was also calmer.

Hermann's father exclaimed, "You know how to help with autism where medication has not worked at all."

After 18 months, Hermann was still functioning below normal, but he was much improved. I think to completely heal would require long-term treatment, including disobsession (clearing negative energies by mediums), as well as psychological therapy. Ideally the family would also have to work on themselves. Unfortunately, the boy's family did not have a good intellectual level to understand the importance of psychological and spiritual work.

In the field of homeopathy, which works with infinitesimal energy according to the law of similitude (or law of similars), it is possible to get a medicine that creates mental and emotional symptoms that are in resonance with the symptoms already present so that the core of the healing can be accessed. Homeopathic remedies are obtained by multiple dilution and succession (forceful shaking in a container), empowering the medication to arouse movement toward healing.

The *law of similars* states that experiencing a minute amount of the substance that causes certain symptoms in a healthy man can also cure him. That means there is an indispensable level of resonance that makes the patient's energy fields and homeopathic medication interact. The greater the similarity, the greater the healing potential mobilized.

Therefore, homeopathy can greatly help the psychiatric patient by providing him with the necessary support to access his healing core. The homeopath searches for the constitutional medicine (the *Simillimum*), the general harmonizer of the personality that promotes the cure according to Hering's law (viz., it should happen downwardly and inside-out).

Flower Remedies

Modern flower essence therapy spread across the world at the beginning of the 1970s. The first researcher was Dr. Edward Bach, a homeopathic physician who, in his search in the 1930s, found that dew of flowers was a source of harmony that assisted him to heal from his ailments. He developed thirty-eight remedies that were the precursors of the flower essences of our time. According to his writings in "Heal Thyself" (1996), disease is a consequence of an action against the unity, which in turn is a result of the personality's search for an independent existence from the Higher Self.

In the records of the spiritual history of humankind, one can read that flower essences were widely used by ancient civilizations such as those in Lemuria, Atlantis, Sumeria, Central America, and Egypt. After studying Dr. Bach, other researchers have developed flower remedy systems worldwide. Consequently, flower essence therapy has been expanding with the harmonizing energy supply from the entire flora on the planet.

I synchronized and co-created the floral essence system Flowers of the Wind in 1995, inspired and supported by the Devic Kingdom and the spiritual guides and mentors who assist me. I am told that this system is a manifestation of a concentration of healing energy that presents itself during the planet's transition periods.

The work of Flowers of the Wind has special features. Due to its origin in the Brazilian serrado, there is a deep connection with the transition period we are experiencing, the emergence of a New Age. The Brazilian serrado flowers have a wealth of the elements of air, earth, fire, and, in some areas, even the water element. The deep relationship with air provides access to the subtle energy level of the heart chakra, which, in turn, is the gateway to the plane of intuition. On another level of relationship, air facilitates the lower mental faculties, which also favors the higher mind by the adequate management of the intellect to facilitate the evolutionary process.

In our time, we are establishing the foundations of mentalism, the belief that everything exists within the mind. This elevates human evolution to a higher level where the mind, deeply connected to the feeling of the Christic Love [a penetrating unconditional love that originates in the source of all life], can guide the new steps of humankind to build a brighter future according to the new spiritual state of the Earth as a planet of regeneration.

The healing potential inherent in the flowers of the Brazilian serrado allows the expression of harmony on all levels of life expressed in humans by the diversity of colors, scents and shapes. We can work with those diversities to provide the human with energy, the vibration of the love of Mother Nature, and the physical expression of Mother Earth, which care for us with extreme care and attention. In this way, no human being is helpless, because all flowers remind us of Mother Earth, love and generosity on an abundant scale, inviting us to turn "lead into gold" so that our souls may be elevated above human passions.

Flowers of the Wind subtly and effectively approach the healing potential of the being. In cases of patients with psychiatric problems, the flowers can serve as excellent therapeutic helpers that promote the strengthening of the major route between the creature and his Creator, an essential process for the restoration of any human being.

These flower essences, as well as essences of minerals, also rebuild and strengthen the power grids of the subtle bodies. Recovery of the human being is magnetically attached to the relationship that each one establishes with the Source of Life. Flower essences work with this level of consciousness and perception. When a psychic field contained in a flower essence makes contact with the psychic field of a human being, several resonance effects may occur, raising its potential for harmony and perfection and the development of inherent positive inner qualities.

Hermes Trismegistos (I) related the law of correspondences: "as it is above, so it is below." It can be deduced that all cosmic processes, as the magic of life itself, are also available on a personal level as a potential belonging to the psychic texture of each being. When we get into contact with this level of perception and experience, there is no limit to the healing process. This is the work that the Flowers of the Wind carry out, facilitating the development and expansion of awareness.

How the Flower Therapy Works

Flower therapy does not work with labels of diseases, but with the human potential to be the inheritor of life and, therefore, to help transform any situation or painful experience into a situation inspiring both wonder and growth. The therapy addresses the mental and emotional suffering ethically and with the extraordinary delicacy inherent in flowers. Taking the drops is like a balm of light that restores our faith even when we are experiencing a personal apocalypse.

In order to have a successful floral essence therapy, we need to focus on the following aspects:

- *The recovery of the power grids of the subtle bodies, which were damaged by trauma, abuse, obsessive processes, or drugs*
- *Mental reprogramming*
- *Harmonization of the chakras*
- *Strengthening and harmonization of the personality, such as the development of love, tolerance and forgiveness*
- *The development of awareness and its connection to the Source of Life*

In the Flowers of the Wind system, we have simple formulas ("essences") that can act in a harmonized manner for psychic ailments. In the case of psychiatric patients, we must observe the following:

- *Treatment is usually long-term.*
- *There must be a spiritual treatment along with psychotherapy and other forms of energy and body therapy. (We recommend jin shin jyutsu, an ancient healing art that harmonizes body, mind, and spirit.) Go to www.jsjinc.net or www. jinshinjyutsubrasil.com.br.*
- *A qualified flower essence practitioner should monitor the case.*
- *The family must also be treated in accordance with the guidance of a supervising primary therapist.*

Below are some formulas of the Flowers of the Wind System and their uses:

- *"Formula for the Mental Body": objective mental balance for regeneration and strengthening of the energy grid of the mental body.*
- *"Formula for Autism": for patients who show disbelief and need isolation*
- *"Swamp Flowers Formula": a powerful antidepressant.*
- *"Formula for the Emotional Body": for regeneration of the energetic tissue of the emotional body.*
- *"Formula for Panic Disorder": helps calm a person who has panic disorder.*
- *"Emergency Floral Formula": for cases of stress, anxiety and emergencies.*
- *"Mineral Emergency Formula": inspires harmony for all the bodies in their relationships with the physical body; can be used in association with Emergency Floral formula.*
- *"Depossession Formula": when there is spiritual interference from a disincarnate that is disturbing the patient. This formula improves the vibratory frequency.*
- *"Superior Light Magenta": helps reprogram the mind, a critical point in the therapeutic process.*

Mineral Essences

The mineral essences are also a great support, as they produce stability, connection to the earth plane, balance and overall vitality. The Flowers of the Wind work with the essences of quartz crystal, citrine, amethyst, pink quartz, sodalite, azurite, sun stone and fucsita.

Medicinal Herbs

Herbs that have the active ingredients of sedative, hypnotic or tonic effects can be used to control psychiatric symptoms in association with other forms of treatment. Some herbal medicines, such as passionflower and valerian, are used by the pharmaceutical industry for stress, anxiety, and sleep disorders.

The flora of the planet is vast, and there are still a lot of plants to be researched for their medicinal effects. The Brazilian serrado is biodiverse, and its plants (including use of the flower and the fruits) can be used in many ways. Life is abundant, and certainly we have everything we need for our personal and planetary progress at all levels of healing. So it is and it will always be, because Love is the life preserver of Energy, "which is willing to accept and embrace a multitude of human imperfections" (Kardec, 2004).

Endnote:

I. Hermes Trismegistos, the Father of Hermeticism, who lived circa 3000 years ago, taught about many laws, including the law of correspondences. Known as "a master of masters," Hermes Trismegistos lived in Egypt and was the founder of astrology and discoverer of alchemy. The details of his life have been lost to history.

CHAPTER SIX
THE TREATMENT OF ADDICTIONS

Editor's Note: When I went to visit Bom Retiro, a Spiritist Psychiatric Hospital in Curitiba, I was given a tour of their Center for Treating Addictions, a separate structure a few minutes walk but on the same grounds as the Hospital, near a stand of large trees. After enjoying a few minutes of watching the monkeys sporting around above us, swinging from limb to limb, my hosts—doctors in street clothes who worked at the hospital—walked into the building and introduced me to a patient, I'll call "Arturo." He was articulate about himself and his course in recovery. Arturo had been addicted to some very potent psychoactive recreational drugs, as well as alcohol. As a result, his life had fallen apart—he could no longer function well in his relationships and work life.

One particularly interesting part of his story: he told me (in Portuguese), *"I got to the point when I can literally see dark entities entering into my room. They used to take me over, possessing me, so that all I could think about was how much I wanted the drugs. They had such power over me that I would do anything to get the money I needed to get my fix….I can still see beings like this hovering around others who are dealing with addictions. We have to learn how to be with them so they don't control us."*

I asked him, *"Have you thought about invoking good spirits who would come to you and help you? Wouldn't it be ideal if they could replace the negative spirits who have been drawn to you?"*

Arturo reflected for a moment, then replied, *"I'm not there yet…I believe what you say is right. Yes, there are good spirits. But, my focus is right now on overcoming the influence of the negative ones. That's what most of us here are doing. I am only unusual because I can see these negative spirits."*

I was impressed with how honest and straightforward Arturo was. I was also impressed with how accepting the doctors were of his visions, which would be labeled "delusions or hallucinations" in the USA. I also wondered, "When will Arturo be ready to use his clairvoyant abilities to seek out and invoke positive beings?" I realized that learning how to do this is generally something transmitted by those who know how to do it. It's a matter of education and readiness; right now he is struggling to maintain his positive motivation.

To describe the inner experience of Arturo, I'll quote Francis Mourao, MD and his associates:

> *According to Spiritist Principles, people can suffer a harmful interference of incarnated and disincarnated spirits, which is commonly called "an obsession." This interference occurs through the obsessor who takes advantage of the mental fragility of the obsessed person, imposing on him pessimistic thoughts of eternal suffering, of anger and hatred, and of violence to the self as well as interpersonal violence. Besides, the obsessor imposes on his victim, depending on his mental sensitivity, threatening and frightening visions. These strategies aim at heightening suffering, by increasing desperation in people subjected to this process of mental domination.*

Kardec (2009a, p.347) wrote:

> *As a consequence of the moral inferiority of its inhabitants, evil spirits swarm around planet earth. The action of malevolent spirits is part of the plagues mankind finds himself struggling with in this world. An obsession is one of the effects of such action, just like sickness and all the tribulations of life. It must, therefore, be regarded as probation or atonement. An obsession is the persistent action that a bad spirit exerts on a person. It presents many different characteristics, ranging from the simple moral influence without noticeable outward signs, up to the complete disruption of the body and mental faculties.*

The Treatment of Addictions
at Bom Retiro Spiritist Psychiatric Hospital

by Francis Mourão, MD, Ivete Contieri Ferraz, MD, Elke Pilar Nemer
Pinheiro, and Janaina Graziela Anzolin Bunese

Bom Retiro Spiritist Psychiatric Hospital was founded in 1924. In the early 1980s, the hospital implemented a Spiritual Care Service in its treatment program with the aim of retrieving religious feelings as a therapeutic source in patients and their families and thus helping them understand their issues as they related to spiritual and religious themes. This service has been added to all treatments offered patients, and despite having the Spiritist Principles as a point of reference, the programs respect all patients' religious beliefs and desires.

The Bom Retiro Spiritist Psychiatric Hospital is a mental-health-care complex that offers outpatient care, a psychosocial care center (CAPS) for those with mental disorders and addictions, a 24-hour hospital, and a full inpatient and emergency psychiatric center. It attends welfare patients from the National Health System (SUS), as well as those with insurance and private patients, with more than 2,000 visits per month. Multidisciplinary teams are composed of psychiatrists, psychologists, occupational therapists, social workers, nurses, physical education specialists, physical therapists and teachers.

> *Spiritual interventions, especially when applied along with other practices, can influence the course of severe mental illness in various ways, including providing support, addressing spiritual concerns and increasing the patients' ability to relate to others…Given the role that religious and spiritual beliefs can have in psychiatric illness, it is important for psychiatrists to give special attention to the patient's spiritual history exploring the beliefs that may be influencing his mental illness and how he is coping with the disease.— Koenig, 2007*

Zilda Sanches (2004) studied 62 young drug users and non-users and identified two factors relevant for prevention of addiction: (1) the practice of any religion and (2) inclusion in a functional family structure. Among non-users, 81% were believers and usually attended religious services.

Among users, only 13% were similarly involved. This fact led the author to conclude that religious practice can be an important preventative factor and may cause some users to abandon the use of drugs. International and national studies have shown that religiosity is an important modulator in alcohol and drug consumption among adolescent students (Dalgalarrondo, 2004).

Motivation

The goal of our therapeutic program is to encourage self-organization, promote socialization, increase self-esteem, and empower autonomy at all stages of treatment. Increasingly, research demonstrates that the determining factor for successful treatment (remission) is the level of patient motivation, since addiction is seen as a "pathology of desire." One of our current challenges in helping those with chemical dependency is to optimize the treatment, aiming for a significant impact on the patient's life in a relatively short period of hospitalization.

The human mind has innumerable functions, including consciousness, thought, emotion, memory, attention, and volition (will). *Will* is a mental function of profound implications for making decisions and choices. Human beings are constantly making choices related to all areas of human life, (e.g., relationships, executive functions, and behaviors in general, resulting in short-, medium- and long-term consequences in one's life).

The current treatment program in the chemical dependency unit is based on the motivational interview technique (Miller, 2001). The motivational interview is an approach designed to help the patient to achieve commitment and to make a decision to change. It is formed by a set of strategies of patient-centered counseling, guided by cognitive therapy, systems theory, and social psychology, combining elements of directive and nondirective approaches.

The treatment aims at working with the patients' motivation and with their state of readiness or eagerness to change. The therapist takes a warm, empathic attitude, giving the patient the opportunity to reflect on the need for a positive change in his or her behavior and way of life. Treatment is not imposed but rather is carried out to promote change.

In order to understand how people change, the motivational interview approach makes use of the *wheel of change*, derived from the Porchaska-DiClemente model. This model describes five motivation stages involved in the process for a change in behavior. They are:

1) **Pre-weighing** or **pre-considering stage**: the stage of denial. The patient is not aware he has a problem and consequently does not see any need for a change.

2) **Weighing** or **considering stage**: oscillation. This is characterized by ambivalence, that is, both considering and rejecting the possibility of change.

3) **Determination stage**: This period is similar to opening a door for change. If the patient recognizes the need for a change, he can walk through that door and go on to the action stage. If not, he continues at the consideration (meditation) stage.

4) **Action stage**: The individual engages in specific actions to achieve change.

5) **Maintenance stage**: The real challenges are to continue with the new behavior (change) obtained by the previous actions and to avoid relapse. If relapse occurs, the individual's task is to identify at which of the four previous stages he or she is and to start again, trying to move to the next stage.

To discriminate the different stages of readiness for change, the therapist approaches the patient according to the current stage. Empathic therapists provide feedback, clarify the objectives to be pursued, and actively work with their patients, directly influencing them to become aware, get motivated and thus positively impact the outcome of their treatment.

The advantage of this approach is that it is appropriate for any patient at any stage in the change process. The content and the strategies of the therapeutic actions may differ, but the general goal remains the same: to motivate the patient to advance to the next stage. Patients need help to move from one stage to the other. The ultimate goal is to help the individual to achieve effective changes in his life, changes that must be sustained over time.

During hospitalization, the most frequent stages are *pre-weighing, weighing* and *determination.* The treatment aims at promoting the patient's awareness of his state of health, as well as of his illness, making it possible for him to develop coping and self-regulation strategies, the continuity of treatment, and preventing relapse.

For implementing the program, a variety of therapeutic resources are used: group therapy based on each person's psychiatric diagnosis; specific individualized activities according to the patient's needs; meeting together cooperatively in outdoor areas, encouraging socialization; eating together in the dining room, in which eating moments are transformed into social events, as well as into organization, socialization and self-esteem stimuli. The outdoor environment has also been used as a therapeutic resource. Caring for the space is achieved through simple actions that make the surroundings attractive, warm and cozy, because we believe beauty is an important factor for increasing individual's welfare, as well as for reducing tension.

Fraternal Assistance

The hospital also provides spiritual care, carried out in partnership with the Bom Retiro "Spiritual Care Society." Volunteers from the Spiritist Community in Curitiba, prequalified by the technical staff, offer complementary activities. Volunteers maintain a holistic vision of humans as an integral human being, understanding each one as a set of complex and synergistic systems that involve bio-psychosocial, cultural, and spiritual aspects.

The Spiritual Care activities can be grouped into two types:

- *one that aims at the development of motivation and social skills through reflection and fraternal conversation*
- *one that has a more therapeutic function. It makes use of techniques recommended by Spiritist principles: fraternal assistance, laying-on of hands and disobsession.*

The *moment of reflection* is a group activity, coordinated by two or three volunteers, and it is free for any hospitalized patients who want to take part. It starts with the reading of texts that address issues of interpersonal relationships as triggers for discussion and reflection on social skills, family life, human values and connection with God. The objectives are to encourage patients to establish social and family relationships based on understanding and respect of their own limitations and those of others, seeking for a more harmonious coexistence and promoting reflection on the importance of having a religious connection, seeing this connection as a factor for encouraging and empowering the individual in implementing the changes, and showing the social support a religious affiliation can offer.

In the *fraternal conversation* activities, the volunteer, in a relaxed way, provides companionship to patients during their leisure time in the courtyards of the hospital, conversing about themes related to being hospitable and dependable and offering guidelines regarding social skills related to other patients' demands. What is sought is encouraging and sustaining the patients in their decision-making process, as well as empowering them to accomplish the actions they set for themselves (e.g., achievement of abstinence).

The *fraternal care* is related to more specific activities developed by volunteers specially trained in dealing directly with patients, providing spiritual support to people who complain of "having visions," "hearing voices," or "feeling harassed and threatened by negatively motivated spirits."

Since these are all generally considered to be delusions and hallucinations (symptoms constantly present in serious mental disorders), they cause great suffering. The volunteer therefore offers a caring "ear," encouraging hope for improvement. The volunteer is simultaneously investigating the possibility that these symptoms are related to interference of mental waves coming from entities (spiritual influences) that could be treated through disobsession. The fraternal care is performed only when requested by the technical team and with the permission of the patient and/or his family.

Patients with severe and persistent mental illness often present for treatment with religious delusions. In the United States, approximately 25% to 39% of patients with schizophrenia and 15% to 22% of those with mania/bipolar disorder have religious delusions. In Britain and Europe, 21% to 24% of patients with schizophrenia have religious delusions, and in Japan the rate is 7% to 11%. As for Brazil, there is less information available, but rates of religious delusions probably exceed 15%. Religious belief and non-psychotic activity are also quite common among people with severe mental illness, and these are often used to cope with the intense psychosocial stress caused by this disease. —Koenig, 2007

Fraternal care is usually performed by pairs of volunteers, working in private, with one individual patient emphasizing respect of the patient's complaints. The volunteers base their observations on the Spiritist knowledge that spiritual interference occurs only through vibrational tuning between the patient and the spirits involved with him. The activity aims at helping the patient understand the importance of establishing new habits as protection against such outside interference.

To illustrate, take the example of an alcoholic that has the habit of going to pubs. In these places, he will interact with people who also possess some degree of alcohol dependence, and the conversation will be facilitated by the alcohol and the shared consumption of alcoholic beverages by everyone present, the foundation for the pleasure generated. To remain abstinent, this person will need to change his habits: to stop going to the pubs and undo his interest in them.

The same pattern of dependency happens with our thoughts. They take us into direct contact with places and people who think like we do. Thus, auditory hallucinations or delusions of persecution (with reports of threatening visions or voices ordering people what to do) may be related to the influence of someone else we have been relating to, whether incarnated (living) or disincarnated (spirits). When the patient's mental attitude changes to one based on hope, appreciation of life and people, and respect and affection, this will provide for the establishment of more positive thought processes, attracting relationships with more positive incarnates and disincarnates.

We understand that mental matter is the subtle instrument of one's will, acting in the formation of physical matter, generating motivations for pleasure or disgust, joy or pain, optimism or despair, which do not effectively reduce the abstractions, once they represent pillars of strength on which the soul creates its own states of inductive mentation, drawing to oneself the agents of light or shadow, victory or defeat, happiness or misfortune. –Chico Xavier and Andre Luiz, 1959

Thus, through **fraternal assistance**, the team aims at helping each patient learn new mental habits, which will force his way out of pessimism and the sense of defeat (which are always present in conditions of dependency) in order for him to arrive at a state of continuous hope and determination in bringing about new attitudes, never forgetting that overcoming difficulties to achieve wellbeing represents the real challenge in a human being's existence.

Editor's Note: The practice of laying-on of hands and disobsession is also used at Bom Retiro. Refer to Chapter 3 for an explanation of these therapies. What distinguishes Bom Retiro's program is their work on motivation and coordination with volunteers (part of many Spiritist Hospitals, but especially strong at Bom Retiro).

At the Bom Retiro Spiritist Psychiatric Hospital, the experience accumulated over the past 30 years has shown that the addition of spiritual care to conventional medical treatment can provide significant help in the recovery process and maintenance of mental health, especially with addiction.

"More research is needed to better understand how the various religious belief systems in Brazil and other South American countries interact with and influence mental disorders." –Koenig, 2007

SECTION 3
RESOURCES IN THE USA

Editor's Note: The Spiritist Psychiatric Hospitals have been in operation since the 1930s, and Spiritist Centers have been active in Brazil since the 1890s. Thus, Brazilians have had access to spiritual healing for health management for a long time.

In 2008 I was invited to visit a healer outside Porto Alegre down an unobtrusive, dead-end side street. Once a week, this gifted man takes over the building dedicated to the Bezerra Menezes Spiritist Center. About 500 people, seated in rows, wait their turn for his attention in the large auditorium. Each will be seen individually for physical or emotional issues. Names are called out one by one, alerting the one called to then enter the healing room. In back of the large room is a smaller room dedicated to the healing, full of natural light streaming in from tall windows. Five gurneys bank the right side and a row of chairs are set up on the left. In front, there is a long table around which mediums sit, eyes closed, to generate energy ("current") to support the healing work. Periodically mediums read a prayer to keep everyone present focused on Spirit. The spiritual doctor moves quickly, almost at a run, from one gurney to the next, diagnosing and treating. Trailing after him were his attending helpers (in the flesh), as well as medical school students there to learn from his extraordinary effective ways. His spirit guides overshadowed his work. Children sat with their mothers, waiting their turn in chairs, free to move about when they were afraid to lie on gurneys. The amount of faith in that room was so palpable that the atmosphere was thickened by it; one not only felt it, but breathed it.

As my two hosts and I jostled from gurney to gurney with the rest of the retinue, they whispered to me about how the healing takes place the great results this man obtains, the diagnosis he was giving in his shorthand, and how the auditorium is always full with hundreds of people seeking healing. "Most of them have also been to conventional doctors but know that they must engage the spirit in healing as well", they said.

Perhaps we don't engage Spirit to help in healing in this manner, but we do have some resources that are moving in this direction. In the future, perhaps we will have gifted healers who can complement biomedical therapies similar to the man I have just described or John of God in Brazil.

The chapters in this section reflect on organizations and individual practitioners in the USA who attend to health through addressing body, mind, and spirit. Remember the phrase "It takes a village to raise a child." At different times, each of us needs to learn from different kinds of people, who have differing skills and resources and diverse personal qualities. At times, a person may also need to be held in the embrace of an institution for residential treatment, a clinic with many cooperating practitioners, or a health provider who can acknowledge and support the steps toward health an individual is taking.

CHAPTER SEVEN
EXTRAORDINARY HEALING AT AN INTEGRATIVE HEALTH CARE CLINIC
by Linda Haltinner, DC

In November 2008, I went to Brazil with a group led by Emma Bragdon visiting and learning about Spiritist Centers and Hospitals. I had been practicing holistic healthcare as a chiropractor for 27 years, the first 19 in private practice. I already was certain that healing is facilitated when patients and health practitioners consciously access spirit.

Larry Dossey's book, *Prayer is Good Medicine* (1996), had affirmed my experiences.

In 1999, I worked with a dedicated team of people from my community in southeastern Vermont to found an integrative holistic clinic with a mission to create a model for change in healthcare. Sojourns Community Health Clinic's core constructs are integration of body and spirit, accessibility, collaboration, and acknowledgement of the need to create a bridge between allopathic and alternative medicine.

The opportunity to learn more about Spiritism in Brazil, both as a healing modality and as a tool for building healthier communities, was in line with Sojourns' vision for social change. I hoped to come home with a better understanding of Spiritist healing and the ways we might use the experience of Spiritist Centers to redefine and expand our work.

I spent two weeks in Brazil—the first in Porto Alegre, visiting Spiritist Centers and a Spiritist Hospital, and the second at the Casa de Dom Inacio in Abadiânia with John of God.

In Porto Alegre, we learned about Spiritism in talks by and conversations with people who were both practicing Spiritists and medical practitioners. We visited Spiritist Centers, studied the core construct of Spiritism, and became aware of some of the differences in interpretations of Spiritist principles. We experienced a center that provided food and clothing for thousands, offered classes on Spiritism that attracted 200 people a day, five days a week, and provided healing and support at no cost to the patients. We watched Spiritists work and participate in healing circles. We attended classes for people learning to become Spiritist healers. We learned about the history of Spiritism and the immense challenges in creating "evidence-based" protocols to evaluate the efficacy of Spiritist healing. We participated in a dialogue with hospital doctors, staff and administrators about the next steps in research and about the resistance of many Western physicians to the possibility of integrating Spiritist techniques into protocols. We experienced Spiritist healings ourselves.

At the Casa de Dom Inácio, we prayed and meditated with the hundreds of people from all over the world who were there for healing. People we met in the shops and at the Casa shared stories of their personal miracles. The deep reminder of the immediate and accessible presence of Spirit in our lives was, in itself, a healing experience.

I came back home buoyed and inspired by the reflection of the common threads between what I had experienced in Brazil and the clinic we had been building over the past eight years. Sojourns was built on principles that have a direct corollary in the spiritual healing tradition I had witnessed during those two weeks:

- *Healing involves active engagement of body, mind and spirit. All healing is really spiritual in nature, even while physical-plane tools define the protocols.*
- *Healthcare is a basic right for everyone, regardless of academic achievement, social class or ability to pay.*
- *Education is an essential component of healthcare. "Patient-centric" care requires that the patient is informed and involved.*

- *We accomplish more when we work together. The tools, teachings and protocols we bring from our individual disciplines can be effectively used to help create a unique healing journey for each patient.*
- *A successful clinic must be integral to the community and culture it serves.*

Healing involves active engagement of body, mind and spirit.

I went to Brazil with the expectation that spiritual healing and Spiritism were essentially the same thing. I learned that although Spiritism is spiritual healing, the converse is not necessarily true. Spiritism is deeply rooted in a faith that includes an understanding and appreciation of the active role that spirits of the deceased play in our lives. The overt acknowledgement of spirit as the source of illness, and as the path to healing, was evident in every encounter we had with Spiritists in Brazil.

The concept of spiritual healing in the United States is less distinct, with a broader— possibly more intellectual, less faith-based—definition. The commonality is the truth that healing our spirits and engaging spirit in healing is essential for true health.

All healing is really spiritual in nature.

Practitioners at Sojourns are challenged to acknowledge that their responsibility for their role in the patient's healing is not only on the physical plane of professional expertise, but also on a spiritual plane—we can offer the patient only the possibility that we see. If we don't believe in the possibility of absolute wellness, we actively limit the potential of the journey that we share with the patient.

Our expectations determine possibility. Sojourns was founded on the core understanding that we can change to the degree that we believe in the possibility of that change. Practitioners at Sojourns meet patients within that context, knowing that their first work is to see the patient as whole and well. From that place of knowing, we can invite patients to see themselves as whole and well. As we partner with the patient to design the protocol that will be the map for their healing journey, we continually reflect our expectation for wellness back to the patient.

This inner work to find the experience of the patient's wholeness may be the most profound spiritual action that a healer can take. Whether the experience comes from our interpretation of channeled information or from another form of connection with spirit, the miracle of healing begins with this. At Sojourns, we have come to equate this recognition of each person's inherent wholeness with love.

Healthcare is a basic right for all people regardless of academic achievement, social class or ability to pay.

One of my deepest impressions of the Spiritists in Brazil was of their selflessness. Spiritists take no money for their services. No exchange is required for the healing; the giving is woven into the fabric of the tradition. This culture of volunteerism underlies the capacity of the Spiritist Centers as well. Many people donate time and money to support the work. The centers seemed imbued with an energy of gratitude, grace and expectation.

Sojourns was founded as a nonprofit. We believe that excellent holistic integrative healthcare should be available to all. Sojourns is located in a small rural community that is not wealthy. We give away more than 10% of our services. To enhance accessibility, we have opted to work with a patient's health insurance whenever possible. Insurance (particularly state or federally supported programming) is often the deciding factor in one's choice of which care to access. Sojourns' decision to accept insurance reimbursement as payment for services is a political as well as a social effort—as more people can access and experience the efficacy of holistic care, a grassroots demand for the care begins to manifest, and change develops a momentum of its own.

We offer primary care and alternative medicine under the same roof in order to increase the awareness and accessibility of alternative services (especially touch that is healing) for all of our patients, not just the wealthy.

Our practitioners meet daily to actively collaborate, and they willingly give of their time—a gift of love—to make this possible.

Education is an essential component of healthcare. Patient-centric care requires that the patient is informed and involved.

Spiritist Centers offer classes as well as healings. People are expected to study, learn and grow from the active participatory work and healing circles.

Patient education is an important part of what we do at Sojourns. We offer classes and workshops on health and lifestyle, and we look for opportunities to teach in our wider community.

Learning opens people to possibility. When we begin to understand the amazing intricacy of the processes that work within us to maintain equilibrium, we begin to see that the symptoms we are experiencing are almost always an indication of our bodies' efforts to restore balance. We open to the potential for true healing, at all levels of our being. As our minds shift from reacting out of fear to acting with informed thought and careful choice, we make space for ourselves to open to the involvement of spirit.

Education is the key to change. Both on a personal level and on a broader scale, education opens one up to new options. Real healthcare reform will include not only a change in the economics of care but also a redefinition of the care itself, as well as a new understanding of what it means to be well. Our conception of good healthcare is changing as people understand and seek services that offer the potential for deeper healing.

The allopathic model of medicine teaches us to think of a body as a battle zone, constantly under attack from "out there," by germs or genetics. At Sojourns, we teach about the body as an ecosystem within the larger ecosystem of our family, community, and world—constantly adapting and striving for balance. As in all ecosystems, the environmental conditions are the primary factor in vitality. If we know that our personal health is dependent on the vitality of our internal environment and that we can change that environment, we become empowered to take effective action to address illness.

We accomplish most by working together.

The tools, teachings and protocols that we bring from our individual disciplines can be effectively used to help create a unique healing journey for each patient.

The Spiritist healing circles that we attended were carefully orchestrated. The intent was clearly defined—to heal a person, cleanse the hospital building itself, or pray for patients. Prayer was always involved. Individual healers often had distinct roles in the circle. At the Casa de Dom Inácio with John of God, the presence of the mediums palpably and essentially supports the healing. People seeking healing at the Casa often sit in meditation with the mediums several hours a day. This participation is a profound part of the healing process; the collective power of focus and prayer creates an environment of healing for all.

The physician's role in patients' healing journeys is to support the patients in returning to a state of balance so they can heal themselves. Our bodies' manifestation of illness is almost always an effort to find a dynamic equilibrium that we experience as health. Whether the challenge is spiritual or physical, the toxicity, deficiency and excess all need to be addressed.

Our practitioner team at Sojourns came together to do the work each of us is passionate about: to facilitate healing by engaging the patient in the journey using the tools made available by our education and experience.

No one approach can meet every need. No one philosophical construct can define a paradigm that resonates with every patient. We use our training to create stories to help us understand how the world of healing works; the story told by an acupuncturist is different than the story told by a biological medicine practitioner, chiropractor, or spiritual healer. Each of the stories we use describes a paradigm that is true, complete within its own context, and effective when it depicts a world that the patient can believe in.

We describe our work at Sojourns using the image of a bicycle wheel, where the patient is the hub, the disciplines we practice and our differing expertise creates the spokes, and the synergy of the collaborative work creates the rim.

Holistic, biological and complementary medicine address chronic disease much more effectively than do allopathic modalities. One of our initial plans at Sojourns was to write protocols for the various chronic conditions that we see in our patients. We found ourselves challenged by the variety of choices we would make in treating patients with similar conditions. A protocol to treat a condition is only partially relevant when our focus is on treating the whole patient. Protocols become reminders, not plans.

They almost always include significant lifestyle changes that necessarily engage patients fully and actively in the journey.

Centering in spirit, meeting the patient with love, knowing the potential for wellness—these first steps determine the next steps. The clinic, then, with this synergy created by patients and staff together, becomes a healing place, a place resonant with our love and intent. One of the comments we hear most often is "I feel better just walking in the door."

A successful clinic must be integrated with the community and culture it serves.

The Spiritist Centers we visited were deeply woven into the fabric of their communities. Each was as unique from the others, as individual neighborhoods in a large city are unique. The people who participated at the Centers came from all over, each choosing a Center that offered the resonance they were seeking.

Some Spiritist Centers become community hubs for social services, recognizing that food, warmth and legal services are an essential part of the healing process.

The success of Sojourns is intimately interwoven with the life of our community. Sojourns was possible because it grew out of and into this specific place and this community of people and relationships. In 1999, after practicing in the area for 15 years, I had a patient base of over 1,800 people and was familiar with many of the doctors and other healthcare professionals. In founding Sojourns, I sought out skilled, experienced practitioners with solid reputations and community connections.

Sojourns meets a need in our community. Our attention to leveraging the strengths of the people and services around us has made us an integral part of making our community a healthier place. We provide more than thirty jobs and participate in health education at local schools and health service organizations and other community events. We "gift care" (offer care for free) when needed. We are gifted by witnessing and experiencing the exchanges people offer by volunteering to help each other in many ways.

Although our work is unusual to some, we are accepted and valued for the roles we play. Our work reflects our fundamental values and those of our clients. As patients and practitioners alike, we seek to be who we yearn to be—real healing affirms and nourishes the essential nature of those who practice and receive it.

Our role in the community and our reputation generate our support, both fiscally and socially. Our primary income is from patient fees. Our initial funding came from a gift that was intended to support keeping the land around the clinic in organic agriculture. Currently, that land is leased at no cost to a farmer who is a pioneer in organic food education, donates to the local food shelf and to local schools, and allows our staff to harvest dinner from his/our field.

We also draw patients from a wide geographical area—creating and participating in community defined not by place but by ideology and choice of care options.

Donations make it possible to take steps toward our larger mission. Our donors primarily come from the patient base. We do apply for grants for our programming and educational outreach, and the possibility of grant awards increases with our reputation and impact.

What are the challenges?

The challenges for Sojourns, and for other clinics that look to bring the essence of the Spiritist model into a clinic in the United States, are both ideological and economic.

The Spiritist model is not easily overtly translated into an American healthcare practice. The Spiritist Centers we visited are much more like healthy, socially responsible, socially invested churches than like clinics. The people participating share a core belief in the power of the Spirits to heal.

In the United States, the active role of the Spirits in the healing process is not an integral part of what we usually call spiritual healing. The deep acknowledgement by Spiritists that spiritual dysfunction results in physical manifestation is reflected by its inverse here: we are more likely to see the physical as the cause of the spiritual discomfort. In spite of the extraordinary increase over the past 20 years in awareness of the nonphysical aspects of healing, the typical patients seeking healthcare in the U.S.— even of a complementary health practitioner—are rarely explicitly seeking spiritual healing.

Our faith in Western medicine is anchored in evidence-based protocols (even though the double-blind study model is not necessarily applicable to healing that is synchronistic and nonlinear and is often in direct conflict with the core principle of spiritual healing). Our challenge as health providers is to pair spirituality with science. On the spiritual side we affirm the power of spirit, the central role of a person's beliefs, and the power of positive expectation. We simultaneously offer the medical and technological tools that support biochemical and mechanical healing.

Economically, the challenges go beyond the current debate about healthcare reform in the United States.

Spiritism is a spiritual practice. Healing services are free; Spiritists volunteer their time to work in healing circles. The volunteering is dependable and consistent, a part of the spiritual practice of the healing practitioner.

Spiritist healers are often extensively trained, yet no tuition is required for the training to become a medium. The commitment of time, attention, study and practice extends over years. The expectation is that one will use the gift freely and wisely, guided by the spirits with whom one has learned to work. The medical practitioners that we met in Brazil maintained a careful distinction between their professional medical practices and their Spiritist healing work.

If spiritual healing is to become a mainstream part of healthcare, we need to address the questions related to how and what we pay for. This dialogue must include both the costs of providing care and the costs of accessing care.

Physicians and other healthcare practitioners usually begin their practices with a significant debt from the cost of their training. We need malpractice insurance. We, or the clinic that employs us, have the day-to-day expenses of maintaining staff and space. We expect our work to provide for our families, while at the same time, we are usually passionate about the service we want to be offering to those in need. Of necessity, we charge for this work that is also our livelihood. How and why we meet our work may be a part of our spiritual practice, but the work itself is not the practice. The work supports our economic needs; the practice supports our spirit.

The typical fee-for-service model assigns the cost of care to the patient. People often pay large percentages of their income for health insurance. Patients, whether privately insured or enrolled in a state or federal program such as Medicaid or Medicare, understandably want to have their insurance cover the cost of the services they need. When a practitioner accepts insurance assignment, the contract with the insurance company defines the care in terms of codes for both diagnosis and treatments. We don't actually get paid for the healing. We get paid for the codes we use, for how much we can find wrong with the patient and how complex an examination or treatment we do.

Complexity defines the expected time required for an office visit. Even after the carefully coded bills are submitted, reimbursement is not predictable—neither when we will get paid nor even how much we will collect for the service. In the chapter entitled "Piecework" in his 2007 book *Better*, Atul Gawande writes, "Doctors quickly learn that how much they make has little to do with how good they are." He notes, "Studies indicate that insurers find a reason to reject payment for up to 30% of the bills they receive."

The practice of billing the insurance company instead of creating a direct exchange with the patient for the service creates an artificial distance between the giving and the receiving of the care and between the patient and the practitioner. This expectation that a patient-doctor interaction can be defined by numerical codes that allot a specific time for specific actions can undermine the potential of creating an environment that allows for true healing.

At Sojourns, we are unwilling to compromise care, and often give much more of our time than we can bill for. Relying on the insurance system (as we do for almost 70% of patient services) challenges our fiscal stability. It also makes it more difficult to be overt about our attention to engaging spirit in healing. We try to mediate this by building community with each other and with our patients and by the active collaboration that reminds each of us as to why we do what we do and how the love we hold and give is actually the determinant of our results.

Why go forward?

In our small town in southern Vermont, we see over 400 patients a week for conditions ranging from acute injury and illness to multiple chemical sensitivities and chronic fatigue. We refer to local psychiatrists and other mental health professionals for direct treatment of mental illness, but we see a wide range of mental and emotional symptoms concomitant to the physical conditions our patients present. Chronic-illness patients are intimately familiar with mental and emotional pain. Pretending that we can separate the parts and just treat the physical is an absurdity.

Two patient stories come to mind.

> • *Nan is a woman in her late 50s, a successful entrepreneur with an internationally acclaimed consulting business. About 12 years ago, she began to experience periods of deep fatigue—physical and mental exhaustion that would confine her to her bed for many hours each day. She had to scale back the business,*

release some of her employees, and struggle to maintain a minimal presence to have sufficient income. She had tried Western diagnoses and alternative healing.

Nan is bright, self-reflective and eager to actively engage in her healing. In her intake, it was clear that her will was her saving grace. Her affect was flat, muscles poorly toned, digestion sluggish, and focus erratic. She described herself as depressed. She ate good food—little sugar or caffeine, no alcohol, adequate protein and lots of vegetables.

We assessed her from a biological and functional medicine perspective. We treated her holistically, with nutrient infusions (suspecting a malabsorption syndrome), homeopathic and isopathic remedies, and herbs and nutraceuticals to effect change in neurotransmitter levels. We spoke of Spirit, meditation, and celebrating moments of joy. She was actively participating in her healing. Sojourns practitioner team frequently held her in our daily circle.

Today, Nan is describing herself as "often happy." She works with enthusiasm, exercises regularly, and is rebuilding her business. She feels healed!

Allopathic treatment couldn't change the symptoms she was experiencing. Alternative treatment hadn't worked. The difference at Sojourns was the synergy of the modalities, our expectation of results, and, especially, our affirmation and engagement of the passionate desire of her spirit to heal.

Lydia first presented as a patient when she was in her early 30s. Her story was of a gradual retreat from many of the things she loved in life because of an increasing sensitivity to foods, fragrances, petrochemical products and certain electromagnetic frequencies. She became fearful of her environment, her world grew smaller, and her sense of possibility diminished. She was afraid of reacting to supplements and was wary of deep touch. We intervened minimally on the physical plane (chiropractic and isopathic remedies), but we consistently held our expectation that she could be well, and we reflected that back to her. Now, she volunteers with a local animal rescue organization and is painting again. She describes leaving a visit with her Sojourns practitioner sometimes feeling so happy that she would just sit outside and paint. Her exquisite watercolors are the tangible evidence of the profound gift of watching a spirit find freedom.

For each of these women and so many others, healing of spirit is at the core of psychological and physical healing. The change in thinking that becomes possible as we free our spirits can change our way of relating with the world. We shift from thinking that our bodies are under attack and that we have to fight for health to understanding that we can choose health by attending to the ecosystem within. We release fear and claim personal power. Peace and a healthy respect for our ecosystem/planet have a much better chance of flourishing when we focus on possibility than when we defend against threat. We find that we actually do have the capacity to heal our world.

In my 30 years of practice, I have seen thousands of patients, sharing many aspects of many healing journeys, celebrating profound changes in many peoples' lives. My training and experience have taught me to be a really good doctor. Working with patients has taught me about healing. Extraordinary healing—true healing—happens only when spirit is actively engaged.

CHAPTER EIGHT
PRIVATE PRACTICE: KARMA HEALING AND BIOENERGY THERAPIES

Where do we go in the USA to find something similar to the laying-on of hands so often used in Spiritist Centers and Spiritist psychiatric hospitals? The ranks of those in private practice offering healing in the USA seem to be expanding quickly as people experience the benefits from quietly receiving spiritual energy from those trained to transmit this gift. Reiki practitioners are now more frequently allowed to practice their energy work in hospital settings—largely to offer comfort to those in palliative care, but also sometimes to help those preparing for, or recovering from surgery. This chapter tells the story of my experiences with a practitioner of karma healing, as well as my perspective on bioenergy therapy and Jin Shin Do, as a result of my training as a practitioner. Finally, I offer a word about Reiki.

Karma Healing

The most evolved spiritual gurus have a gift borne of their profound compassion and love: when you are with such a guru, your spiritual evolution is accelerated and you are supported in letting go of complexes, issues and problems gathered over lifetimes (your "psychic baggage"). This has been called a purification of the Soul, or karma clearing. Spontaneous healing of physical problems may result, as well as becoming more compassionate and wise. Satya Sai Baba and Amma-Bhagavan's followers have documented dramatic healings of this kind in India, as have visitors to Mother Meera in Germany and those participating in events with the Dalai Lama of Tibet.

Is it possible that trained spiritual guides or psychotherapists could clear away karmic knots that have led to dysfunctional patterns in health and relationships?

Olga Louchakova, a medical doctor, professor, and researcher, introduced me to Sergei Slavoutski, a handsome, fit, fiftyish man, born in Russia, who practices healing in the San Francisco Bay Area. He began his training in 1992 with Galina Arbatskaia, an extraordinary clairvoyant in Moscow, Russia, who uses her gifts to facilitate healing for others. Later, Sergei and Galina developed their form of "Karma Healing" together. Sergei is an exceptional clairvoyant—a necessary qualification for this form of work.

Clearing the Biofield through a Phantom: Phase One, Stage One

"I'll just put a phantom of you out here in front of me," he said, reaching his right hand out at arm's length in front of him, and drawing it down to indicate that a mock up of me now "stood" in front of him. I sat and watched from the comfortable green velvet couch, as instructed, arms and legs uncrossed so as not to obstruct my energy. Sergei was scanning my body using his right hand as his X-ray device, looking for problems on three levels in my body's informational fields, also know as subtle bodies, or biofield. These refer to the subtle energies that Spiritists call the "perispirit".

After informing me about the formal protocols to expect in the session, Sergei looked psychically for negative thought forms that had stuck to me, which I carried around as baggage–the collection of "I don't like you for this or that" kind of stuff. He said, when people judge and their judgments don't roll off our back, the negativity corrupts the biofield. In my case, he saw seven people and identified them by hair color, weight, dress, age and other characteristics so that I could readily recognize them by name. I was impressed—he was "seeing" accurately and had no other way of having acquired this information, so intimate to my life story. I relaxed into more trust in him.

Then, one by one, Sergei peeled the energy of the negative thought forms from me, returned the energy to the originator, and then, with intent, dismissed the "person" to be on their way—no longer to be part part of my psychic baggage.

I looked in his work for elements of religious ritual: prayers, mantras, beads, gurus, saints or amulets. Such elements were not used, except the single flame of a small beeswax candle burning, and some universal symbols of compassion from various religions adorning the walls: Tara, Kuan Yin, Buddha, and the triangle from John of God's Sanctuary in Brazil. The special candle had been sent for from a particular Russian Orthodox Church in the former USSR and had been lovingly made by devotees with a prayer that the light of each candle bring purification. This clearly made it a tool for spiritual work—but did not limit us to the confines of any particular religion.

Second-Sergei scanned my phantom for more intense negative thought forms, something along the order of deliberate curses directed to me (e.g., "May she experience being trapped by the misery I now feel," "May the lineage of women in her family line never be happy"). Such zingers have the force of bombs and can change the face of the psychic landscape for generations. He found two such "curses." He identified who had sent them and when and why, and he cleared them. Again, I dropped deeper into trust in him, as he had seen so many elements of my story without prior knowledge.

At this point I had to wonder, I've been working with clearing of negative thought forms since 1990 for myself and others. Was I so blind to myself that my worst baggage in this area, the proverbial elephants hiding under the living room rug of my soul, had evaded me? Or, is Sergei so good at this clearing that he can see into a deeper level than I had been able to access for myself? Certainly, he's a skilled miner of the subtle realms. His mastery as a clairvoyant and clairsentient, a kind and ethical guide, became more apparent as the minutes ticked by.

Finally, he scanned my phantom for signs of professional black magic—an oddity in our culture but found in other lands. Nothing there to clear. Well, that's good news! We are complete for the day.

Riding home on Bay Area Rapid Transit (BART), speeding through the Oakland hills and then zipping through the tunnel under the San Francisco Bay, I compared the difference between spiritual healing I have experienced in Brazil, such as laying-on of hands, intended to clear negativity from the layers of subtle energy surrounding the body, and Sergei's surgical precision exorcising negative thought forms from the biofield. It's not the style that's essential but rather the skill and intent of the practitioner. His presence even more than his style is initiating me to new levels of understanding, hard to put in words.

Phase One, Stage Two: Clearing the Chakras

As I approached the office, I looked at Mt. Diablo ("Devil Mountain"), which defined the Eastern horizon. Its flanks were burnished with the tawny dry grasses of late summer; it's peak was blanketed by a halo of clouds. "Yes, this work is clearly about clearing out inner demons that bedevil us," I thought, "First I need help to see through the cloud cover."

Sergei uses L-rods for dowsing with great familiarity, as if they are an extension of him. He taps them twice to bring them into neutral. He may then ask for confirmation that he has completed his work thoroughly, that his client has cleared something fully, or if there is more to do. At times, he asks the rods to move right or left to signal an answer to a yes or no question.

Today our work was to clear the seven main chakras, from crown to sacrum. He again worked through a phantom of my body, observing and reporting to me the health of each chakra. Then, as necessary, he cleared each chakra, removing defects in color and shape and restoring its spin to its natural rhythm. Finally, he aligned my chakras. Again, his observations resonated with my sense of my own health and the way my history had left me weakened in some areas—some petals of the lotus flower bent, or pulled in. As Sergei worked, I felt I was in the presence of an ancient shaman, but one that used no incense, unusual rituals, hallucinogenic drugs, gestures or cult prayers, and one that does not mimic the old ways—definitely a modern-day shaman.

Finally, Sergei taught me two ways to energize my body, one in nature and the other involving active imagery in a meditative state, which I can do anywhere I am.

Phase Two: Untying Karmic Knots

"How are you?" he asked in our next appointment, wanting to know how the work was affecting me. "OK, a bit more vulnerable and quick to tear over emotional things. But, I feel very alive and good," I said.

Next, he asked me, "What do you want? The intention of our work must be crystal clear," he said. "No room for fuzziness. This is of the essence." "I want to clear any obstructions I have so I can make good choices in the partners I choose," I said. We discussed the meaning of this in more detail and then proceeded.

Sergei looked into my auric field and clairvoyantly "saw" three karmic knots. He described them as if they were sculpted beads: the first is round, smaller, and narrower. The second is the biggest and will be the most challenging. The third is stretched out and somewhat rounded. The density of all three is the same. He then clears this image away with one hand, as if cleaning a screen. "We'll need three sessions for the work," he informed me.

First knot untying: Sergei instructed me to close my eyes, and sit in a relaxed position on the couch. "Let's look first through a window to see the story the first psychic knot represents," he suggested. I entered into a light trance, similar to meditation—disengaged from my left brain's critical thinking. Next, Sergei recounted the story he saw, slowly, detail by detail, while I listened and engaged the story—as it did feel somehow familiar, as if he had pulled a file out from my deepest memory banks. Sergei did not ask me to give him any input. He was reporting his psychic impressions. Then, when the story of that life concluded, Sergei asked for guidance from his spiritual guides, about what story would be best to replace the original with, to create a positive end. Then, he told that story in detail, slowly, so deep levels of my consciousness could absorb it. (He follows his guidance regarding the speed of delivery.)

With Sergei as my guide, I observed a life in which I was a Japanese woman, in the 1600s, sold by my mercenary father to a brute of a man to be his "wife"—really a concubine. I was never respected or loved by him—or allowed my own life interests. I was his sex slave—always ready for him when he wanted to take me—confined to a room in his walled estate, with only a window to look out of to engage the world. Period. Sergei's guidance then replaced this story, transforming "that life" into one of being a young woman who connected deeply with an artist who loved her dearly, with whom she had a loving family, and a simple, pure way of life in a community of friends and family. This (life) story filled me with a knowing of what it is to be loved, to love a good man, and to be part of a good life. I absorbed it in my bones and registered it deeply, making it truly mine.

Sergei calls this process "cognitive restructuring" (done in altered states of consciousness) in order to reframe (or rather replace) old stories stored at a deep level that have structured our belief systems and thus laid down our patterns of behaving in life.

I asked him, "Are you looking for emotional responses in the process?" He does not feel there has to be a big catharsis as one observes the first story and observes the tragedy of that story. But one does have to see what happens (viz., the death and the profound events that shaped consciousness) and let go into the feeling of the alternative route provided by guidance.

I felt a bit sleepy during the session. I wondered if I slept awhile during it. It was late in the day, and I was a bit tired. Or was I in a hypnagogic state—the perfect state of consciousness to absorb new information at a deep level?

After the stories were complete, Sergei used his dowsing to ascertain if the knot was gone. "Yes!," he confirmed.

Second knot untying: Holland. 1700s. I am a man with a wife who loves flowers but is not exciting. I decide to seduce women and, without offering them love, have sexual liaisons with about as much heart as a butterfly collector counting newly-speared items in his boxed collection. My wife feels terrible—boring, unloved, and not respected. She is unable to have children. Sergei's guidance then initiates a different story: my wife and I have two boys and a baby girl. I become deeply engaged in the lives of the kids and the evolution of my family. My wife is exciting to me in that she is the one who makes family life possible. We enjoy a rich and rewarding life together.

Third and last knot untying: Before the untying, Sergei (ever thorough) checks my biofield and sees some obstruction. He advises me to go through a process of forgiveness he has taught me, and he clears my biofield to prepare for the work of the day.

We discuss how I have been: I speak of a sore throat and swollen glands that rolled through me for a day. No doubt I was integrating the ugliness and heartlessness of my last lifetime explored in session.

In the last life we went to in order to untie a knot: It was in the early 18th century. I am an East Indian Buddhist woman with an abusive husband. A bronze statue of Buddha, two and a half feet tall, his head covered by a fully-open 1,000-petal lotus, occupies a prominent place in my home. The cognitive restructuring happened when I chose to leave this home and the abusive relationship.

What does this inner work elicit in my day-to-day life? First, Sergei affirmed that personalities of significant others from my past lives had shown up again in this present life, and my thinking about them in this life was enhanced, as if I could see more of who they are, and thus make better decisions about my relationships with them now. Secondly, that week I met several people who offered new opportunities for personal and professional relationships.

My inner life? The night after this session, I was up in the middle of the night with a lucid dream about rolling a large stone back from a doorway, allowing me time to move out of the zone where I had been trapped. In this new realm, there are a whole new field of possibilities for relationships and partnerships. I could feel "the word" getting out that "there is a new vibration in town". I was aware of new energies approaching and opportunities approaching me.

In sum Sergei is a healer, first and foremost. No psychic fairs for him. No past-life readings. He is available if someone wants to go through transformation—a process of psychospiritual growth that enhances wellness. Can you find this form of karmic healing in other places? You may find components of what Sergei does in others' work, but I doubt if you will find the thorough system that Sergei and his teacher have created together.

Bioenergy Therapy, Jin Shin Do and Reiki

Sergei is one of a kind, but so are all healers. Fortunately, we are living at a time when there are many kinds of energy work to draw from, and many superb healers. Our recognition of the effectiveness of this kind of work has penetrated mainstream thinking: Some teaching hospitals are requiring nurses and doctors to take some training in laying-on of hands—to be able to either offer it to patients, or (at the least) respect the practice when it is performed by others. Healing traditions from cultures around the world are spreading quickly into the USA as the Internet and international travel make exposure to these traditions and training more accessible. Reiki (described below) is perhaps the most well-known.

The two forms of energy work with which I am most familiar are Bioenergy Therapy which developed recently in Slovenia by Zdenko Domancic, and Jin Shin Do, a modern translation of the older Japanese, Jin Shin Jyutsu—believed to predate Buddha and Moses. Both of these paths bring balance to the body's energies, promoting optimal health and wellbeing. Both assist in the flow of an infinite supply of universal energy, but the process does not deplete the practitioner's personal supply of energy. Either form of work can awaken a felt-sense of complete harmony within the self and between the self and the universe—certainly conducive to reducing stress and improving mental health.

Domancic has been highly effective in healing all manner of physical illnesses at his center in Slovenia (Hochstatter and Cote, 2007). Patients come for a morning or afternoon session and sit as a group encircling Domancic and others on his team, who work with one patient at a time as that person sits, fully clothed, in a chair inside the circle of other patients. The energy generated by the group adds to the healing energy available in treatment. Practitioners focus the bioenergy that surrounds and supports life such that the receiver gets a boost of energy, which improves the functioning of his or her innate self-healing abilities. The language used to describe this energy transfer has nothing to do with spirituality or religion, only a reference to the "bioenergy," which sustains life. Domancic believes that each person has the innate intelligence to use the energy coming to them in bringing healing to the areas of their body/mind that need it most. Little physical pressure is applied to the body; instead, energy is directed from outside of the body into the body (similar to laying-on of hands in Brazil), or the practitioners full hand is applied with light pressure to the problem areas, warming them. Sessions last approximately 20 minutes, and ideally, a series of four sessions are done on four days in succession.

Jin Shin Jyutsu is similar in that it works with energy, but in this form, the inherent energy of the body is stimulated by the practitioner, who holds particular focal points on the body's energy pathways (meridians) for a particular length of time to stimulate harmonious functioning of the body. Sessions generally take place privately with the receiver lying fully clothed on a cushioned table. A session usually lasts for an hour.

The website www.reiki.org describes Reiki:

> Reiki is a Japanese technique for stress reduction and relaxation that also promotes healing. It is administered by "laying-on hands" and is based on the idea that an unseen "life force energy" flows through us and is what causes us to be alive. If one's "life force energy" is low, then we are more likely to get sick or feel stress, and if it is high, we are more capable of being happy and healthy.
>
> The word Reiki is made of two Japanese words—Rei which means "God's Wisdom or the Higher Power," and Ki which is "life force energy." So Reiki is actually "spiritually guided life force energy."
>
> A treatment feels like a wonderful glowing radiance that flows through and around you. Reiki treats the whole person including body, emotions, mind and spirit creating many beneficial effects that include relaxation and feelings of peace, security and well-being. Many have reported miraculous results.

Reiki is a simple, natural and safe method of spiritual healing and self-improvement that everyone can use. It has been effective in helping virtually every known illness and malady and always creates a beneficial effect. It also works in conjunction with all other medical or therapeutic techniques to relieve side effects and promote recovery.

While Reiki is spiritual in nature, it is not a religion. It has no dogma, and there is nothing you must believe in order to learn and use Reiki. In fact, Reiki is not dependent on belief at all and will work whether you believe in it or not. Because Reiki comes from God, many people find that using Reiki puts them more in touch with the experience of their religion rather than having only an intellectual concept of it.

Note that within the above description of Reiki there is mention of the Spirit and God. This may not appeal to everyone; however, it is more consistent with the Spiritist laying-on of hands.

CHAPTER NINE
COLLABORATION: ACUPUNCTURE, MEDICAL INTUITION AND ORTHOMOLECULAR MEDICINE

In previous chapters, we have considered resources outside Brazil that provide some of the components available in Spiritist Psychiatric Hospitals in a residential treatment facility, a complementary healthcare clinic or with an individual practitioner. This chapter reveals how individual practitioners in private offices are collaborating to serve their mutual clients. This is a patchwork-quilt model, with the patient and practitioners patching together the treatment plan, which may involve coordination with travel, especially if the practitioners are far away from each other and the patient cannot drive. The practitioners are also left with the extra work of maintaining contact to coordinate treatment plans, as needed—not such an easy thing to do when you are not working in the same physical space. Playing phone tag can absorb a lot of time, as can emails.

A working model for collaboration is illustrated in a story in which I participated with an acupuncturist and an orthomolecular psychiatrist who live in western Washington state, USA.

Jessica Randall

On June 6, 2011, I interviewed Jessica Randall, a licensed acupuncturist and seasoned medical intuitive, about how she works with patients with serious mental illnesses.

I met Jessica in 2009 when she accompanied one of her patients in a group I was leading in Brazil. The patient, "Gerry" (referred to in the Introduction), had come to consult John of God about "episodes" she was having. These episodes had been diagnosed by her psychiatrist and others in a psychiatric hospital where she had twice been a short-term resident for "mania," but she did not fit the typical definition for bipolar disorder or schizophrenia. MDs had also referred to her illness as psychosis. Her story began in 2007 when her parents first called me for help, as they felt Gerry was having a spiritual crisis. Gerry subsequently came under John of God's care for two weeks in 2007 and six weeks in 2009. Ten days before her 2009 visit with him she had finished tapering off all psychiatric medications, as they seemed to be aggravating her condition. They had been gradually decreased in order to re-evaluate her condition. Soon after stopping all psychiatric medication, Gerry was functionally catatonic for six weeks: hardly sleeping, barely eating or drinking, and rarely speaking. She preferred to stand upright, in one place, not communicating, staring into space. It is difficult to know if the catatonia was part of her detoxification from the drugs or a time of profound working through of the roots of her condition. As of mid-2011, she is living independently, driving a car, looking forward to going to law school, and planning her wedding.

Jessica Randall describes herself as a grounded person who is deliberate in the use of her well-honed intuition. She compared the difference between the way she uses her intuition and the way Gerry sometimes gets in trouble with her psychic boundaries:

> *I can be open when I need to be, to understand and see into a client. Otherwise, I try to stay out of my patients' space, in order to let their own process unfold. A part of me is allowing a natural interaction to take place, including the spontaneous feelings, body gestures and conversation that occur during the session. Another part of me is operating intuitively: consciously observing myself, my patient, and our interaction. This requires being connected and separate at the same time. My boundaries are very good."* Gerry, on the other hand, has had problems opening and closing her boundaries at the appropriate times. Gerry is also gifted with incisive intuition, but she tends to get stuck in a purely open position, then gets very spacey, forgetful, and easily triggered emotionally. (At her worst, she was impulsive, taking inappropriate risks, and could not take care of her basic needs.)
>
> We discussed how Gerry was doing. Jessica said, "She has not had an episode for six months. I give her an acupuncture treatment once every three weeks. If she doesn't receive the treatment regularly, she tends to get somewhat spacey, a light version of what her episodes were like. The treatments appear to reinforce her individuality and sense of boundaries, as well as reorient her energy so that her system is running smoothly. When she has more stress, more frequent treatments are beneficial.

Jessica has collaborated with Brad Weeks, an orthomolecular psychiatrist, in helping Gerry stay grounded and stable. Jessica reflected:

> *It's as if Gerry previously had potholes in some neurological pathways. Information would attempt to travel down these pathways and then get lost in the pothole and never reach its destination. Therefore her biological systems could not be in constant communication—necessary to maintain balance, or equilibrium, in body and mind. Acupuncture, one-on-one interaction, family support to promote a healthy lifestyle, and spiritual healing helped to forge new pathways. As the new pathways were being forged, the nutritional supplements Dr. Weeks provided Gerry gave her the precursors her neurological system needed to reinforce these new pathways and avoid the potholes in the dysfunctional pathways. He also assisted in the detoxification that was necessary for her nervous system to recover. These*

nutritional supplements and the lifestyle changes Gerry made worked hand in hand with acupuncture to first stabilize her and then help her function optimally. This "rewiring," or change in her neurological functioning, will likely take a decade or so to be complete. It requires consistent effort.

Most of the patients who come to me have a problem that is draining energy (qi) from their systems. This is true of those with physical issues as well as psychological imbalances. We are all containers of qi and need that energy to function. It is the working of qi that creates equilibrium in all the systems of our body. Ideally, we want all our systems to communicate and collaborate with each other, as they are mutually interdependent. Many things can cause the breakdown of this communication: pathogens, inherent weaknesses, poor lifestyle, and trauma are common causes. Psychic forces in the environment are also issues that can cause this breakdown of the body's natural equilibrium.

When a patient first arrives I take a medical history, hear how they articulate the problem, and then I try to find the leak in his/her qi. It could be on a physical, emotional, intellectual, relationship, or spiritual level. I use my abilities as a medical intuitive as well as my abilities as a diagnostician from the point of view of Chinese medicine. The treatments I do may include using acupuncture, Chinese herbal medicine, Chinese massage or Chinese energy work.

I have found that these forms of traditional Chinese medicine [TCM] provide a very good way to achieve emotional stabilization. They reinstate a healthy balance in the whole system, where all the systems are in tune and helping to rebalance each other constantly. Traditional Chinese medicine's ability to diagnose and treat this is very sophisticated—probably more so than conventional Western medicine is at this time.

Gerry is a good example of how healing takes place in those who have serious illness. First she received spiritual healing from John of God and other mediums who could attend to her spiritual issues. Then, Gerry had the benefit of acupuncture, nutritional supplements and detoxification. These are a complement to the spiritual work, which is primary, because it goes to the core of the problem and can clear it up.

The tricky part is that we have to negotiate our own roles and cultural biases in order to deliver the best treatment to the patient. While in Brazil, I had to give way to John of God and his Brazilian way of healing through Spirit. To do this, I had to step out of the way. I was given his permission to treat Gerry with acupuncture *while we were in Brazil, but I knew this was only to complement the work that was being done at his sanctuary. I considered that my job was to help stabilize her physical body. Then, after we left John of God, I helped Gerry from a Chinese medicine perspective with the regulation of qi, being respectful of the work John of God had done so as not to obstruct it. Finally, we collaborated with Dr. Weeks, an orthomolecular psychiatrist, who overrode the initial bipolar diagnosis given by the Harvard-trained psychiatrist who had given Gerry psychiatric medications. Dr. Weeks' opinion of Gerry: "She's not emotionally ill, she just has a finely tuned system, so she needs extra help with the best of care and feeding. Her system is more like a Maserati (a finely tuned luxury car) than a Ford. Like a Maserati, she demands extreme attention to details and has to expend more energy caring for herself with the help of a team.*

I was impressed with the way Jessica has been able to be flexible and work with her own paradigm while also respecting the paradigm of others. She shared, "I frequently collaborate with psychotherapists who want me to help stabilize their clients and recognize the physical issues that may be contributing to their psychological problems. Clearly, collaborating with Dr. Weeks has allowed Gerry to get the best of care."

Brad Weeks, MD

Dr. Weeks also has the flexibility to work within different paradigms, combining the best of conventional biochemical knowledge with other streams of thinking. The following is from his Website http://weeksmd. com/?page_id=2 (accessed May 30, 2011):

Dr. Weeks completed undergraduate studies at Dartmouth College then, prior to medical school training at the University of Vermont, Dr. Weeks worked in the Harvard system doing two years of research at Massachusetts General Hospital's mineral metabolism unit. In addition, he studied nutrition (including macrobiotics with Mishio Kushi in Brookline, MA), acupuncture, massage (shiatsu), music therapy, Anthroposophical medicine, and classical homeopathy. Medical school at the University of Vermont was followed by medical internship (1 year) and psychiatric residency at Dartmouth Hitchcock Medical Center (3 years). He is a specialist in psychiatry and developed the field of "corrective medicine and psychiatry."

He has been a charter member of the Physicians Association of Anthroposophical Medicine (PAAM) since 1983 and is most active in the following professional associations: the American Association of Physicians and Surgeons (AAPS), the International Schizophrenic Foundation (ISF), American Holistic Medical Association (AHMA), and the American College of Advancement of Medicine (ACAM). He is licensed to practice medicine in the state of Washington.

Who does Dr. Weeks treat?

Dr. Weeks treats people of all ages and all illnesses dealing with the physical, emotional and spiritual aspects of health. He is particularly interested in the treatment of chronic illnesses including all varieties of mental disorders. These include psychosis (schizophrenia, manic depression/bipolar), depression, anxiety, autism, and other thought and mood disorders.

As no illness occurs in a social vacuum, Dr. Weeks offers family therapy, couples' therapy and individual counseling whether for adults, child/adolescent and the elderly.

Protocol Paradigm

Dr. Weeks loves music and thinks of health in terms of musical metaphor— playing a musical instrument. In order to play an instrument well (to be healthy) one needs four factors: (1) a well-built and well-maintained instrument, (2) a tuned instrument, (3) someone who loves playing the instrument, and (4) someone who has composed or can create de novo *(improvise) a musical piece.*

Those four factors represent, respectively, 1) the physical body (the instrument), 2) the vibrational or etheric body (being tuned), 3) the soul's delight in life (the joy of the musician) and 4) the birthright of all humans to participate in the spiritual act of creation of their life (the composer). For this reason, all protocol recommendations from Dr. Weeks are designed to correct imbalances in: 1) your biochemistry (physical body), 2) your vitality (energetic, vibrational, etheric body or "Qi"), 3) your emotional being (the soul) and 4) your self-esteem (your spirit).

Dr. Weeks believes that all four of these "bodies" interweave and affect each other constantly.

That said, he also believes that the predominant process is a trickle-down effect meaning that your spirit (thoughts, values and attitudes) affects your soul (feeling, attachments, urges) which in turn affects your vitality (sleep processes, growth and regeneration forces, stamina) which finally affects your physical body (substance and biochemical matter). Therefore he pays particular attention to the spirit since he considers that to be the best target for correcting illnesses or states of "dis-ease."

Each patient is given a specific "Corrective Protocol." It has four categories of intervention in order to strive for balance and integration of the four "bodies." Those interventions include dietary changes, nutritional supplements and medicines for the physical body, energetic or vibrational homeopathic remedies for the etheric or energy body, exercises to develop will forces and the ability to visualize for soul strengthening and meditative or mastery of thought behavior for the spirit. Furthermore, Dr. Weeks does not see health as a goal sufficient unto itself, but rather as a means toward an end. He hopes you will wonder about what changes you will make in your life once you are healthier.

Dr. Rudolf Steiner, father of Anthroposophy, taught that we learn in two manners—we learn through thinking about our experiences (e.g., "that burns, I won't touch that again") and, on a deeper level, that which we can't learn through thinking, we learn through suffering. This is the path of compassion or heart-warmed thinking. In this second realm of learning, illness often serves as our best teacher. In that sense, we are well advised to seek the gift within the pain in order to harvest the fruits of out illnesses (see Dr. L.F.C. Mees' book Blessed By Illness*).*

Steiner, who also created the Waldorf School system (see Education towards Freedom*), would also agree that the goal of the doctor is to help people grow towards freedom. Why is that? Perhaps we might all agree that the most important goal of human beings is to love one another. Love, we all know, cannot be coerced or forced in any manner. Therefore, if love is to exist, it must be given freely.*

Dr. Weeks has witnessed many incidences of illness teaching people to love—be it the cancer patient who acknowledged that only when he faced death did he finally learn to express his love for his children, or the woman who only was able to lovingly forgive whole-heartedly when she faced her health challenges. It is so common as to be cliché—illness often brings out the best in us. So, to the degree that illnesses help us

113

focus on our imbalances or self-destructive patterns and offers to make better lovers of us all, the doctor is well-advised to not miss the opportunity to use the illness to enhance the entire well-being of the patient on the four levels discussed above.

Treatment Methods: Although he is licensed as an MD to prescribe antibiotics and life-saving medicines, Dr. Weeks does this only when medically indicated. He prefers "pro-biotic" remedies as opposed to "antibiotic" medicines when appropriate. "Probiotic" remedies include vitamins, minerals, amino acids, hormones (all things which are natural to your body) as well as other remedies also from natural sources which stimulate the body's own healing forces. Techniques to integrate the relationship between the healing forces of the mind and the biochemical mechanisms of the body are also employed (visualization, biofeedback, exercise, diet).

Treatment Philosophy: A relationship with Dr. Weeks involves not only enjoying his commitment to offering his best medical advice and care, but equally his effort to teach clients about health care principles and disease prevention. In this way, clients become empowered with regards to their health.

Description of Treatment Options: CORRECTIVE MEDICINE AND PSYCHIATRY: Corrective medicine and psychiatry involves the collaborative experience of listening with, educating and advising patients about how to correct imbalances in their four realms of life: their physical bodies, their vitality, their emotional life and their spiritual path. This encompasses education and counseling concerning the lifestyle "NET" (Nutrition, Exercise and Thought—see this illustrated as the Weeks Health Pyramid with Lifestyle as the foundation, Supplements as the next step, Medications only when supplements are inadequate and, of course, when required, Hospitalization or Surgeries when medications don't suffice.)

NUTRITIONAL BIOCHEMISTRY: This is the process of identifying deficiencies or excesses (toxic) in the body's own biochemical workings and then either supplementing what you are low in or, on the other hand, detoxifying what have too much of. Enzymes, amino acids, minerals, essential fatty acids (oils) and vitamins so overlooked by conventional medicine are essential to health. (Even their name, "essential nutrients," cries out for attention!) If you buy a new sports car, you will spend $50,000 of which half might be the engine cost and half the chassis and marketing expense. But if you forget to buy a simple quart of oil ($1.89) the engine will seize up and be irreparably destroyed within 10 miles. . .never to run *again! Don't forget to "change your oil" and supplement or detoxify as necessary for optimal health.*

ORTHOMOLECULAR MEDICINE: A big word meaning "same molecule." The point is to identify which molecules (enzymes, vitamins, minerals, amino acids, hormones) you are short on (deficiency syndromes) or long on (toxic syndromes). We then simply re-balance you by using supplements to make up for deficiencies and/or detoxification techniques to get rid of excesses. However, the key point is to accomplish this using natural molecules which occur in your body (i.e., orthomolecular) not foreign, unnatural molecules (allopathic) which are designed and patented not for health and bio-compatibility but for profit. (Remember, you can't patent a naturally occurring substance but you can alter it "significantly" and then patent it. These alterations are often toxic).

ANTHROPOSOPHICAL MEDICINE: This is a fertile, world-wide system of healing derived from the research of Dr. Rudolf Steiner (1861-1925) involving mineral, plant and animal substances prepared in a manner that, by featuring the forces inherent in these substances, offers potent, non-toxic remedies. These remedies are offered in the context of mind/body health work and a spiritual perspective which strives to see health challenges as important lessons.

CORRECTIVE PSYCHIATRIC SERVICES: Many people labor under the stigma of a psychiatric diagnosis which is undeserved and misapplied. In the cases of "psychiatric illnesses" those diagnoses may include ADD, psychosis, schizophrenia, manic depression, addictions (including illicit drugs, alcohol and nicotine).

Frequently organic causes are overlooked because careful biochemical detective work was not performed. Dr. Weeks is specially trained in identifying those people who are incorrectly diagnosed with a mental illness and helping them to re-attain normal function. For this reason, even if you come for psychotherapy or counseling, Dr. Weeks offers a physical examination and nutritional work-up to rule out an organic cause. Better to fix that biochemical dis-ease than to spend years "on the couch" having not addressed this aspect of your health.

For those folks who struggle with psychiatric illnesses, Dr. Weeks uses his training as a psychiatrist to monitor their need for antipsychotic, anti-anxiety or antidepressant medications. At the same time, however, he offers complementary remedies that frequently lessen the need for strong psychiatric medications.

It seems to me that orthomolecular medicine may be an important part of treatment for anyone suffering from serious mental disturbances. Therefore, I've appended a short article by another orthomolecular psychiatrist who describes more about this medical specialty in Appendix F.

CHAPTER TEN
MANAGING LOSS WITH
THE HELP OF A MEDIUM

One of the most traumatic experiences we can have is losing someone or something we are attached to: a parent, a child, a lover, a job, a home, or physical functioning. Getting older is a loss of energy and function, and some people choose to suicide because they simply don't want to go through that loss—or other losses, like the death of a loved one. Support from caring family members and community can be of great help, as can focused support groups and psychotherapy,

If people are treated for grief after a loss with anti-depressants that dull the emotional pain, they will be denied the full experience of going through the natural grieving process and obstructed from the resolution that comes from going through the process to its natural resolution. They may also establish a routine of using antidepressants to avoid feelings of sadness and grief and, as mentioned earlier, long-term use of psychiatric medications has been shown to shorten lifespan and lead to numerous kinds of breakdowns in the systems of the physical body, as well as cognitive impairment. Going through the natural grieving process—feeling the loss—and not taking drugs may be a more healthy choice.

This is not to say that people who are crazed with grief should not have a modest amount of drugs to help them sleep and thus be able to function. For a short period of time, this can be the wise and compassionate response. I (along with others) wish only to flag a warning that when we treat the natural grieving process as a mental disorder, we go against the natural processes of the body, mind and spirit. The consequences of disowned grief can appear later in a different form, crying for attention, as a cancer, a heart condition, or other complication.

Mediums who facilitate contact between a person and the spirit who has passed on can be of great help in moving toward resolution of grief.

Stories of How Mediums Help with Grief

I. **Susan Casey** is the Editor in Chief of *O: The Oprah Magazine*. For two years after her father died, she was inundated with a grief, which she described in the December 2010 issue of O as "life threatening." "[The sadness] scoured everything, leaving my nerves and emotions exposed and raw, it was an actual physical weight that I dragged along. I wore grim-colored glasses, looking out and seeing nothing but gray days, angry at the universe for taking away my father."

Susan felt pulled to go to see John of God in Brazil, hoping this extraordinary medium and healer could take away the grief. She wrote, "I wondered if John of God could patch up the hole inside me and help me love my life again, a life that did not contain my father."

Zsolt Pap de Pestény, an Austrian physician about 60 years old, was also visiting John of God's sanctuary and spoke to Susan about his experience. Before coming to John of God, Zsolt had received conventional surgery for his colon cancer, which had metastasized to his bones, liver and bladder. His surgeons removed his buttocks, 75% of his colon, 85% of his sacrum, and parts of his liver and bladder, but the cancer still progressed. John of God was his last hope; after several visits, he was in full remission. John of God told him, "If everybody had as much faith as you, then they would be healed."

Susan learned that an important part of the healing process is sitting in meditation ("Current"), sometimes close to the medium as he does his work (often counseling more than 1,000 people each day). She was in fact invited by John of God to sit in his consultation room for several hours, where she experienced "part of a buildup of a river of benevolence."

Like Zsolt, Susan also asked for a full healing of her condition. John of God told her to "represent her father" when she sat in meditation, and he would take care of things for her. In her three-hour meditation, with eyes closed, she found herself visually back at the family summer cottage in Canada. She found herself spontaneously slowly reliving precious moments and conversations she'd had with her father long ago. She came to feel a sense of certainty that her father was now in a blissful state, capable of sending her waves of love, in a sense "being love," absolutely present, and eternally there; she even heard his voice innerly speaking to her loud and clear. Weeks later Susan fully recognized that the grief had disappeared and been replaced by peace.

Conventional thinking is that people go a bit mad when they are experiencing grief and may imagine hearing voices or seeing the loved one who has died—but it's not real. Peter Fenwick, an English psychiatrist, has a different viewpoint. In his book *The Art of Dying*, he referred to the 1996 book *Hello from Heaven*, which published an interview survey of more than 3,000 North Americans. The survey suggests that one in five bereaved Americans have experienced contact with loved ones after that person has died. This sense of the presence of the person tends to occur when a person is in a relaxed state: drowsy, going to sleep, awakening, or meditating.

Fenwick writes that a hallucination is, by definition, "a subjective experience that is not shared." To counteract the opinion that all experiences of a presence of the dead are hallucinations, he tells stories of people, miles apart, that experience the same presence at the same time either in waking life or in dreams. These defy the definitions of hallucination and bring into focus the real possibility of after-death communication. In Fenwick's opinion, we cannot so easily dismiss hallucinations that comfort as simply having a psychological cause, which opens the whole world of ghosts and mediumship.

2. *The Mothers of Chico Xavier* is a major motion picture released in Brazil in April 2011. The film tells the poignant stories of three mothers who experience a psychological hell in relationship to their children (two of whom die unexpectedly). These mothers are comforted by hearing from their deceased children through one of Brazil's finest mediums, Chico Xavier. The story begins with Ruth's teenage son facing problems with drugs; Elisa, who is attempting to compensate for the absence of her

husband by giving full attention to their son Theo; and Lara, a teacher who faces the dilemma of an unplanned pregnancy. Toward the end of the film, the deeply disturbed women are together in one room as Chico passes on messages to them that clearly identify markers (like particular pet names) of each child that could be recognized only by the parents of the children.

How did this fine medium know what to say to these mothers? From the age of four, Chico was able to see the spirits of the dead and communicate with them. He did this to bring comfort to many people who came to him personally. He also channeled more than 400 books, many of which are translated into English, which describe in detail life after death and the ways spirits communicate with the living. The books he channeled were complete as written, with no editing needed. They purportedly came directly from highly articulate spirits using Chico's arm as the tool for writing and communicating what they had learned from "the other side of the veil."

At the end of the film, each woman has clearly reclaimed inner peace and said good-bye to the most terrible part of her disturbance. Each knows, through the personal message given by Chico, that her child is at peace and carries no blame, only love for the parents. The viewer of the film leaves the movie theater more able to understand how a good medium can help a grieving person move on in life, after accepting an agonizing loss.

This film was a box office hit in Brazil, making history, as more people attended this movie than any other prior film. Is this a signal that we are more ready to consider that mediums might play a significant role in the lives of those reaching for resolution of their grieving?

3. **Forty years ago** in 1971, I was seven-and-a-half-months pregnant, preparing for natural childbirth, when I was told of my mother's unexpected sudden death. Naturally, it threw me into profound grief. I had expected her to come to be with me and help me after the birth. How could this have happened to her?

I flew across country with my husband to my family home in Vermont. Our spiritual teacher, Suzuki Roshi, flew in to officiate at the funeral ceremony. I went to the funeral parlor to see the body, to make it real, somehow. My siblings and their spouses and my husband and I sat together with Suzuki and prayed for her liberation, several times, over three days, following Buddhist tradition. Still I had deep questions: "Why now?" "Where is she?" I was unresolved: I never got to say good-bye.

Six weeks later, the delivery date my doctor had given me came and went. Days went by as my husband and I became more and more anxious. I was ten days late, when I finally said to myself one late afternoon, "I have to make a decision." I went out to the garden and lay in a hammock to confront the questions "How am I holding up the birthing? Am I resisting?" The answer sprang from my inner heart: "You need to put aside the questions you have about your mother's death for now, and then return to them after the birth." I then resolved, "OK. I'll be here just for childbirth and the baby. Then, in six weeks, I'll go to the best medium I know, and ask her my questions." Within minutes, the contractions began and my precious baby was born, naturally, within hours at French Hospital, as planned.

Keeping the contract I had made with my own heart, I went to see Anne Armstrong six weeks later. (At that time Anne lived in the suburbs of Sacramento, California with her husband, Jim, a highly respected engineer. He was not only accepting of his wife's unusual abilities, but came to later teach alongside of her, helping structure their presentations, so that others could learn how to develop the resources of their own intuitive abilities at the famed Esalen Institute.)

But the day I first met Anne in 1971, she was poised on the frontier, doing a job that carried little credibility in the mainstream. She had surrendered to using her psychic abilities to counsel others only after a terrible history of migraine headaches, which stopped after hypnotherapy helped her acknowledge her mission in life. Anne's home was simple and well lit. Children played across the street at the local elementary school playground. Anne was kind and gentle and dressed as any suburbanite might dress in a comfortable pantsuit. There were no crystal balls or incense, none of the accoutrements of gypsies. She invited me to simply sit together quietly; then Anne closed her eyes and, within a minute or two, seemed to "locate" my mother. She told me:

> *I see her washing her face in a stream, refreshing herself, as one would after a long, hot hike carrying a backpack. She is happy and relieved to be away from the*

stresses and burdens of her life on earth. She is beaming and full of love. She is acting
as if she has been liberated. She feels free!

Instantly, I felt a river of relief moving swiftly through my whole body, a peace and relaxation I had not had for the three months it had been since her passing.

Anne then transmitted messages from my mother to me in just the kind of language my mother would have used, as if she was speaking directly to me. It was such a comfort to hear that wherever my mother was, she still loved me and wanted my life to be happy and good.

I came away from that session saying to myself, "I don't have the ability to understand exactly where Mom is, but that's ok. She is somehow eternally present, in some location, loving me. I get it."

Since then, I have periodically had a strong sense of her presence at times, confirming what Anne transmitted to me back in 1971. I have also had waves of grief at specific times: a birthday, Christmas, the anniversary of her passing, a thought about wishing she was there to behold the beauty of my son. These would come and go naturally during a situation—uncomfortable, sometimes inconvenient, but never more than that. I never had a lasting depression that was rooted in her passing. I was able to give myself fully to nurturing the life of my baby, and get on with life.

4. In 2001, I was invited to visit **a Spiritist Center in Sao Paulo, Brazil**. On the first evening of the visit, I was ushered in to meet the lead teacher of the center, Dona Marta. She greeted me with great presence and a twinkle in her eye: all 5 feet 4 inches of her (in high heels). She asked, "Do you know anyone who has died?" I replied, "Both my parents." She said in Portuguese, "Write down their names on separate pieces of paper, and the date of each one's passing." I did, and handed her the slips of paper. She put them in a neat pile of papers on a table.

Next, I noticed her greeting people as they came in the door, inviting them to write down names, receiving more slips of paper, stacking them carefully in discrete piles. Soon, she had at least 50 names in 8 piles.

For the scheduled evening event, a séance, we went, along with a hundred others, into a large hall and sat in chairs facing a large table around which sat 8 mediums. There were no religious symbols on the walls, no incense, no crystal balls. Each medium had been given his or her own separate pile of names by Dona Marta, who had assigned them through the help of her own inner guidance. Dona Marta was there, dressed in a business suit; the other mediums had come in after their day's work and were also dressed in their street clothes. A prayer was said by one of the mediums to invoke the presence of Christ consciousness and the blessing of beings who represent Light and Love. The audience, seeking consoling messages from those who had passed on, was asked to sit quietly.

For the next 45 minutes, the mediums would pick up a piece of paper from their stack, look at it, close their eyes, and then begin writing a message quickly on a larger piece of paper. After that message was complete, they would go to the next until all the small papers had been addressed. Alongside this amazing display, as the mediums were ostensibly in contact with the dead in an orderly fashion, they showed no waves of emotion, just the neutrality one would expect of court stenographers. Finally names were read out by an assistant, who then gave the written messages to those present who had made requests for contact. On receiving messages, many cried.

I was thrilled to get a response from my father through Dona Marta. He said, "Your mother and I are together. We have resolved the problems that led to our separation. We are so sorry you were burdened by these problems. We are doing everything we can now to back you up and help you."

No one—not Dona Marta, not my host–knew that my parents had separated when I was sixteen years old. No one knew of the burdens I had carried because of the problems they had when I was growing up. How was it that Dona Marta, an elderly lady in Brazil, had written this the first night she met me? Could she be making it up? How could she be giving me what I most wanted to hear? I had questions, but just as I experienced with Anne Armstrong, something deep within me relaxed, as if I felt wings of light above me, giving me loving direction and help.

I was also impressed by the fact that none of the mediums charged money or was reimbursed for their time. They feel, "That which is given

RESOURCES FOR EXTRAORDINARY HEALING

for free to us should be given to others for free." This means that they see their mediumship as a God-given gift, and they need to give that gift to others in order to empower them and to help them on their ways.

Mediumship has been researched in many countries, following in the footsteps of such respectable, well-known psychologists as C. G. Jung and William James. James began his study more than 110 years ago and served as president of the American Society for Psychical Research. Great strides have been made in ascertaining the difference between a fake medium and a valid medium, as well as discerning which mediums are honest and psychologically balanced. As in any profession, one has to realize that not all mediums are great, just like not all medical doctors are great. Just because one has a certification does not mean that one is good. As with selecting a physician, it is always wise to learn who comes highly recommended before seeking out a consultation with a medium.

5. **An old friend of mine, I'll call "Betsy,"** has decided not to see a medium, even though she faces a situation that a medium could resolve. Betsy says, "I just don't want them playing with my head." Her 23-year-old brother "Rick," a student at an Ivy League college, was the lover of a famous person in the art scene, but that man had turned cold towards him. One summer weekend, Rick went home to be with his family at their beach house. He seemed to be in fine spirits and warmly connected with Betsy, his other siblings, and his parents. After dinner, he told his mother he was going "out for fresh air," but hours later he had not returned. The family was concerned. They wondered "Had he gone back to his college to be with friends? Had he taken recreational drugs and become disoriented?"

The next day the family was on the phone to his friends, but there was no sign of Rick. No one had seen him. Finally, the police were called in, and a short time later his clothes were found next to the water's edge. But, there was no sign of his body. The family questioned: *"What happened to him? Had he swum out to sea? Been eaten by a shark? Had he been murdered by an agent of his famous lover? Did he want to disappear and start a new life without any ties, or his history with his lover? If it was a suicide, why hadn't he written a suicide note? Is it possible he had drunk more alcohol and had some pot, or another drug, then simply drowned as a result of hypothermia? What might he want to communicate to his family?"*

These are all questions a good medium could answer, but Betsy wanted no part in that. "I've made my peace," she says, "I don't want to dig it all up again. Who knows what happened?...There was a time a few years ago when our mother died and we wondered if Rick would show up for part of the estate. We never heard from him. So, I believe he died in the ocean. I just leave it at that."

I respect Betsy's choice. This must have been a traumatic experience for her and her whole family. How could she really know if what the medium said was correct? She didn't want to run the risk of her mind being played with. That's okay. It's important that we keep our heads. Some want to explore; others say no. After all, it is a territory that still represents the vast unknown to most people and is just plain too weird for others.

Questions about the dynamics of mediumship are currently being researched by finely trained people who are asking: Do mediums contact the dead? Or, do they contact a repository in the "universal mind" where all information resides? As mediums give readings about the dead, how much are they actually reading the mind of the person in front of them or that person's companion? How much are they feeding the client what that person wants to hear? While researchers like Julie Bieschel, PhD, of Windbridge Institute delve into these questions, some of the best mediums are available during weekends in places like the Omega Institute in Rhinebeck, New York, giving readings and teaching others how to delve into the resources of their own intuitive abilities.

CHAPTER ELEVEN
THE SAFE HOME MODEL

[In the field of mental health]...there exists a suffocating sprawl of technical knowledge that none of us can comprehend or assimilate. Trying to repair people as if they were faulty machines adds to their suffering because the scientific approach objectifies and alienates. Alienation and estrangement is the disease, more of the same is not going to help.

The most important factors in healing via psychotherapy are truth, meaning, and attention to particulars rather than explanations, theories and generalizations. We all long for attentiveness from others. The essence of abuse (physical, mental, sexual) is not being taken seriously. Many of us will remember fondly forever the one who listened to us for the first time.

...R. D. Laing wrote about his approach to patients: "Therapy requires, on my part, the development of rapport, of reciprocal communication that moves toward communion. My attempts to address myself with skillful means to the specifics of the other's difficulties calls on all the resources of my repertoire of learned and acquired techniques of effectiveness-through-harmlessness." In communion no one dominates, no one submits; no one leads, no one follows. There is surrender, but not to each other: to the dance, to the music, to the situation. We have to learn how to be with each other, how to hang out, how to enjoy conviviality, co-presence."

Harmlessness implies not doing anything to the other. The Hippocratic Oath (2,500 years ago) includes the following: "I will prescribe regimen for the good of my patients according to my ability and my judgment

*and never to harm anyone"...Forming a relationship takes time. Loving
someone is time-consuming work. It's not efficient. When I attend to
you, I give my life to you, I live my life with you.*

—Andrew Feldmar, 2001

*"If you treat people with dignity and respect and want to understand
what's going on, want to get in their shoes, you can do it."*

–Loren Mosher, MD

*"In every instance, people treated psycho-socially did as well or better
than those treated conventionally."*

–Robert Whitaker, investigative journalist

It has become evident that providing a safe place is one of the most
effective means of facilitating healing. In a "safe house" a person in crisis
can be attended to by empathic companions who share food and shelter
and cooperate in household maintenance duties. The support team can
assist the person in crisis to find meaning in their experience, gain clarity
regarding what overwhelmed them in the first place, confront and resolve
the stressful situation he/she did not have the skills to confront, and begin
to take steps towards a more positive future.

The effectiveness and economy of these safe houses was shown in the
Soteria House in the 1970s—Soteria was a pilot program sponsored by
the National Institute of Mental Health (NIMH) through Loren Mosher,
MD (Mosher, 1999; Mosher and Burti, 1994; Mosher, Hendrix, and
Fort, 2004). The original Soteria House project (1) had the same or better
recovery outcomes than conventional hospitalization with medication, (2)
had substantially better recovery outcomes than conventional treatment
in longer-term outcome studies, and (3) demonstrated a cost savings of
43% over conventional treatment in longer-term cost-comparison studies.
A succinct description of the saga of Soteria and the neglect of it as an
effective model is included in Robert Whitaker's book *Mad in America.*

The history of compassionate care in residential treatment in the
USA began with Gould Farm almost a century ago and has been carried

on by residential facilities that respect the individuals receiving care and make every attempt to empower them. However, many of these residences, unlike Soteria, often consider psychiatric medication to be a central part of treatment.

The efficacy of Soteria-type residences has been demonstrated more recently in diverse programs in Finland and Sweden, as reported by Robert Whitaker (2010) in *Anatomy of an Epidemic*, and documented in film by Daniel Mackler in *Healing Homes* (2011). Safe homes whose professional staff delay the use of medication, or avoid it altogether, can facilitate better long-term outcomes than the doctors and therapists who immediately and persistently rely on psychiatric medication for treating those with serious mental illness.

In the safe homes modeled after Soteria, psychiatrists are available for monitoring medication, as needed. However, they use medication with caution; it is not the first step in treatment. Rather the preference is to wait and see if the person in crisis can safely get along without the medication. In some cases, short-term medication is used, especially to support adequate sleep, but lifelong usage of any drug is not considered the most advantageous route to health.

Being off medication, patients can be more present with their feelings; can better process them; and can go through their sadness, anger, and confusion rather than cover up these feelings, which can blunt access to intuition as well as aliveness. A true healing can then take place.

In the United States there are homes set up throughout the country to offer sanctuary to those in "psychotic" (or extreme) states. These programs differ in their attitudes toward psychiatric medications. Some consider it part of stabilizing patients, and others try to avoid all psychiatric medications. The Soteria model is cautious in use of psychiatric medication.

A safe house in Anchorage, Alaska uses only the model of a group home and is modeled after Soteria House. It is specific to Alaskans but provides another model that collaborates with city, state and federal government agencies that can help with funding, making it available to those who could not otherwise afford it. Soteria-Alaska hopes to become a model for future similar home-like and flexible environments both in and outside Alaska.

Soteria-type homes, like the one in Alaska, have been replicated in several countries in Europe, although these homes may now be making more use of psychiatric medication—a departure from the original model.

Soteria-Alaska

[The following section paraphrases "Soteria-Alaska: An Alternative to Hospitalization for People Diagnosed with Serious Mental Illness—Business Plan for Start Up and Sustainability," Submitted to the Alaska Mental Health Trust for FY 2008 and FY 2009] http://soteria-alaska.com/Grants/FY06-07PreDev/SoteriaSept06BizPlan.pdf (accessed June 2, 2011).

Soteria-Alaska is an alternative to psychiatric hospitalization for adults newly diagnosed with serious mental illness. It differs from conventional treatment in that it uses a psychosocial approach and incorporates alternative modalities such as meditation, yoga, music, and traditional native methods. Treatment is dependent on a unique environment that is homelike, self-directed, flexible, and in the community. Residents can continue with life activities as is appropriate and possible. Soteria House staff helps residents maintain community roles such as worker, student, spouse, and family member. Family members are welcome to visit at any time. Although residents may take certain types of medication, the treatment modality rests primarily in the environment and personal relationships and supports, which are fostered there. Using this approach, the trajectory of chronic disease, disability and costly hospitalizations can be averted for many people.

Mission: Soteria-Alaska provides a safe, non-coercive, home-like environment where people in Alaska who are diagnosed with serious mental illness recover from acute and long-term symptoms and avert the trajectory of chronic disability and poverty. Patients have choice about medication. It is an evidence-based, cost-effective alternative to hospitalization that is responsive to individual needs, desires and cultural values.

It is useful to distill its mission into the following six values:

- *Non-coercion*
- *Recovery-orientation*
- *Individual choice*
- *Easy access to appealing behavioral health services*
- *Informed self-determination*
- *Flexibility*

Vision: Alaskans diagnosed with serious mental illness have access to a full range of environments and services that change their trajectory from one of chronic disability to health and community inclusion. Soteria-Alaska will be one piece of the behavioral health system that supports this vision.

Soteria-Alaska is staffed by paraprofessional residential advisors who are supervised by an independently licensed clinician and a medical director.

Evidence Based: Soteria-Alaska, Inc. follows the principles established by Dr. Loren Mosher in the Soteria House project he developed in California in 1971 for newly diagnosed patients (Mosher, Hendrix, and Fort, 2004). That project and similar projects around the world have been the subject of rigorous scientific research and qualitative study. Much has been learned about the positive effects of implementing an intervention that primarily relies on psychosocial principles and interpersonal relationships.

Projected Outcomes: Soteria-Alaska projects that it will (1) serve approximately 40 individuals per year, (2) have a daily rate that is about one-third of the cost of conventional hospitalization, (3) provide longer-term residential treatment than is currently available in the hospital at approximately the same cost, (4) have recovery rates of 40-70% for adults who receive or would receive a diagnosis of serious mental illness, and (5) demonstrate a cost savings of 43% over the lifetime of an individual.

There has been evidence for some time that people recover from even the most serious of mental illnesses, yet we continue to provide services as if we believe people do not recover (Anthony, 2001).

At least ten world studies demonstrate that people with even the most serious of mental illnesses recover (Harding, 2001). 23-45% of people with schizophrenia are considered fully recovered (Siebert, 1999). One predictor of nonrecovery is living in a wealthy country such as the US (Whitaker, 2002). Some things associated with higher rates of recovery include:

- *an expectation that people will recover,*
- *a top-down-system vision that people are likely to recover, rather than a vision of maintaining people in the community on medication,*
- *vocational rehabilitation (Harding, 1996).*

Affluent countries that tend to rely primarily on medication maintenance have been found to have poorer recovery outcomes than countries that are less affluent and that incorporate other non-medicine alternatives (Whitaker, 2002). This information is rarely offered to people who are newly diagnosed with mental illness, thus preventing them from making an *informed choice*.

The Soteria Environment: Soteria-Alaska is a "home-like" facility where residents have their own rooms and privacy. In addition, there are community spaces, including a kitchen, dining room and living room. The facility has a maximum capacity of eight residents. Based on research on the original Soteria and its second generation, the projected length of stay is 1-4 months.

The residents, staff members and volunteers maintain the operations of the house together. Daily decisions and the flow of daily life within the community are determined by the residents. The role of the staff is to create a safe environment where residents are safe, feel safe, and can conduct their daily life activities while recovering from their acute symptoms. (See Appendix A for guidelines for staff.) Residents are encouraged to help each other in whatever ways they can.

Soteria-Alaska makes alternative therapies including massage, physical therapy, diet and other modalities available to residents. The safe, supportive healing environment is the primary care. Residents choose from a variety of tools and design their own program with guidance and support of staff under the supervision of a psychiatrist and another mental health professional.

Staffing: Soteria-Alaska follows the guidelines that were established by Loren Mosher, MD and that are followed by successful Soteria replications. One essential element related to the effectiveness of Soteria is the utilization of paraprofessional staff members who are trained in the philosophy, values and techniques of Soteria, but who do not come with preconceived notions that mental illness must be a chronic and lifelong disabling condition. Staff has clinical oversight by a masters-level clinician and psychiatrist.

The following are Soteria staff positions: (1) program/house director, (2) residential assistants, (3) administrative assistant, (4) medical director/psychiatrist, (5) expert consultants and contract workers, (6) volunteers and trainees.

In Keeping with Federal and State Government: The federal government and the entire country are focused on ways to transform behavioral health systems so that they are effective. Soteria is one example of a service that demonstrates effectiveness in recovery with people who have symptoms of serious mental illness. If we are to transform our system, we need to incorporate effective services, consumer choice and blend funding streams.

The President's New Freedom Commission on Mental Health: In 2003, the President's New Freedom Commission identified examples of emerging best practices and promising practices in the area of recovery and resilience. These include consumer/peer- or family-provided or -operated services (that are provided or owned by qualified recipients or family members of recipients of services), employment services, and housing. Soteria fulfills several of the characteristics identified by the Commission. It is evidence-based, it involves peer-provided services, and it incorporates housing and employment.

Myers v. Alaska Psychiatric Institute: The Alaskan Supreme Court found (June 30, 2006) Alaska statutes pertaining to the involuntary administration of psychotropic drugs to be unconstitutional (1) for failure to require proof that it is in the best interests of the person and (2) when there are less restrictive alternatives. To fulfill the Supreme Court's decision, the courts must review the benefits and negative effects and explore the possible use of alternatives prior to forcing one to take psychiatric medication. Soteria-Alaska is one such evidence-based alternative to hospitalization. It is a timely addition to the system.

Soteria in Europe

From http://www.soteria.hu/index.php?lang=en&page_id=2 (accessed on June 2, 2011)

Soteria Bern in Switzerland celebrated its 25th year of operation in 2009. Today, noncoercive, minimal-drugging family approaches to schizophrenia treatment are flourishing in two Scandinavian countries.

Luc Ciompi, MD, a professor of social psychiatry in Bern, Switzerland, is primarily responsible for Soteria's renaissance. Operating since 1984, Soteria Bern has replicated the original Soteria study findings. That is, roughly two-thirds of newly diagnosed persons with schizophrenia recover with little or no drug treatment in 2 to 12 weeks (Aebi et al., 1993; Ciompi, 1997; Ciompi et al., 1992a, b, 1993, 2004). As original Soteria Project papers diffused to Europe and Ciompi began to publish his results, a number of similar projects were developed. At an October 1997 meeting held in Bern, a Soteria Association was formed, headed by Professor Weil and Machleidt of the Hanover University Medical Faculty. Soteria lives, and thrives (admittedly as variations on the original theme) in Europe (http://www.moshersoteria.com/soteri.htm)

In 1995, Andrew Feldmar and Dr. Éva Csom established the Hungarian Soteria Foundation in Budapest. Their original aim was to establish a "crisis house" in Hungary similar to the original Soteria House in San Francisco. However, because of the lack of community-based mental health services in Hungary, Soteria steered itself to provide such services and furthermore address Hungarian mental health reform. In 2001, their Foundation launched Hungary's first drop-in mental health center, the "Kilátó Clubhouse," in the third district of Budapest. More recently, in early 2006, they opened "Materia Clubhouse" in Budapest's thirteenth district.

Their clubhouses run services that enable users to live in an environment of choice, avoiding the risk of being labeled or excluded from the local community. In other words, users may avoid living their lives in large, closed, secluded institutions and transition safely to mainstream life. In addition to the clubhouses, virtually every service introduced by Soteria–including family counseling, legal advocacy efforts, and employment training–has been pioneering within the largely institutionally-based Hungarian mental health system. As of now, Hungary's social welfare system still does not provide mental health users with crisis intervention facilities or other alternative solutions to hospitalization.

Recent Soteria projects in Europe available to view on the Internet:

Soteria Bern (Switzerland): http://www.soteria.ch
Soteria Zwiefalten (Germany):
http://www.zfp-web.de/K3/html/artikel.
php3?path=0:3:32:138&a_id=83
Toll-haus project (Germany): http://www.toll-haus.de/index.html
Soteria Frankfurt an der Oder (Germany): http://www.lunaticpride.
de/SOTERIA.HTM
Soteria Budapest (Hungary): www.soteria.hu

Residential Facilities: ARTA

(from www.ARTAusa.org/benefits.html; accessed on June 14, 2011)

While varying in style, residential facilities share the following core practices, each practice proven to promote healing that is more likely to be sustained:

- *Every resident is seen as a unique individual with strengths and weaknesses (like the rest of us) and is accepted and appreciated for who they are, rather than being viewed as a "case" or "a patient."*
- *Growth occurs in small steps, the product of individualized goals. A major goal of all residential facilities is to develop a wide range of habits of self-care, from personal hygiene and taking meds to resting and asking for help.*
- *A high level of supportive structure is built into daily life. All residential facilities help residents establish normal, stabilizing routines for day and night.*
- *Residents take responsibility for their behavior since it affects others.*
- *Residents contribute to the community in some way, which boosts self-esteem.*
- *Residents support one another, forming relationships.*
- *Quality of life is stressed, which includes meaningful activity and nurturing relationships.*

Taken together and working synergistically, these practices create a powerful therapeutic community—a healing environment that only exists in a residential setting. The alternatives to residential care often don't work.

Residential psychiatric care is a positive alternative to the less productive route that typically starts with a hospital stay. After managing the acute crisis that triggers the admission, hospitals usually do not offer patients enough structure, despite the fact that the majority of people with serious psychiatric disorders do best with a high degree of structure. Equally important, the typical psychiatric hospital stay is not long enough for a patient to develop the necessary skills and habits to function well.

It is well documented that, following discharge from the hospital, many ex-patients do not take advantage of outpatient mental health services, tending to withdraw from these services over time. Nor do the services, themselves, provide the level of structure and protection necessary for a person on the "outside."

Once discharged, the person typically returns to an isolated lifestyle, either at home, in the community, or on the street. While social isolation may feel comfortable and familiar, it is a negative force that not only impedes the person's growth toward mental health, but often sends them sliding backwards.

For many people, there is also the issue of medication. Chances are, the patient was discharged from the hospital when they were not yet willing or not yet able (or both) to take their medication regularly. But outpatient services often do not effectively monitor the taking of medication, certainly not over the long haul. Now add the fact that former patients engage less and less with these services over time—and monitoring becomes non-existent.

When a person returns home from a psychiatric hospitalization, the burden of responsibility often falls on the family to provide daily structure and to monitor the taking of medication. Since there is often a history of stressful relations between the family and the troubled person over these very issues, the family's attempts to help can add to the strain on all involved.

In this isolated and almost treatment-free state, the person's level of functioning deteriorates. Medication use grows sporadic and often stops. The stage is now set for another hospitalization. In all this time, little or no progress toward growth or recovery has taken place.

There is a high dollar cost for this unproductive cycle. But the human cost is huge—a person who could have quality of life and make a contribution to society is caught in a loop that prevents them from functioning better. . .or even flourishing.

Residential care offers you a way out of this unproductive cycle. It offers you proven resources and approaches for leading a better life.

The ARTA (American Residential Treatment Association) can help you make the best match. They are composed of more than 30 member facilities in the USA offering residential care to adults with serious mental challenges, including schizophrenia, bipolar disorder, depression, personality disorders, and disorders combined with substance abuse. They deliberately keep their membership low in order to have personal knowledge of each facility, which allows them to offer informed recommendations. They also give you professional guidance in choosing among the many options so you can make the best match.

On their website (ARTAusa.org), you will find general information on residential treatment. They also keep an updated Directory of Residential Facilities with links to individual websites offering detailed program information. There is a great range of approaches among their facilities. This is good—you have options. An example of one facility follows along with the compelling story of how it was founded.

CooperRiis (CR)
"Lisbeth & Don Cooper: Turning Adversity to Healing"
by Judy Heinrich
(Reprinted from the *Tryon Daily Bulletin*, November 2005)

In its November 15 issue, Woman's Day magazine *named Lisbeth Riis Cooper one of its four "Shining Stars of 2005." She was honored for creating, with her husband Don, the CooperRiis (CR) Healing Farm for the treatment of mental illness located in Mill Spring, North Carolina. Considering its 20 million readers and the many nominations* Woman's Day *received, Riis Cooper's selection is surely worthy of celebration. But most of us would gladly forego the award if we could also avoid the circumstances that led to it.*

An Expert by Necessity

If you're lucky, your family is among the 75 percent who will not have to deal on a first hand basis with serious mental illness—severe depression, bipolar disorder, schizophrenia, or other disorder—according to statistics from the National Alliance on Mental Illness (NAMI). Riis Cooper found herself on the other side of that equation when it became clear some 15 years ago that her daughter's behavior was more than typical teenage rebellion or mood swings. With that realization, Riis Cooper began a journey through a mental health system that seemed more like a maze than a path toward help and recovery.

At the time, Riis Cooper was an apparel industry executive and divorced mother of three living in New York City. "I was a mother like anyone else," she recalls. "I had no knowledge or background with mental illnesses or treatment."

Her family's need for mental health support unfortunately coincided with social, political and insurance changes that were greatly reducing the availability and quality of care.

"Because of funding cuts and new managed care plans, hospitals were offering fewer beds for the mentally ill. They would only accept patients on a crisis basis and then discharge them in a few days," Riis Cooper says. "You would think your child is getting help and then would come the call from the social workers which made your heart sink because they want to talk about a discharge plan. How can you discharge someone who needs help? The system depended on psychotherapy, drugs and halfway houses with locked doors, yelling and keepers with keys. Even a well person would start feeling paranoid."

While she was learning to navigate the mental health system and any other resources she could find, Riis Cooper's job also had her traveling regularly to the Carolinas to visit textile companies. During that time she married Don Cooper, an Atlanta-based financial executive. The couple moved to North Carolina in 1993. Meanwhile her daughter had reached adulthood and was living with periods of improvement and decline. She was in North Carolina when she suffered a severe episode in 1999, and the Coopers needed help.

"Everywhere I turned I was met with obstacles and the things you can't do," Riis Cooper remembers. "I found a facility that had beds but wouldn't accept my daughter because she was not already in the system. I couldn't apply for her; she had to do it in person. She was hospitalized but was supposed to go in person and complete an application so she could be in the system and then be on a waiting list—even though there were beds available. How do you make sense of that?"

From Crisis to Crusade

That Catch-22 situation turned out to be the final straw for Lisbeth: it's when she first approached Don about creating a treatment community. "If someone tells me I can't do something, that's when the fun starts," she says. "I'm not good about taking no for an answer because if there's a problem, it's an opportunity to find a solution." With an idea in mind for a healing community similar to ones they knew of in New England, the Coopers began looking for land in the fall of 1999. They *found and purchased 80 acres in Polk County near the intersection of Highways 9 and 108. The next step was to qualify for 501c3 nonprofit status with the IRS—which took 11 months to achieve. "We knew from Day One that we wanted this to be nonprofit," says Don. "We couldn't sleep at night knowing we were making money from other people's illness and sad circumstances."*

The first contribution to the new nonprofit was the farm the Coopers bought. "It was my children's inheritance and our legacy," says Lisbeth. "Many years ago I made myself a promise that when I die, I don't want to have any regrets in life and I don't want to leave a lot of money for people to fight over. If I have extra money, I want to share it now and be part of the joy and benefit gained by it."

Convincing others to lend financial support wasn't always easy. Don and Lisbeth reached out to contacts they'd made throughout their careers as well as to individuals and foundations in the Carolinas. "We had never done anything like this before individually or together and there were times we wondered if we could really see it through," says Lisbeth. "But then we'd remember all the people who had already supported us and realized we couldn't let them down either. We made a pact to tell at least two more people every day about our mission—people at the bank, in the supermarket, wherever we could find an audience. It became our daily affirmation and kept the adrenaline flowing: 'We can do this.'"

In the end, the Coopers were able to raise $10 million through private donations. The fundraising was just part of a three-year whirlwind of permits, design, setbacks, construction, learning and excitement that culminated in the June 2003 opening of "CooperRiis, A Healing Farm Community".

To create the campus, the CooperRiis team added to an existing arts-and-craft style home that became the farm's 12,000 square foot Main House, with administrative offices, a dining hall, a living room, meeting areas, and a state-of-the-art commercial kitchen and bakery. Three 10,000-square-foot residential lodges mirror the architecture of the Main House, and each provides housing for 12 residents and has recreation areas. A dilapidated 5,000-square-foot hay-and-storage building was restored to become the Arts & Crafts Barn with a fully equipped shop for woodwork, arts, crafts and music. There are five acres under cultivation and two large greenhouses tended by residents who grow organic vegetables and flowers. A restored horse barn, animal pastures, chicken coop, tennis court and lake round out the pastoral setting.

"We have a certain standard here and we designed this place to be special," Lisbeth explains. "If you put people in nice surroundings, they live up to the expectations. We want our residents to feel special and, so far, they haven't let us down."

The CooperRiis Vision

The CooperRiis goal is to support residents in mind, body and spirit through a combination of community setting and strong clinical programming. The entire experience is overseen by the executive director team of Virgil and Lis Stucker, respected mental health professionals who met, lived and raised their children at the Gould Farm in Massachusetts, one of the community models CooperRiis has followed. Dr. Sharon Young leads the CooperRiis Enhanced Recovery Program. Forty-eight full- and part-time staff and eight part- and full-time volunteers serve the needs of 36 community residents. All residents perform some job at CooperRiis as part of the recovery process.

"All residents start work on the farm, since those jobs are lower-skill, but they also provide a very healing experience," says Lisbeth. "When they feel better, they can ask to work in the kitchen, in housekeeping, on the maintenance crew or with the animals. Our current residents also produce a CR [CooperRiis] television show and a community newspaper."

"Our residents are some of the smartest, most talented and interesting people you would ever meet," says Don. "A lot of them haven't been encouraged to show that previously. It is so punishing to go out and not meet people's expectations so they often just stay home. Here everyone is encouraged to re-engage and it brings out such talent."

Most residents stay at the farm for six to nine months and then enter the graduate program, living off-campus in a group home or apartment, with a level of staff support depending on need.

"The objective is for everyone in the graduate program to have developed enough capability and stability to work 30 hours a week, with 'work' being going back to

college, volunteering or a paying job," Don explains. "The intention is that from the CooperRiis experience, graduates will move back into society but with support—not just turned out as happens with hospitals."

With the quality of clinical care and staff support that CooperRiis provides, the community is not an inexpensive proposition. Each resident is responsible for their first two months at the full rate of $6,500 per month. "That's not covered by insurance, so it's an out-of-pocket expense for the residents and their families," says Don. "Some can simply pay it, while others may take out a home equity loan or put it on a charge card. It's an amount that allows us to break even on our expenses while also indicating the individual's commitment to the process." After the initial two months, CooperRiis works with residents and their families to provide a range of scholarships based on need. "We have yet to fail," Don says. "We have been able every time to do what was required to support the resident."

Thus far CooperRiis has served 130 people from 27 states. The community doesn't plan to expand beyond 36 residents, but the potential for the graduate program is unlimited. CooperRiis uses a sophisticated management information system to track program statistics and measure the progress of residents and graduates. Successful practices are shared with others who are already in the mental health field or who are interested in creating a similar setting to serve the mentally ill in their own areas.

We hear from parents, especially after the Woman's Day award, asking "How did you do it? How did you start?" says Lisbeth. "We know that CooperRiis is making a difference and my dream is that, in my lifetime, I will see something like a CooperRiis in every state. We don't have the ability to go out and build another one but we are here to consult with others who have the desire."

Toward that end, the CooperRiis leadership team dedicates time to sharing their experience, knowledge and hard-won expertise with other mental health facilities, industry organizations and parent groups. Don talks about financials and philanthropy, Virgil about programs, and Lisbeth about a parent's perspective. A "how-to manual" is another goal of the Coopers for helping others start similar programs.

Part of the Larger Community

The Coopers say they've been very gratified by the response of their Polk County neighbors.

"We've been terribly blessed with the welcome we've gotten from the community," Lisbeth says. *"The fire department and police department have been wonderful both in helping us design our facility for safety and in coming out to do courses. Our residents have been accepted in the community, with many working for local organization as volunteers or at paying jobs."*

"Sometimes society has a stigma against mental illness," Don adds, *"with people being afraid and shying away from contact. But that hasn't been our experience here. We are so pleased that we located in this area."*

"A person with mental illness is not so different from you and me," says Lisbeth. "If you come to our dining room, you wouldn't be able to tell the residents from the staff. Dr. Sharon uses the analogy that if a person loses a leg, it doesn't change who they are inside: they just have to learn to do things differently. Mental illness is the same way—it's biological. Those affected by it are still the same wonderful people inside. Here we are teaching them ways to do things differently, to manage their symptoms and cope with their own needs so they can have self-esteem and be part of society. It's what we all want: to be accepted for who we are and be with people who care about us."

The Foundation for Excellence in Mental Health Care

In February 2011, Lisbeth Riis and Don Cooper gave a two million dollar grant as seed money to start the Foundation for Excellence in Mental Health Care, a not-for-profit charitable foundation. This donation will empower the Foundation to hire staff, sponsor future symposiums, and fund research. They want to support studies and pilot projects that aren't being funded today (e.g., using psychiatric medications in a selective, limited way.) This would contribute to a new paradigm of care that promotes long-term recovery and wellness.

The chairman of the board, Virgil Stucker, wrote in early 2011:

> *The tasks before us are awesome and will require many millions of dollars to accomplish. We are actively looking for other philanthropic partners, like Don and Lisbeth Cooper, who are willing to donate significant resources to help us make a difference.*

CHAPTER TWELVE
PEER SUPPORT, SPIRITUAL EXERCISES, AND WITHDRAWAL FROM PSYCHIATRIC DRUGS

June 23, 2011, the *New York Times* ran a cover article and showed an original two-minute video interview with Marsha Linehan, a respected psychologist and professor, who has practiced for years at McLean Psychiatric Hospital—associated with Harvard University. Dr. Linehan had decided to reveal her personal story, as well as the self-inflicted scars on her arms, legs and midriff that were testimony to her having been diagnosed and hospitalized more than once for attempted suicides. Her doctors had diagnosed her with borderline personality disorder earlier in life. It's not every psychologist who has the courage to reveal this kind of history.

The following days, hundreds of people wrote to her via the *New York Times*, thanking her for providing them hope, as they had been diagnosed with serious mental illnesses and had faced despair and a serious desire to suicide, just like she had.

Dr. Linehan, a specialist in behavioral therapy, seasons her treatment of patients with Christian contemplative exercises and mindfulness exercises from the Buddhist tradition. The source of her own healing had begun, she said, in an uplifting spiritual experience when she one day unexpectedly perceived her church filled with a gold light, which she associated with the Divine. That same day her mood shifted from abject despair to the joy of fully taking in, for the first time in her life, that "I love myself." Success in life skyrocketed from that day onward, and she was able to return to school, get her PhD, and effectively help others who were suicidal. She became a source of inspiration to other health professionals.

In a similar way, Ed Knight, PhD—who, like Linehan, was also hospitalized for psychiatric issues—found personal help for his serious mental illnesses in the practice of Zen Buddhist meditation and the study of diverse spiritual texts. Dr. Knight writes that he learned skills through meditation to "be with" the unusual extreme states he experienced and now copes with them along with a busy schedule. Currently his life is engaged with being a psychologist, teacher and researcher. He sometimes leads meditation retreats for those diagnosed with serious mental illness in order to transmit the skills he learned that helped him find freedom from being imprisoned by his mental imbalances.

He writes on his website (www.professored.com): "The path of 'zen dharma' recovery includes not only anxiety but 'hearing voices' and other hallucinations, mania, depression and addictions. The use of meditation for anxiety recovery is a key to all mental health recovery. Anxiety in my experience is part of the experience driving all symptoms. Recovery from all of these conditions is not only possible but probable."

Neither Knight nor Linehan promotes a particular form of spirituality or religion. Instead, they have adopted spiritual exercises that can be easily performed by people of any religion, even agnostics. The exercises simply develop a different relationship with the mind, helping liberate individuals from the hold of imbalances. As in the Spiritist approach, all religious loyalties are respected, and the patient is the one to choose what spiritual or religious practices fit him or her.

Mental Patients Find Understanding in Therapy Led by Peers

Carey Goldberg, a staff reported for *The Boston Globe*, wrote about the power of peer support in June 8, 2007, at the time this kind of support was beginning to take up some of the slack brought on by mental health patients not having enough resources for help. Carey wrote:

> *Years ago, Jess Zaller came to the "Pathways Mental Health Program" as a day patient. In and out of institutions, he had fought mental illness since childhood. His life felt like a nightmare of chaos and despair.*
>
> *Zaller, 45, was back in a Pathways therapy group last week, but this time as a leader, listening carefully as members laid bare the pain of their fears and compulsions. When he delicately pointed the way, it was often in the first person, using his own hard lessons learned: "Our lives are at stake," he told members. "It takes a lot of courage to walk a path of recovery, and each one of us develops our own path."*
>
> *Massachusetts is beginning to develop a corps of people like Zaller who have been through the depths of schizophrenia, bipolar disorder, or depression, and recovered enough that they can help others with mental illness.*
>
> *Such comradely aid has long been exchanged informally, or scattershot at mental health venues. But now the state has launched a new job category—certified peer specialist—meant to formalize these relationships and gradually, they hope, get peer counseling reimbursed routinely by insurers and Medicaid.*
>
> *"There's something about receiving support from someone who's gone through exactly what you're going through now that people find invaluable," said Michael O'Neill, the state's assistant commissioner for mental health services.*
>
> *A few handfuls of Massachusetts residents, including Zaller, have completed the eight-day training session and exams to be certified as "peer specialists"... The new field must work through many possible problems, from the potential for relapse among specialists to the potential for resistance from more traditional mental health staffers...*

147

Massachusetts is redesigning its mental health system to be more user-friendly, O'Neill said, and "peer support is a fundamental element of that redesigned system." In the coming months, Massachusetts will be setting up six regional centers where peer specialists will work with clients and support each other in their fledgling vocation, O'Neill said.

The concept has taken off in 30 states. In half a dozen, Medicaid, the public insurance program for the poor and chronically ill, pays for the services, said Paolo del Vecchio, associate director for consumer affairs at the federal government's Center for Mental Health Services.

"Over the past five years, we've really seen the development of a new mental health profession emerging," he said. The growth of the peer specialist profession comes against the backdrop of a sweeping national shift toward greater optimism that those in dire condition may improve or recover, and toward giving people with mental illness more control over the help they get. People with mental illness are not passive patients, the thinking goes; they can help themselves and as they get better, they can help others.

In their work, peer specialists are expected to share their stories of recovery when relevant to their clients. They may have learned skills worth sharing, or simply inspire hope by being much better than they once were.

The work goes beyond a typical speaker at a 12-step meeting. It can include helping a patient in a psychiatric hospital make the shift back to living at home, or supporting an emergency room patient in crisis. A specialist might remind a team of clinicians that their patient is in a kind of hell, or take a lonely client out for pizza.

Early research, which is just beginning to accumulate, suggests that peer specialists may be particularly useful with patients who would normally resist help from the mental health system, said Larry Davidson, a Yale professor who conducts studies on peer specialists.

People with mental illness sometimes feel disliked by the professional staff who treat them, he said; it appears that with peers, "they feel less disliked and more understood." Studies show that "people in recovery can provide services at least as well as people who don't have that experience," Davidson said. Hard data are being collected now on whether they offer "value-added," he said.

Anecdotal reports of successful work by peer specialists abound. In Georgia, which has 340, they have proven particularly useful in helping discharged state hospital patients build new lives at home, said Gwen Skinner, the state's top mental health official.

Though the new field is growing, resistance remains, Davidson and others said.

They worry that staff and clinicians without mental illness could feel threatened by the influx of newcomers whose experience with illness is considered an asset. Traditional staff could also worry about being replaced by peer specialists. Certified peer specialists are supposed to earn a typical mental health staff salary of $12 an hour to $15 an hour on an entry level, said Deborah Delman, executive director of M-Power, the Massachusetts mental health advocacy group that runs the peer training courses. But some peer workers who are not certified may earn less, she said.

After they are certified, Massachusetts peer specialists will continue to be overseen by The Transformation Center, a statewide training organization that is supposed to ensure they maintain ethical standards and continue their education.

The peer specialists also pose staffing issues. What if, for example, a peer specialist works with patients at a state hospital, then has a relapse and is re hospitalized there, then resumes the job? Boundaries and definitions may get fuzzy; confidentiality may become a concern.

Also, Davidson said, if supervisors view their patients as problems, then adding peer specialists to their staff is asking for more problems. The challenge, he said, is for them to shift to thinking about all people with mental illness as "having assets and strengths to help solve problems."

Judging by responses in Zaller's small therapy group in Taunton, some people with mental illness immediately see the benefits of being helped by a peer. "He's not looking at us through a book," said one group member, Diane Silvia. "He can relate to us, and we can relate to him."

Peer Support: Brazil vis a vis USA

> "Christ has no body now on earth but yours,
>   no hands but yours, no feet but yours.
> Yours are the eyes through which Christ's compassion
>   looks out on the world.
> Yours are the feet with which he is to go about doing good.
> And yours are the hands with which he is to bless us now."
>   —St. Teresa of Avila, 1580

One of the most impressive, pervasive and powerful components of Spiritist treatment both in the Spiritist Psychiatric Hospitals and in Spiritist Community Centers is "fraternal assistance." This occurs without any financial exchange when a Spiritist is in contact with someone who is upset by life problems. The "fraternal assistance" provides fellowship and empathic human connection from paraprofessionals who position themselves not as authorities but as equals. In Brazil, fraternal assistance might involve listening, providing moral support, sharing personally about what gives life purpose and meaning, and possibly reading an inspiring passage from a book together and discussing it. It is often set up by the Spiritist Psychiatric Hospitals and volunteers who come into the hospital at scheduled times to be with the patients. (There is some training given by the hospital staff to prepare volunteers for the task.) Often specific volunteers are suggested for specific patients, and a supportive relationship grows out of numerous meetings. This can evolve into an important part of the treatment for someone hospitalized, and the volunteers consider the time they spend to be a component of their own spiritual evolution. Keep in mind this type of fraternal support is a mainstay within the Spiritist Community Centers when mental health issues are taken care of outside of the hospitals.

In the United States, we call this "peer support," and it might incur a small fee or might be a free exchange. Generally, if people are participating in peer support, there is a sensitivity to the fact that the person receiving support may not have money to pay, so the support is made affordable and accessible. Peer support for those with serious mental illness in the USA can happen over the telephone, in homes, and in group meetings. It may happen if someone is hospitalized and a peer support person comes to visit; however, it is rare for any hospital to set up peer support in the hospital for patients as they do in Brazil. This hospital-sponsored peer support is something that we might bring into being that would support patients and the mental healthcare system, as well as volunteers who see value in doing charitable work.

Peer support may be the only kind of support that some people with serious mental illness ever receive. Even though there are many who could benefit from residential treatment, most of them will never be given the opportunity or be able to afford to stay in a safe home. These people may be hospitalized in a state hospital when they are in crisis and then be released within days to return to a life of isolation, often now suffering with the burden of a psychiatric diagnosis and the stigma that accompanies it, as well as adapting to the use of psychiatric medications. Peer-support people can assist them to overcome isolation and locate affordable psychosocial resources in their community that support their endeavors moving toward wellness and finding a job and home.

Another group—those who have been in residential treatment and then return to their communities in more stable condition—not only find support, but often *provide* support within peer counseling communities: classes in yoga, art therapy, music, etc.

Peer support can be especially useful in helping those who have decided to stop using psychiatric medications. This process—often lasting months—can be a physical and emotional ordeal, with patients feeling unable to sleep, delusional, fearful and apprehensive about fitting in. Peers can be available for emotional support to the person in withdrawal and possibly be part of a team support system, with health professionals monitoring the medical aspect of the withdrawal.

In Appendix C are two models of organizations that provide peer support and training in giving peer support in Massachusetts. Both organizations perceive recovery as a real possibility for those suffering from serious mental illnesses. Toward the end of this chapter are resources for support in withdrawing from psychiatric medication.

In comparing the Spiritist model of volunteerism and the peer support model, keep in mind that in the Spiritist model, volunteers may have had no life experience in being mentally ill, but they have developed empathy and stability and a desire to help others. They also have supervisors they can turn to for extra support as needed. In the peer support model in the USA, peers are in the process of recovering mental wellness after lived experience with severe mental challenges. Their supervision comes through facilitators support groups, led by more experienced facilitators.

Open Dialogue

Another model of quasi-peer support, in place since 1990, is Open Dialogue. This has been developed in western Lapland (in northern Finland, 60 miles south of the Arctic Circle), with offices in Tornio. Although this technique uses professionals (psychiatrists, psychologists and nurses) specially trained in family therapy, the therapists bring themselves into the lives of the patients and try to stay out of the hospitals, clinics and offices altogether and use medications only when requested, and then for only a brief period, and typically in minute dosages. Contact phones for Open Dialogue services are within the local hospital. Every attempt is made to respond immediately to the problem in the first 24 hours of being called in, then to meet each day for 2 weeks or more in the homes of the patients. Effort is made to be respectful, generate dialogue, and share openly. Emerging out of this open dialogue—where everyone is on the same level (thus like a peer)–solutions evolve.

This program has the best outcomes in the world for those with psychosis. From 1960 to 1980, before Open Dialogue, western Lapland had the highest incidence of schizophrenia in the world. Now that Open Dialogue is used, it has the lowest, two cases per 100,000 people.

Their perspective is that the dilemma that created the psychosis likely originated in the emotional life of the patient, call it a "tear within the fabric of relationships," rather than originating from a biochemical problem. Treatment therefore engages the patient's social networks in order to mend the tear and bring change and healing. The best outcomes are seen when no one is exposed to psychiatric medications. In a five-year follow-up study (Seikkula et al. 2006), 83% of patients had returned to their jobs or studies or were job-seeking after 5 years (thus not receiving government disability), and 77% did not have residual psychotic symptoms. Such outcomes led the Finnish National Research and Development Center for Welfare and Health to award a prize recognizing the Keropudas group for "the ongoing development of psychiatric care over a period of ten years." There is a solid base of research studies about Open Dialogue. Jaakko Seikkula, MD has been the most prolific author of these published articles.

Picture 2-3 therapists, dressed in normal street clothes, attending to a disturbed individual by visiting the person in his or her home, inviting open dialogue with all family members. If necessary, one therapist will also stay in the home overnight, to maintain more safety in a crisis situation. The therapists openly dialogue with each other about their concerns for the disturbed individual in front of the person and his/her family. (In fact, they are not allowed to talk about the person unless the open dialogue is taking place.) The therapists' modeling of open dialogue encourages others to also speak openly. The so-called patient, from the beginning, is taking an active role in his/her treatment and the fabric of relationships becomes the focus of attention. This kind of behavior diminishes the hierarchical system in most therapies and engenders more of an attitude of "we are all part of the same community and can help each other." This is well adapted to the semirural area of Tornio (a city of 70,000), served by Open Dialogue. It has been such a success that individuals in the community now also call when stress is heightened by anxiety or depression but there is not a full-blown crisis. These people receive the same level of care.

Because Finland provides free medical care through socialized medicine, the therapy is provided free to the family in need and paid for by federal government. The intensive program is still cost effective, as patients rarely come back for treatment, treatment is relatively brief, and patients return to the workforce and do not need welfare. (Remember that in the USA, recidivism is common, and those with schizophrenia continue to take drugs, usually do not return to the workforce, and most often are drawing on government welfare programs for living expenses.)

Because those with psychosis heal so quickly in the Open Dialogue system—before six months—their psychosis does not qualify them to be subsequently labeled with "schizophrenia." This diminishes the stigma of having "mental illness" for the patient and family. Staying out of the hospital also diminishes the stigma that comes from being an inpatient in a mental ward and facilitates patients' to consider their brief psychosis as a mental breakdown that is manageable.

Robert Whitaker (2010) wrote about Open Dialogue in *Anatomy of an Epidemic*. In 2011, Daniel Mackler, a psychotherapist, created a 75-minute documentary, *Open Dialogue: An Alternative, Finnish Approach to Healing Psychosis*, available through www.iraresoul.com.

Safely Withdrawing from Psychiatric Medication

This Resource book takes a rational approach to the use of psychiatric medications; it is neither anti-psychiatry nor anti-drug. However, we realize that psychiatric medications are not right for everyone, and given the success of such programs as Open Dialogue, we understand that there is some evidence that medications may in fact not be useful for some people. We advocate that patients be given the information they might need to make informed choices about the use of medications and the side-effects they might have in the short term and long term.

It is a good idea for anyone who is on psychiatric medications to become educated about the drugs' short- and long-term effects, in order to become conscious of the side effects and be able to make responsible choices in self-care. In this way, we can stay out of harm's way or extract ourselves responsibly from a situation that may at some time be destructive to our wellbeing.

Marcia Angell, MD, the former Editor-in-Chief of the *New England Journal of Medicine*, who now teaches ethics at Harvard University Medical School, reviewed several books on the shadow side of psychiatric drugs in the *New York Review of Books* in 2011. The titles are "The Epidemic of Mental Illness: Why?" (June 23) and "The Illusions of Psychiatry" (July 14). Angell refers to the accuracy of the research of Robert Whitaker, a medical journalist (with no commercial ties to the pharmaceutical companies or a clinical practice), in *Anatomy of an Epidemic* (2010), his book about the long-term effects of psychiatric medications. Angell concurs with Whitaker that psychiatric symptoms have reached epidemic proportions and tend to be used loosely to describe behavior or attitudes, making it easier for people to seek out medication and then be negatively impacted by it. For example, sometimes, quite automatically, people feel in need of medication when they are simply sad or stressed about a life situation and are not wanting to cope with the feelings associated with the situation.

This informal use of diagnostic categories and symptoms leads patients to ask for medications for depression or anxiety from their general practitioner, but the ease of getting medications can have terrible consequences when a patient "hears voices" or has unusual experiences, such as a loss of the ego-self. Naming that experience to an MD can result in a diagnosis of "psychosis," and the patient may be immediately given antipsychotic medication as well as a poor prognosis (e.g., "You will need to take this medication the rest of your life").

Think about it–if the voice the individual heard was positive (e.g., the voice of his higher self telling him not to commit a crime), it should not be considered a symptom of disease, nor should a loss of ego-self that brought the person into a greater communion with God or nature. Jesus Christ heard voices. Moses heard voices. Yes, it might initially be scary; however, hearing voices or dissolving the ego- self can be extremely positive, as it was for Christ and Moses. What is important is what messages are being received. Are they consistently positive messages that inspire one to take care of oneself and be charitable to others? Or, negative messages that inspire one to cause harm to oneself or others? We cannot begin to diagnose successfully unless we know the answer to these questions.

The pharmaceutical companies are financially benefiting as more and more medical doctors are prescribed medications in automatic response to a patient reporting a symptom or in response to requests from people who see advertisements on television encouraging them to feel better by taking pharmaceutical drugs. The downside for society, as Whitaker reports, is that since the time that pharmaceuticals were introduced we now have millions of people qualifying for Supplemental Security Income (SSI) or Social Security Disability Insurance (SSDI) because they are unable to work or function as a result of the long-term disabling effects of psychiatric drugs. Between 1987 and 2007 those qualifying for SSI and SSDI increased two-and-a-half times from 1 in 184 Americans to 1 in 76. For children during this same two decades, there has been a 35-fold increase.

Another alarm is sounded by psychiatrist Peter Breggin (2008), who writes about the "spellbinding effect" of psychiatric medications in his book *Medication Madness*. The spellbinding effect refers to the potential of a psychiatric drug to cause patients to behave badly. The effect can be so strong that it seems rational to a patient to steal, hurt others, or plan to suicide even when the patient would consider that unthinkable in a nondrugged state of consciousness. Fortunately there is an official diagnosis in the DSM-IV-TR for "Substance-Induced Mood Disorder." This neurological disorder is caused by drug-induced disruption of neurotransmitter systems and can be easily identified by measuring the amount of drugs in the bloodstream shortly after a crime is committed. Naming this disorder has allowed some patients to be excused from the worst kind of legal judgments (e.g., homicide) when the judge and jury came to understand that the patient was out of his mind as a result of the drugs causing neurological impairment—not insanity.

The legal system looks more sympathetically on people who become intoxicated against their will or without foreknowledge of the drug's potential to cause them to behave badly. This is considered involuntary intoxication. (Breggin, 2008, p 13)

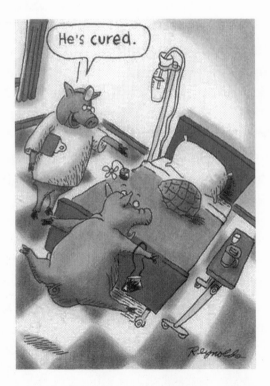

We need to be aware of both the spellbinding effect of psychiatric drugs and the long-term effects of using drugs, often rendering patients unable to work or carry on family life and becoming a burden to both our legal and welfare systems as a result of medication madness and dysfunction.

Judi Chamberlin is Co-Chair of the World Network of Users and Survivors of Psychiatry and Director of Education and Training for the National Empowerment Center. She wrote the preface to *Coming Off Psychiatric Drugs* (2004) edited by Peter Lehmann. She wrote,

> *Much of the conventional wisdom about psychiatric drugs is wrong. [Many] psychiatrists and the pharmaceutical industry have successfully convinced much of the public, through the media, that psychiatric drugs are "safe" and "effective" in "treating" "mental illnesses." Let us look at each of these words in turn:*
>
> *Safe—generally accepted to mean that they cause no harm, despite many known negative effects such as movement disorders, changes in brain activity, weight gain, restlessness, sudden death from neuroleptic malignant syndrome and many others.*
>
> *Effective—generally accepted to mean that they reverse or cure the symptoms for which they are prescribed, despite the fact that much research has shown they have a generally sedating effect that masks not only the targeted behavior, but all activities.*
>
> *Treating—generally accepted to mean that the prescribed agents have specific effects on specific disease processes.*
>
> *Mental illnesses—generally accepted to mean that there are specific clinical entities known as "schizophrenia," "bi-polar disorder" etc., despite the fact that there are no known structural or chemical changes in the body that can distinguish people who have these so-called illnesses from those who do not.*
>
> *How is it that these myths have been so successfully accepted as fact? For one thing, those promoting the drugs are authority figures, doctors and scientists who are generally accepted to be presenting value-free experimental results. Another factor, perhaps even more significant, is that those who are given the drugs and who are the ones who have spoken out about their negative effects, are automatically discredited by having been labeled mentally ill.*

The diagnosis of mental illness carries with it a host of associations, particularly that the person so labeled has impaired judgment and is not a reliable reporter of his or her own experiences.

A free online book, *Harm Reduction: Coming Off of Psychiatric Drugs*, can be downloaded for those interested in learning more about drugs, their side effects, and help for stopping: http://www.freedom-center.org/freedom-center-icarus-project-publish-coming-psychiatric-drugs-guide.

The book's sponsors describe it: "The Icarus Project and Freedom Center's 40-page guide gathers the best information we've come across and the most valuable lessons we've learned about reducing and coming off psychiatric medication. Includes info on mood stabilizers, antipsychotics, antidepressants, anti-anxiety drugs, risks, benefits, wellness tools, withdrawal, detailed Resource section, information for people staying on their medications, and much more. Written by Will Hall, with a 14-member health professional Advisory board providing research assistance. This fine booklet is available in Spanish and German as well as English."

A 352-page book titled *Coming off Psychiatric Drugs* can be ordered online from book retailers. It addresses family members, health providers and people who want to withdraw on their own decision. Twenty-eight people from 15 countries write about their experiences with withdrawal, and eight support people report on how they helped in the withdrawal process." Dr. Breggin's book, *Medication Madness*, also includes a few chapters on safe withdrawal from psychiatric medication.

Increasing numbers of individual psychiatrists are becoming aware of the issues of the overuse of medications. Fifth Ave Psychiatry in New York City writes on their website:

Many people (children and adults) being treated for a variety of psychiatric symptoms, are often overmedicated. In fact, many psychiatrists routinely treat depression and anxiety with complex medication combinations that are not evidence-based. Many medications commonly prescribed for these disorders are not even indicated or FDA approved for that particular use. Another common practice 'polypharmacy' is when someone is put on multiple medications, usually there is no evidence at all that these combinations are effective-this can be costly, debilitating, and has no proven therapeutic effect. People can be on these medication regimens often for years only to be exposed to many side effects and potential long-term risk, with minimal relief of symptoms.

Some patients may choose to use psychiatric medication in a crisis and then withdraw once the crisis is over. Some may choose to stay on medications; others may choose to withdraw after months or years.

We feel that information on safe withdrawal is important to include in this resource book to address those people who want to consider safe withdrawal. Does it fit into the theme of considering the spiritual nature of care, especially what is offered in Spiritist Community Centers and Psychiatric Hospitals in Brazil? Not exactly, but that is because the psychiatric medication is not overused in Brazil. In the USA, we are living in a culture that is actively promoting the use of psychiatric medications, and it is quite normal for patients to be advised by their health provider to continue taking these powerful medications for life. This is not done now in Brazil. Therefore, Brazilian patients do not tend to think of themselves as needing medication for life, nor are they exposed to the suggestion via television that psychiatric medication might be beneficial to use when not in crisis. Brazilians use the medications more sparingly than we do, and thus have less experience with the debilitating circumstances that come from the overuse of the drugs.

See Appendix E for organizations that can help with the withdrawal of psychiatric medications. (Note: Those engaged with writing and consulting about this book have no philosophical membership or financial ties to any of the organizations listed; I have selected these organizations mainly as sources of information for the reader.)

An Example of Rational Use of Psychiatric Drugs in a Private Practice: Fifth Ave Psychiatry (from http://www.psychiatrynyc.com, accessed June 21, 2011)

Research shows that the gold standard of treatment for depression, anxiety, and ADHD in both adults and children is combined psychotherapy with medication used judiciously.

This private practice puts a strong emphasis on psychotherapy as the foundation of treatment. Treatment is best if provided by the same person, or by a team of professionals collaborating closely. Their team believes that each individual is unique and that differences among patients should be considered in guiding treatment. Though it seems simple, this concept is often not applied. At its core, personalized treatment is the systematic use of information obtained from the patient to dictate the type and course of treatment.

Two psychiatrists, Drs. Glazer and Megwinoff, carefully evaluate and discuss the current treatment regimen with a patient as it compares to evidence-based practice guidelines, and most of their treatment plans minimize medication use.

In order to stay objective and true to evidence-based practices the staff at Fifth Avenue Psychiatry do not meet with pharmaceutical representatives. Drs. Glazer and Megwinoff do not consult with nor receive compensation from the pharmaceutical industry.

Samuel Glazer is nationally recognized for his treatment of professionals with addiction.

Olga Megwinoff is a board certified psychiatrist with extensive experience in the treatment of childhood disorders. She is an expert in treating ADHD, anxiety disorders, mood disorders and families affected by addiction. Along with being a psychopharmacologist and psychotherapist, Dr. Megwinoff is an expert on alternative treatments such as meditation, diet, and supplements, and she prefers to integrate these into her traditional treatment plan.

Tracey Bassett is a clinical psychologist and expert in several modes of therapy for children and young adults. She has unique experience in the treatment of addiction in adolescents.

An Example of Rational Use of Psychiatric Medications in a Community Clinic: Advocates, Inc. in Framingham, Mass. (www. advocatesinc.org, accessed July 18, 2011)

Founded in 1975 by a group of volunteers providing patient rehabilitation services on the grounds of Westborough State Hospital, Advocates is one of the largest human services organizations in Massachusetts. This not-for-profit organization employs over 1,000 staff and serves 20,000 individuals at over 100 sites across eastern and central Massachusetts. Advocates' mission is to help people achieve their hopes and dreams within the fabric of their communities. They partner with elders and people with disabilities and other challenges to overcome personal obstacles and societal barriers so they can obtain and keep homes, engage in work and other meaningful activities, and sustain satisfying relationships. They work to inspire communities to create opportunities for contribution and participation by all.

At the heart of all Advocates services is a commitment to partnering with the individuals they support and with their family members, so that they can lead full, satisfying lives of their own design. They practice a person-centered approach that respects the unique needs, wishes and abilities of each individual.

The work of Advocates extends beyond the walls of their programs and into the heart of the community. Through a range of public lectures, professional trainings, conferences and cultural events, they strive to build strong, inclusive communities that value the contributions of all members.

Chris Gordon, MD, is vice president of clinical services and medical director of Advocates, Inc. Dr. Gordon is able to prescribe medications and monitor those who want to safely withdraw from the use of medications. He has a special interest in spirituality and mental health.

CHAPTER THIRTEEN
TRANSFORMATIVE SANCTUARIES
by Barbara Findeisen, MFT

Editor's Note: Although transformative sanctuaries are not specifically designed for people diagnosed with serious mental illnesses, they do serve those who are motivated to change their behavior, thoughts and attitudes. This chapter is included because we believe there are many people now looking for ways to be supported in changing to a more positive way of being. They may have been diagnosed with a psychiatric illness, or not. They may have been taking medications, or not. Profound inner transformation is what they want.

Something beyond traditional therapy is included in the concept of transformation. It requires a radical change, a change among professionals, a change in the environment, and an openness to move beyond established procedures and attitudes. The availability of a sanctuary is an advantage for those in the process of transformation. I have been a part of creating two retreat centers combining psychology and spirituality. It has been an exciting and challenging adventure.

The word *transformation* is heard more frequently as our consciousness evolves and expands. We read books and papers; attend seminars and workshops; and talk about transforming lives, relationships and careers. Even the government referred to the term *transformation* in the formation of the New Freedom Commission on Mental Health in 2003.

Unfortunately, there is also strong opposition to the inclusion of a spiritual reality in the training and practice of psychology, psychiatry and allied fields of mental health. Transformation, which requires a change of old, comfortable ways of thinking and behaving, can be disruptive to systems and individuals. Resistance to change is common. Deeply personal nonordinary states of consciousness do not lend themselves easily to inclusion in professional textbooks, technical terminology, or the limitations of vocabulary and rigid theories. They can be easily dismissed as delusional or "just imagination," even when profound healing occurs. My personal experiences confirmed their reality and prompted me to want to create a safe environment for others during transformational changes. I came to believe that great opportunities of healing could be hidden within a crisis, especially when there is time, support and respect for the process.

In my forties, my carefully constructed life fell apart, and I experienced myself in a nightmare. I was a practicing, licensed psychotherapist with years of personal therapy, so I had some professional awareness of my situation, but it did not help. I found that I could still work during the day wearing my professional persona and using the skills I had mastered. The nights were hellish. I felt wrenching emotional pain, which I could not control. I had experiences so far removed from ordinary life that I felt I was losing my mind. During this chaotic time, I clung to some belief that I would get through it and somehow would be blessed. I cried and screamed and prayed. I had times that I seemed to be floating above my body. I had whipping surges of energy up and down my spine. I had no understanding of what was happening; that would come much later. I did not seek professional help. I did not want to be labeled, diagnosed, hospitalized or medicated. I clung to my fragile connection to Spirit. One part of me wanted to go through it, whatever the outcome. Another part of me prayed for it to stop. Fortunately, several wise individuals appeared in my life with healing and understanding. As my internal world began to gather some coherence, my nightly catharsis diminished. I began to sleep again and had moments of peace and clarity. Over time, I had a wisp of an idea, which became more persistent. Despite my resistance, it grew stronger. The message I received was "create a sanctuary for people like you." I began to talk to others about it. Based on my own crisis, I believed I had an idea of what would be supportive. I wanted to turn "breakdowns" into breakthroughs by providing a safe, nurturing place with people who had faith in people's journey toward wholeness. I did not know how, where, or when, but I believed the dream. Then I met psychiatrist Stanislav Grof and his wife Christina (1989). I met Stan and Christina at a transpersonal psychology conference in Santa Rosa, California. The genius of their work gave me a context for what I had been experiencing. It was well documented. Like many others, I was going through a purging, an awakening, a dark night of the soul, a rebirth. Called by many names, this transformative breakdown was not rare or unusual for those on a spiritual path. It was part of the journey. I became part of the Spiritual Emergence Network created by Stan and Christina. I learned about nonordinary states of consciousness and learned how to be with others in similar situations. My dream of finding a place was shared by many others. Someone came into my life and said to me, "let's find it"–a place to do your work. It felt like a miracle. It was a miracle.

We began looking around, mostly in Northern California. We looked at vineyards, big houses, ranches, and old hotels, but nothing felt right. Then in 1986, we followed a long, seven-mile winding dirt road, across a wooden bridge over a bubbling creek into an old rather ram-shackled cluster of buildings. Located on 400 acres, the ranch was nestled at the foot of Pocket Peak in Sonoma County, north of San Francisco. It had not been used for several years and needed a lot of fixing up, but it had the potential to meet all of our requirements. It seemed like the ideal place. Buildings were scattered around a dining room and old lodge. The décor needed to be changed. No more animal heads and costumes hanging on the walls. There were cabins, several complete houses, and a relatively new swimming pool in which to cool off during the dry, hot summers. Best of all, there was a lot of space, and privacy. There were mature, large California oak trees dotting the hillsides and meadows and a pine forest. There was a separate house on a hill overlooking the main complex that we could use as our acute residential care center. In this little mountain valley, we could manifest the shared vision of a place where individuals and groups could come for healing. It was purchased for that purpose. We wanted to keep the name "Pocket" because we remembered that as children we kept treasures in our pockets. The people who came here for sanctuary were the treasures. Pocket Ranch became a reality.

We moved in, rolled up our sleeves, and went to work. The dining room and kitchen were remodeled and brought up to code. Cabins were refurbished; the lodge was cleaned up and eventually remodeled. We smudged everything. The crisis residential house, called the Woodlands, was modified to fit all of the state and county regulations for our license. The cabins were cleaned up and made more comfortable. In time, we built an octagonal meditation room deep within a grove of trees. There were rooms for art, sandtray therapy, massage, psychotherapy, and a large group room. The land provided areas for walking, hiking, dabbling in the creek, or just sitting and relaxing. Our intention to create a safe, welcoming place had happened.

It was essential to hire a professional staff that shared our vision of honoring the spiritual path of each individual. Even the nontherapy staff members who were often the first to speak with and welcome guests needed to be in alignment with our purpose. The importance of staff cannot be understated. We all needed to be flexible, able to resonate with clients, warm, and mindful of boundaries. Most of our therapy staff came from traditional mental health environments and were eager to leave it behind. Most had extensive personal, professional and spiritual experience. Most agreed with our vision of dealing with crisis as an opportunity for transformation.

Surprising additions to our staff were the animals on the ranch, especially the dogs. For some individuals, one of the beautiful Labrador retrievers became a vehicle for change. The four-footed "therapists" seemed to know exactly who needed extra loving attention. From time to time, one of the dogs would stay by a client who was in a fragile state for days. They provided a source of safety and comfort. For others, one of the cats became a soothing presence. Massage was an important part of the program. Sensitive and respectful healing touch—be it body work, a pat on the shoulder, a hand to hold, or dog to pet—played a major role in healing. The Ranch was large enough for groups to come without disturbing our residential clients. Everything became a part of the process of transforming suffering into a sense of wholeness and compassion for self. Driving up the winding dirt road across the wooden bridge and under the Pocket Ranch became part of the journey of transitioning from the world of traffic, noise and stress to a secluded, sacred space of peace. We had the luxury of time and space, taking walks, and sitting with our bare feet in the creek or the hot tub. Therapy rooms, where emotions could be safely released, were available when needed. There was time to listen and to be heard. Everything was part of the process. We worked with people, not "on" them. Ours was not an authoritarian, hierarchical system. We avoided diagnosis and rigid schedules and a "one way fits all" thinking. We learned to look beyond symptoms for root causes and hidden meanings, remaining open and flexible yet responsible. We looked for healing signs and opportunities for transformation. It required cooperation and trust with each other and within ourselves. A repeated phrase was "trust the process." In the ten years we were at Pocket Ranch, more than a thousand people came to us yearly for rest and renewal. In the early 1990s, our benefactors purchased an adjacent property. We now had 4,000 acres. There were no close neighbors. We felt secure and protected. We were not.

We began to hear complaints about our presence in the area, particularly about the road, which we shared with a few other property owners. We maintained the road, making repairs as needed, especially after storms. Complaints were filed with the county; we were investigated for code violations, and some were found. Actually, the road issue was covering another agenda.

Our policy at the ranch was not to discriminate on the basis of race, ethnicity, sexual orientation, or religious persuasion. We met with officials, groups, local churches, neighbors, and hosted anyone who wanted to come up and visit the ranch firsthand to see what we were doing. Still, rumors grew and threats were made. Friends in the County reported the rumors people were spreading. I was labeled a witch. It was said that we had gay bathhouses; that dangerous, naked people were running around in the woods; and that we tied people up. We were seen as a threat to public safety. It was ugly. The rumors were not true, but few people came up to find out for themselves.

One of the most dangerous threats in dry California is the wild fire. A group of local high school kids talked about coming up to Pocket Ranch and setting fires to burn us down. They were restrained, but they reflected the misperceptions and hatred that were being spread about us. Clients and friends who had benefited from treatment at Pocket Ranch told us privately how much they wanted to support us. Some did, but others were afraid to speak up. After a long struggle and high legal fees, we lost. Not one supervisor voted for us. The focus again was on the road. It became impossible for us to continue to work at the Ranch. The restrictions imposed upon us made it impossible to stay. I was shocked at the viciousness of some of the opposition. Even though we were on 4,000 acres at the end of the road, nestled in a valley with no close neighbors, we were seen as a threat to the safety of the area. It was heartbreaking for clients and staff, many of whom had left mainstream jobs to become a part of what we were doing. It was their dream too. The property was eventually sold. Some of the buildings were abandoned. We moved on. The dream seemed to be dead, but it wasn't.

Individually, we continued to work with groups and clients with the same belief in the healing power of including mind, body, and spirit. We carried the vision forward in our personal and professional lives. Places may change, but the work continued and expanded. The dream of creating a sanctuary seemed lost, and I had no desire to repeat it.

Reflections on Transformation

There is no transformation without change. This is where resistance surfaces. I have noticed that the closer that individuals, organizations, agencies, and even cultures get to changing (or needing to change), the more opposition and fear arises. Entrenched ways do not usually yield gracefully, even in the face of new information and research. Habituated ways of thinking and behaving restrict us from moving ahead. I have also learned that holding fast to viewpoints of past experiences keeps us stuck. Genuine present-time experiences, often referred to as epiphanies, have the power to bring about significant change. An accident, illness, death or other stressful event can serve as a wake-up call to see things in a new way. They can also be very disruptive, even traumatizing. Simple changes like adding a reading corner or fresh flowers are appreciated and may actually enhance the environment supporting more profound shifts.

Substantive transformation requires an altered state of perception. It can be frightening. Like turning around a huge ocean liner, turning a system around can be a slow, arduous process. This is especially true when an individual or a system is entrenched or is needing to control or to be right and defends against alternatives. Change is unwelcome and often brings about an angry response.

All of these reactions can rise up even when all legal, ethical and traditional methods are honored, as we learned when we created Pocket Ranch, an alternative spiritually-based treatment facility.

The traditional medical model for mental health has resisted the inclusion of alternative modalities. Most conventional treatment is intended to contain and control symptoms, which is sometimes necessary although there may be better options. Medical and pharmaceutical advances have been stunning and immensely valuable. Technology, research, and medicine ease symptoms but they do not necessarily result in transformation. Something else is required.

Many places have integrated what is best of traditional and complementary and healing approaches, as we did at Pocket Ranch. Research into consciousness and body-mind connections has given us new information and insight. Traditional religions are often included and practiced in treatment facilities. Spiritual experiences, which have been frequently dismissed, are becoming more acceptable. There is a growing desire of individuals to seek and ask for alternatives outside the medical model. This has been substantiated by Leitner and Phillips (2003) and Leifner and Adame (2010) who reported the increasing prevalence of clients using nontraditional treatments. Can mental illness be seen as a wake-up call for the need to transform our lifestyles? Transformation occurs on a continuum. What is transformational for one individual is not necessarily transformational for another.

Real change entails an internal shift in attitudes and perceptions and a change in heart, mind, and focus. It may be a simple acceptance of a present-time condition or a cessation of resistance. The mental, emotional, and physical environment, including the attitudes and projections of others, can restrict or promote healing. Rarely is one so blessed as to receive a significant experience powerful enough to cause instant enlightenment. Transformation comes in increments, large and small, profound and mundane, giant leaps or tiny steps. Any step along the way may serve as a wake-up call or affirmation, depending on the awareness and intention of the seeker. Caregivers who hold the vision of unfolding opportunities for awakening and transforming serve as holders of the light in times of stumbling in darkness.

Complementary and alternative medicine (CAM) authors report that approximately 40 percent of people diagnosed with severe depression or panic attacks use some kind of an alternative treatment. Many clients seek complementary modalities but do not tell their professional helpers. Increasing numbers of people use acupuncture, yoga, meditation, mindfulness, self-help treatments, spiritual practices and a host of other approaches to healing mind, body and spirit. Traumas, losses, and changes in a relationship and life's situations can create issues that are improved by alternative modalities.

Moving on to Kenyon Ranch

After Pocket Ranch, I continued seeing clients, writing and renting other places for my groups. I found an old ranch in southern Arizona to rent for our transformational STAR workshops. Occasionally I would receive a frantic call from a person, often a therapist, who wanted to send someone to Pocket Ranch. I explained the situation and made other suggestions. It was not easy. There were few places like the sanctuary at the foot of Pocket Peak. Phone calls continued to punctuate my life from clinicians, families, and individuals going through a spiritual emergency. Occasionally, I would hear the same old voice repeating "create a sanctuary or people like you, for others whose lives are falling apart," but I was not eager to repeat the experience of Pocket Ranch. I was being encouraged to at least look around for another place. I kept an eye open but did not mount a serious effort.

California was too expensive and was almost strangled by regulations. I rented an old ranch in southern Arizona to hold my transformational STAR workshops (Findeisen, 2005; Chaudhary 2009). A friend remembered an old ranch near Tucson, now 96 acres. Like Pocket Ranch, there was space, peace, privacy and possibilities. Lots of them. We made an offer, and it was accepted.

Kenyon Ranch was built in the 1930s out of rocks and adobe from the land. Originally it had been a 2,000-acre *dude* ranch where guests came to escape cold winters, ride horses, have cookouts, rest, play "cowboy," and enjoy themselves. The original brochure stated that you could bring your own gun and requested that you send your trunk ahead on the Southern Pacific Railroad, and you could have "Levi's" trousers made locally.

The ranch is on ancient Native American land at 4,000-foot elevation between two mountain ranges. The vistas are beautiful. Compared with Pocket Ranch, the sky seems bigger. The nighttime stars are spectacular. The desert is dotted with mesquite trees, which are much smaller than the California oaks. There are more horses and wild critters but fewer cars. The dogs still take seriously their work of comforting, and so does the staff. There is a swimming pool and cabins, called "casitas."

We have restored almost all the buildings, built a lodge, rewired and replumbed the casitas, painted, hung artwork, and created a sandtray room. We have two massage rooms and a wonderful "hang out" room converted from an old four-car garage. One group created a labyrinth. There are special places located around the ranch where people sit quietly, meditating, writing, talking or swinging gently in a hammock enjoying the sun and the shadows on the mountains. In 2004, we opened the ranch as a sanctuary and place of healing for individuals and groups. The essence of the work and the commitment of the staff remains the same. The dirt road into Kenyon Ranch is much shorter than the one in California, though guests report a similar shift in their state of mind as they cross over the cattle guard into the complex of adobe and stone buildings.

As in California, we are careful to adhere to local and state regulations. There is considerably less bureaucracy in Arizona than in California. The local county offices are small, and people are on a first-name basis. The ethnicities in Arizona include Native American, Hispanic and Anglo. One can feel the spirit of the ancient native cultures who lived, roamed, and worshipped in this desert expanse of valleys and mountains. When we decided to build our lodge, we consulted a nearby shaman to help us determine the best location.

Treatment options include opportunities for artistic creation, physical exercise, bodywork, drumming, dancing, sandtray, and group and individual therapy. Best of all, there is space and time for reflection and regeneration.

There have been many changes in awareness since we opened Pocket Ranch in 1986. The reality of spiritual experiences has become more accepted and validated in treatment centers, conferences, research, literature and the media across a wide spectrum of treatment modalities. Research continues to verify the power of seeing the wholeness in each person, including brain, mind, body, emotions and soul, which is gradually transforming our attitudes and ways of dealing with psychological issues.

We even see traces in governmental agencies. One example of this is the 2002 formation of the Presidential New Freedom Commission on Mental Health. Designed to improve state mental health and addiction services, 11 states were chosen to participate in the program. Maryland was one state identified as a "transformation state." Government grants were awarded to provide financial support and opportunities to enhance and expand services. One successful Maryland project created consumer self help centers across the state. These sanctuaries are available throughout the state and are often a preferred alternative to hospitalizations. Staffed by trained fellow consumers under the guidance of professionals, they provide badly needed safety, comfort and relief. They also save the State of Maryland's resources, which can be used elsewhere. The opportunity to explore spiritual paths is an integral part of this program. The program empowers people to become more educated in understanding their illness and recovery options. Organized consumers are a growing force throughout the state and country, not in opposition to established practices but in cooperation and expansion of treatment choices. With federal and state financial support in the hands of dedicated state staff, Maryland serves as an inspiration and model in the inclusion of self-help and available options in mental health treatment.

Paradigms are shifting. Changes have and will continue to happen. Providing sanctuaries such as Pocket Ranch and Kenyon Ranch and other nontraditional treatment centers are a part of the new paradigm. They require determination and willingness to stand in the face of opposition. Each person needs to be seen as a unique individual member of the human family. From that perspective, respect and compassion for others emerge, not in codependence but in recognition of our interdependence. We discover our deep yearning to find purpose and meaning in our lives. One individual or facility or community can provide sanctuary. One by one, in community, we are transformed.

CHAPTER FOURTEEN
THE ROAD AHEAD

Barbara Findeisen (1993, 2010) deepened her dedication to helping others after going through a period of deep disturbance and subsequent transformation. Selene Almeida, MD, was awakened to her purpose through her deepening connection to the energies of plants, trees and rocks near her home, as well as her spiritual guidance. Linda Haltinner came to renew her life purpose through travel to distant lands and self-reflection. These exemplary women ultimately found purpose and meaning by assisting others to find balance.

After reviewing many of the perspectives and resources in integrative mental health, let's reflect again on the Spiritists' recipe for mental health: finding one's life purpose is essential for making healthful lifestyle choices, and implementing one's life purpose is one of the most certain paths to wellbeing. This is how people find meaning in life, and a life of meaning and purpose fits our definition of a "spiritual life." I think Spiritism has been so successful in its treatments because it facilitates individuals acting with compassion, clarifying their purpose in life, and aligning with that purpose.

As written earlier, a Spiritist considers that pervasive and long-lasting mental imbalance may manifest because a person is rebalancing themselves after a life experience that was traumatic, where he or she did not act out of compassion, or where he or she lost his/her purpose in life. What needs to happen? The "unbalanced" person needs to balance the books. This may include finding out what was done without love and compassion in the past. This can be uncovered by means of meditation, self-exploration through an personal inventory of past actions, consulting with a therapist or peers, or receiving the insight of mediums. Next, a kind of rebalancing is necessary, that may include both forgiveness and some form of atonement.

The fastest path to balancing the books (and few of us have been saints, so we all have work to do here) is not self-punishment, but rather charitable acts towards others. In Sweden or residences like CooperRiis in the USA, this can start at "safe homes" that are farms, where the "patients" participate in responding to "moos," barks, squawks, and droopy leaves by milking cows, feeding dogs and chickens, and watering gardens. In Finland, it can be facilitated through Open Dialogue. Giving and receiving dependable, personal, compassionate connection consistently shows up as an essential ingredient to healing mental illnesses. Fraternal support is intrinsic to care in Spiritist hospitals and centers. The peer support offered there (and in some centers in the USA, like Soteria-Alaska) patiently acknowledges the pain of the person who is suffering, eventually sets aside past hurts, and charts a course toward relationships of mutual respect and collaboration. Sometimes we need extra support to find our way out of a complexity in our personal relationships. Going out to milk the cows with a friend is more fun than doing it alone.

Someone once defined *persistent serious mental imbalance* as "a lack of willingness to do your own work." All of the paths to mental health out of mental illness we have explored require work. Self-reflection, contemplation, opening up to new angles on life, meditation, assessing relationships, open dialogue, listening to others even when it hurts, and charitable acts towards animals and people—they all require action and focus. The shifting of lifestyle choices Gerry had to do—eating differently, abstaining from recreational drugs and alcohol, sleeping more, exercising, choosing her friends more carefully—these did not come naturally but rather required persistent effort on her part. This is another level of personal "work."

Asking oneself "Why am I here?" and "What gives my life meaning and a sense of purpose?" are questions some people resist their whole lives long. It takes concentration and humility to focus on these questions and sort through the answers. Eddie, who went to visit John of God after a lifetime of mental anguish, asked the questions and got his answers—and replaced his persistent overwhelming anxiety with peace. This involved work. Individuals in extreme states who resist the "work," and opt for psychiatric medications, like Sylvia in Chapter One, obstruct their own healing.

An important question looms: Can those taking the psychiatric drugs daily motivate themselves to do "the work" if they are under the influence of psychiatric medications that often drain emotions and motivation? The question of the true usefulness of psychiatric drugs is one currently under discussion, as the answer is not clear.

Spiritism, like Open Dialogue and Soteria-type treatment, takes the middle road. Drugs are available but are not considered the most obvious and central part of treatment; rather they relieve symptoms such as inability to sleep especially in the beginning of the crisis. Mending difficult relationships is central, and fraternal counseling/peer support can be extremely helpful in that endeavor. Much of that work with peers can be done outside a hospital setting, in a home or community center that is a safe environment. One or more compassionate, empathic people being with the person in crisis soon after the crisis starts is one of the determinants of successful healing, preventing deeper trauma, and facilitating an effective and relatively short treatment.

In the end, it is hard to compare the successes of Spiritist treatment to other established, well-researched models, like Open Dialogue. As mentioned, there are few qualitiative studies of Spiritist treatment for serious mental illness. However, those that have been done by Ferreira (Moreira-Almeida and Almeida, 2008) and Herve (2003, 2006) reflect that at least 30% of seriously ill patients have a complete remission of symptoms without psychiatric medication. This merits further study, as it appears to be better than what our current system offers in the USA.

We know the following from Spiritism: First, the karmic accounting books need our attention; we are here to become more compassionate and wise. When we forget this, we have to balance the books. Secondly, we need to stay aware of life purpose, or calling, and make it real. When one follows that "destiny path," and gets about doing it, one finds the deepest satisfaction in life, whether one is still taking some psychiatric medications, as Sascha Altman (in Chapter One) and Marcel do (Chapter Two), or not. Gerry (first mentioned in the Introduction) is supported by orthomolecular supplements and acupuncture, as well as her family, and gets along well without psychiatric medications.

This understanding makes mental health achievable and full recovery possible. We need only to be willing to dive deeply into our own hearts, negotiate the tsunami waves if and when they come, and bring our passion to the surface.

APPENDIX A
SELECTIONS FROM TREATMENT AT SOTERIA HOUSE: A MANUAL FOR THE PRACTICE OF INTERPERSONAL PHENOMENOLOGY

Final National Institutes of Mental Health Report: Grants Number R12MH 20123 and R124H 25570. Prepared by Loren R. Mosher, MD, Project Research Director; Robert Fanzine, PhD, Research Co-Director; and Alma Zito Menn, A.S.C.W., Principal Investigator. This report includes material from Soteria: A Manual (1972), compiled and edited by Mosher and Menn.

Soteria and Emanon were not observational experiments with controls. Staff were not Audubons sketching schizophrenic birds in protected parts of the forest. They were Janes or Joes trying to relate to, *be with, attend* and understand persons whose means of communication and behaviors were often unlike anything the staff had encountered before. In most cases staff came to have an experience that would leave an indelible imprint, an experience that would be reciprocally formative, on which they would have an impact. Staff were explorers in an uncharted frontier; they were **in a** place where few people without preconceived notions had ventured before, and they were there without the usual trappings of power to control madness.

Staff did not carry the highly symbolic keys to freedom: There were no locks on the doors; there were no syringes and few medications; there were no wet packs, restraints, or seclusion rooms.

Four prohibitions: Soteria had four prohibitions which comprised their original rules:

1. In so far as we were able to prevent it, violence to self or others was forbidden. From the outset, Soteria planners believed it important to make this expectation explicit. Providing the safe, quiet, protective, containing, predictable environment we found essential to natural recovery from psychosis demanded freedom from violence.

2. "Tourists" were not allowed without prearrangement and agreement of the current residents of the house. (Family members and friends of residents were of course, welcome, although the community preferred to know in advance that they would be visiting.) Just as no one *can* invite a stranger into my house without asking me, the community exercised a similar veto. In addition, clinical experience taught me that persons disorganized enough to be labeled psychotic frequently reacted poorly (for example, they withdrew, ran away, or became angry and assaultive) when confronted by strangers.

3. No illegal drugs were allowed or were to be consumed in the house. When Soteria and Emanon were in operation, much of the nation was involved in drug use and abuse. Both to continue to be in good standing with the NIMH, however, and, more importantly, to coexist peacefully with the local community, the facilities could not afford to be seen as drug scenes. Furthermore, we were attempting to conduct a drug-free experiment. We had no clear guidelines as to what effect illegal drugs would have had on the course of recovery from acute psychosis. We did not wish to muddy further the already opaque waters of madness.

4. The Soteria community affirmed an "incest taboo" on sex between staff and residents—not between staff members or between clients.

The rule against using illegal drugs—itself a felony—was a universal rule. Obviously, members of the Soteria community were also expected to refrain from acts forbidden by civil authorities—murder, rape, robbery, etc. The rule requiring that the kitchen's box of knives be locked for a set period after a new resident arrived was limited to certain situations, as needed.

Relationships were central to Soteria's therapeutic environment. Said one staff member, "When I was first hired for the job at Soteria, I felt as if I had been adopted into a family." Her experience resulted from the community's style of interpersonal relationships. Its aim was not only to provide tangible examples of and personal participation in honest, affectionate, caring, and trusting interactions, but also to instill the skills necessary to initiate such contact with others. Soteria created the opportunity for such relationships for both the staff and the residents. If this base did not develop, a resident's progress could be greatly inhibited, and much of what was unique to the Soteria experience, which rests on interconnections and a sense of community, would be lost.

Staff members were selected because of their strength of character, compatibility with the others, tolerance, and flexibility. Identification and emulation were major components of change at Soteria; therefore, staff members were chosen for their abilities to serve as good role models as well as to be comfortable with the maelstrom that often characterizes acute psychosis. Although everyone was allowed an individual view of the nature of reality, the staff and program director were the purveyors of Soteria's culture. Thus the *program* conformed in many ways to conventional realities while it at the same time recognized the *individual's* right to harbor an idiosyncratic one. Soteria's process, thus, allowed its members to establish a community that had the support and protection of a group identity to guide it through the broader social context.

Because interpersonal relationships among community members were key factors at Soteria, the house strove to establish a milieu conducive to such lasting interactions. This concept deviates significantly from traditional modes of treatment and calls for several operational factors:

- *a willingness on the part of the staff to view a client as a potential peer,*
- *a process that allows and/or encourages both clients and staff the opportunity to establish and maintain a shared, equal relationship,*
- *available networking space for people to connect with each other.*

The last point is of critical importance.

The Vigil

The "vigil" was both a treatment and a training tool. For treatment, it was seen as a way to intercede in the psychotic process and have an impact on its course. As training, it gave staff members experience in being with someone in psychosis both as observers and as participants, a concept [Harry Stack] Sullivan pioneered.

Because of the variety of demands and the large number of disturbed people on the small psychiatric ward at Agnews State Hospital, administrators for this special ward had defined and allotted extra staff to deal with severely disturbed persons in order to avoid medicating them. Paired male and female staff and volunteers stayed with the person in crisis in consecutive shifts of from four to eight hours in a medium-sized, comfortable room designated as the "vigil room." In this way, attendants were able to provide continuous individual help for four or five days at a time. During the vigils, the staff members involved had no duties and were expected only to *be with* the person in crisis in any way that seemed to make sense. Other personnel provided necessary life-sustaining functions such as meals. While the acutely ill person was encouraged to remain in the room, the staff did not prevent exits and could, if indicated, use all of the hospital grounds as an arena for *being with.*

To train staff for the Agnews' Hospital vigils, a mock vigil took place without a person in crisis. Assigned pairs simply remained in a room with nothing to do for extended periods of time. During group meetings held after each vigil– real or feigned–all staff and volunteers discussed their experiences in detail.

The vigils were successful. One patient, who fought six times and broke four windows on the ward the day preceding his *vigil,* was not violent either during his vigil (four-and-a-half days and nights) or–towards people— after it. He went through an acute schizophrenic crisis to full reintegration in three months. Not only did all patients given vigils improve, but also there was much lighter property damage, less emergency medication, no injuries, and fewer transfers to the maximum security ward.

Being With in Three Stages

The three stages of *being with*, as the process occurred with most Soteria residents, were:

- *the major crisis, when the client most needed basic care*
- *the reconstitution, when the client re-established his/her personality in relation to the new surroundings*
- *the extension, when the client began to expand boundaries of relationships*

These stages weren't completely separate; they overlapped, did not always occur, and were manifest in different sequences.

Stage One

Stage one began when a staff member picked up the client at the screening center. The person who made the first contact initiated through *being with* the Soteria process of interpersonal bonding. While relationships generally develop over a long period of time, some basic ties take less than an hour to develop when the environment is new and the faces, unfamiliar. A friendship an hour old can seem firm and important, especially if it rescues the sufferer from a frightening place.

Stage one took advantage of this condition: Thus, the person who brought the new client home made the introductions to the group and stayed with him or her continuously until s/he connected sufficiently to someone else. Once such a connection had been established, the vigil can continue to establish the interpersonal connections that have to develop before meaningful change can occur. The primary care giver during stage one, therefore, must be the person(s) who are most able to interact comfortably with the new resident.

Stage one was the "tight" vigil, as differentiated from the "loose" vigil of stage two. In most cases, the tight vigil took place in one room—usually the client's—but on many occasions it happened in other places in the house or the yard.

During stage one, staff tried to make and maintain contact with the person having difficulty interacting. The tight vigil also initiated a basic support network. This kind of involvement became the bonding material for long-term personal relationships. Through common experience, two individuals can quickly create a closeness similar to that among family members. These relationships are the building blocks of change at Soteria. And material generated in the tight vigil led to the second stage of *being with*.

Loren's comment: Soteria's provision of a low-stimulation, consistent, quiet milieu, which offered interpersonal support, acceptance, and predictability, was especially important to a successful journey through stage one.

Stage Two

If the first stage of *being with* was bonding, the second stage was development. During this part of the process, a variety of relationships began to form, relationships that became the core of change Soteria-style. Without basic interpersonal relationships to establish supportive networks, clients were unable to support identities separate from their families of origin. This failure guaranteed the eventual return of the crisis in these young, recently psychotic individuals, usually coming to Soteria fresh from their childhood homes.

The content of *being with* in this process was creating normative interactions. The degree to which the members of Soteria could achieve such relationships was the degree to which positive change was possible. During the second stage, the content of activities encouraged symmetrical relationships, and residents were allowed a myriad of choices *as* to how they would spend their time. Staff avoided scheduling too many organized functions for clients in stage two, encouraging such residents to take the initiative in organizing their own time in relation to the community's activities.

In this stage, validation of their experiences in the context of a safe, protected environment away from the site where the trouble had its roots began to effect change. This was, in turn, reflected in increased socialization and involvement in the Soteria community.

Stage *Three*

The complaint that "I'm bored, and there's nothing to do" often meant that stage two was moving toward stage three. Such a complaint is usually a sign that the client is interested in doing *something—but* something that s/he finds interesting rather than distasteful. Dishwashing, no, for example; a walk or a drive, yes. Having to come up with an alternative rather than simply complaining offers an opportunity for developing internal motivation.

At this point, *all* community members including but not exclusively the staff—tried especially to reserve time to devote to the client entering stage three. In fact, an important part of this last stage was the breaking of boundaries among groups in community activities and the expanding of relationships within and without the house. In the third stage of *being with*, people at Soteria related to each other as individuals, not as staff, residents, volunteers, and so forth. For example, a former resident remembered a time when she wanted to go skiing and hadn't quite known how to organize the activity. She turned to another resident for help, and he *was* able to meet her needs:

You remember that week when we went skiing at Dodge Ridge? I really appreciated Henry [another resident) for going through all that trouble getting everybody to come to the meeting that day. I think that if he didn't help me I would never gotten the group to go by myself.

On a similar note, Voyce recalled that after Chuck (a participant) had entered stage three, his relationships with members of the Soteria community changed dramatically. Rather than having his crisis occupy *the* house as it did during his first week, he helped the house psychiatrist tend to other residents. His relationship with Voyce changed as well: Chuck and I would go play tennis a lot and do things together on a daily basis. In fact,

I went to Disneyland that summer with my kids, and Chuck went along with us and had a good time. It was a lot of fun for all of us.

Of this friendship, Loren wrote, How Chuck's very real, down-to-earth relationship with Voyce altered his stay at the house is unusual for traditional psychiatric treatment (but not for Soteria). While not defined as psychotherapy, it was clearly therapeutic. Voyce provided Chuck with a model of efficacy and competence (especially self-control) to emulate, and their shared life experiences and positive emotional ties seem to have been critical in Chuck's change over time.

Continued Loren: "Stage three within the milieu involved extensive collaboration, planning, and negotiation in the context of involvement in a— by then—familiar, trusted, and tightly knit social group whose members played a variety of roles with differing statuses. Stage three was much more complicated than the first stage."

APPENDIX B
SUPPORTIVE ORGANIZATIONS

Associated Psychological Health Services (APHS)

Our non-residential treatment facility is one of only a few of its kind in the United States that specializes in and supports a patient's wish and right to be treated without the use and reliance upon psychiatric drugs. For this reason, we often find great working relationships with patients often labeled "treatment resistant" and "non-compliant." We welcome clients finding psychotropic medications useful, and hold no religious or other forced aversion to a patient's wish to use such interventions. Medications are very successful for controlling thoughts, feelings and behaviors; however, we specialize in fundamental long-lasting psychological treatment.

2808 Kohler Memorial Drive, Suite I
Sheboygan, WI 53081
Phone: (920) 457-9192
Website: http://www.abcmedsfree.com

Center for the Study of Empathic Therapy, Education & Living
Director/Founder: Peter Breggin, MD

Empathy *recognizes, welcomes* and *treasures* the individuality, personhood, identity, spirit or soul of the other human being in all its shared and unique aspects. Empathic therapies offer a caring, understanding and empowering attitude toward the individual's emotional struggles, aspirations and personal growth. They promote the individual's inherent human rights to life, liberty and the pursuit of happiness. They respect the autonomy, personal responsibility and freedom of the person. They encourage the individual to grow in self-appreciation as well as in the ability to respect, love and empathize with others.

Website: http://www.empathictherapy.org

Foundation for Excellence in Mental Health Care

This Foundation's mission is to promote better mental health outcomes. It will do so by identifying, developing, and sharing knowledge with the public about mental health care that best helps people recover and live well in society. It will promote improvements in mental health care by sponsoring research and the development of programs designed to help people thrive—physically, mentally, socially and spiritually.

Chairman, Virgil Stucker, Virgil@MentalHealthExcellence.org
Vice Chair, Gina Nikkel, Gina@MentalHealthExcellence.org
Mailing Address:
The Foundation for Excellence in Mental Health Care, Inc.
P.O. Box 600, Mill Spring, NC 28756
Website: http://www.MentalHealthExcellence.org

Freedom Center

Freedom Center is a support and activism community run by and for people labeled with severe "mental disorders." We call for compassion, human rights, self-determination, and holistic options. We create alternatives to the mental health system's widespread despair, abuse, fraudulent science and dangerous treatments. We are based in pro-choice harm reduction philosophy regarding medical treatments, and include people taking or not taking medications.

Address: 60146 Florence, MA 01062
Email: freedomcenterinfo@gmail.com
Website: http://www.freedom-center.org

The Icarus Project

We are a network of people living with and/or affected by experiences that are often diagnosed and labeled as psychiatric conditions. We believe these experiences are mad gifts needing cultivation and care, rather than diseases or disorders. By joining together as individuals and as a community, the intertwined threads of madness, creativity, and collaboration can inspire hope and transformation in an oppressive and damaged world. Participation in The Icarus Project helps us overcome alienation and tap into the true potential that lies between brilliance and madness.

Website: http://www.theicarusproject.net

INTAR: The International Network Toward Alternatives and Recovery

INTAR gathers prominent survivors, professionals, family members, and advocates from around the world to work together for new clinical and social practices towards emotional distress and what is often labeled as psychosis. Based in leading edge research and successful innovations, INTAR believes the prevailing biomedical overreliance on diagnoses, hospitals, and medications has failed to respect the dignity and autonomy of the person in crisis, and that full recovery must be at the center of ethical care.

Website: www.intar.org
General inquires: intar@intar.org

International Network of Integrative Mental Health (INIMH)

Their mission is to advance a global vision for an integrated whole person approach to mental health care via education, research, networking and advocacy, by bringing together the wisdom of world healing traditions and modern science.

623 River Road, Suite I
Fair Haven, NJ 07704
732-747-2944
Email: info@inimh.org
Website: http://www.inimh.org

International Guide to the World of Alternative Mental Health

Up to date directory of organizations, individuals, clinics and hospitals on the world's largest site on non-drug approaches to address mental health problems. This site has testimonials, and over 100 articles. You can also get information from their bookstore, support groups, email lists, and their free monthly newsletter.

Website: http://www.alternativementalhealth.com/
directory/experts.htm

Madness Radio: Voices and Visions From Outside Mental Health

An hour-long interview format, Madness Radio focuses on personal experiences of "madness" and extreme states of consciousness from beyond conventional perspectives and mainstream treatments. Madness Radio also features authors, advocates, and researchers on madness-related topics, including civil rights, science, policy reform, holistic health, history, and art. It is a regular FM show produced through WXOJ-LP in Northampton MA, and aired on KWMD in Anchorage Alaska, KBOO in Portland Oregon, and several other stations. Madness Radio is syndicated through the Pacifica community radio network and shows are picked up by stations around the country and internationally. The show is also available online and through iTunes.

Website: http://www.madnessradio.net/

National Empowerment Center (NEC)

The mission of the National Empowerment Center Inc. is to carry a message of recovery, empowerment, hope and healing to people who have been labeled with mental illness. We carry that message with authority because we are a consumer/survivor/ex-patient-run organization and each of us is living a personal journey of recovery and empowerment. We want people who are mental health consumers/survivors/ex-patients to know there is a place to turn to in order to receive the information they might need in order to regain control over their lives and the resources that affect their lives.

NEC has a toll-free information and referral line, Monday through Friday, Eastern Standard Time, during regular work hours. A Spanish speaking information specialist is also available. We have a great deal of information about topics such as advance directives, shock treatment, schizophrenia, self-help groups in your area, legal services in your area, meditation and self-help techniques, coping with depression, etc. If we don't have the information you need, we will work with you to find it.

We are not a crisis line and do not provide counseling over the phone. We can refer you to help and supports in your area. The NEC keeps updated lists of consumer-run organization and advocacy groups in all 50 states. We are also active in the cross-disability movement and can help you network with independent living centers and disability rights groups across the country.

Address: 599 Canal Street, Lawrence, MA 01840
Toll free: 800-POWER2U (800-769-3728)
Outside the U.S.: 978-685-1494

Local: 978-685-1494

Website: http://www.power2u.org

Orthomolecular Medicine

ISOM: The International Society for Orthomolecular Medicine is a site for information on orthomolecular organizations and societies throughout the world.

Website: www.orthomed.org

ISF: The International Schizophrenia Foundation has been a leader in the orthomolecular treatment of schizophrenia. It is a national, non-profit, charitable organization federally chartered in 1968, with international affiliates dedicated to raising the levels of diagnosis, treatment and prevention of the schizophrenias and allied disorders. The ISF has developed programs which include professional and public information, working with mental health care professionals and governments, and research.

Website: www.orthomed.org/isf/isf.html

Portland Hearing Voices

Portland Hearing Voices is a community group to promote mental diversity. We create public education, discussion groups, training, and community support related to hearing voices, seeing visions, and having unusual beliefs and sensory experiences often labeled as psychosis, bipolar, mania, paranoia, schizophrenia, and other mental disorders. We aim to reduce fear and misunderstanding, question stereotypes, promote holistic health options, overcome isolation, and create a more inclusive community.

Website: http://www.portlandhearingvoices.net/

PsychRights

The public mental health system is creating a huge class of chronic mental patients through forcing them to take ineffective, yet extremely harmful drugs. (http://psychrights.org/Research/Digest/NLPs/neuroleptics.htm).

The Law Project for Psychiatric Rights (PsychRights) is a non-profit, tax exempt 501(c)(3) public interest law firm whose mission is to mount a strategic legal campaign against forced psychiatric drugging and electroshock in the United States. They see this as a thrust for civil rights akin to what Thurgood Marshall and the NAACP mounted in the 40s and 50s on behalf of African American civil rights.

Currently, due to the massive growth in psychiatric drugging of children and youth and the current targeting of them for even more psychiatric drugging, PsychRights has made attacking this problem a priority. Children are virtually always forced to take these drugs because it is the adults in their lives who are making the decision. This is an unfolding national tragedy of immense proportions. As part of its mission, PsychRights is further dedicated to exposing the truth about these drugs and the courts being misled into ordering people to be drugged and subjected to other brain and body damaging interventions against their will.

http://psychrights.org/Research/Digest/Effective/effective.htm
lists articles on alternatives to neuroleptic therapy.
More articles by Nathaniel Lehrman, MD are at
http://psychrights.org/Research/Digest/Effective/Lehrman/
Lehrman.htm
Website: http://psychrights.org

Recovery Innovations

Our mission is to create opportunities and environments that empower people to recover, to succeed in accomplishing their goals, and to reconnect to themselves, others, and to meaning and purpose in life. Our vision is a transformation in the service delivery system grounded in the belief that people with mental health and substance use challenges do recover and move on with their life. The principle ingredients of this transformation include hope, education, employment, peer support and self-help. New programs are now available.

Website: http://www.recoveryinnovations.org

Websites on Mental Health Recovery and WRAP

recoveryfromschizophrenia.org

New understandings of the mind and of madness can open new doors to full recovery–thoughts from way outside the straightjacket of the "medical model."

www.mentalhealthrecovery.com

Getting well and staying well is the focus of Mary Ellen Copeland–author, educator, and mental health recovery advocate. Mary Ellen's work is based on the study of the day-to-day coping and wellness strategies of people who have experienced mental health difficulties.

www.peershelpingpeers.org

The Depression and Bipolar Support Alliance (DBSA)

Technical Assistance Center (TAC) is one of five consumer and consumer-supported assistance centers funded by SAMHSA, the Substance Abuse and Mental Health Services Administration. The purpose of the centers is to promote the involvement of consumers of mental health services in the transformation of mental health systems nationwide and to assist consumers in gaining the necessary skills to enhance consumer, peer-run programs.

www.nolongerlonely.com

A welcoming community that understands the trials and pitfalls of managing a mental illness. Find friends or seek romantic relationships knowing that everyone on this site has some form of mental illness.

www.patdeegan.com

Pat Deegan & Associates, LLC is a consumer/survivor/ex-patient run organization. Their mission is to improve the personal, social, economic and cultural wellbeing of people with psychiatric disabilities through ex-patient directed study and research.

www.mouthmag.org

A bimonthly magazine, usually only in print, but here's an online sample. We're now the only disability rights-oriented magazine put to printed page, and that is our focus.

www.intervoiceonline.org

If you hear voices (aka auditory hallucinations); if you know someone who does; if you work with people who hear voices; if you want to know about more about this experience. Then this site is for you.

www.recoverylearning.com

Vision Statement from the Final Report of the President's New Freedom Commission on Mental Health: We envision a future when everyone with a mental illness will recover; a future when mental illnesses can be prevented or cured, a future when mental illnesses are detected early, and a future when everyone with a mental illness at any stage of life has access to effective treatment and supports—essentials for living, working, learning, and participating fully in the community.

www.recoveryxchange.org

The Recovery x-Change was founded on the belief that with the appropriate supports and resources recovery is possible for anyone.

www.dailystrength.org

Home to over 500 support groups for physical and mental health challenges, this website provides valuable information on treatment choices for both short and long-term needs, like helping people get through to their next therapy appointment.

APPENDIX C
MODELS FOR PEER SUPPORT
(MASSACHUSETTS)

The Transformation Center is a peer-operated center in Roxbury, MA. Staff are in all stages of recovering mental health wellness and freedom from addictions and trauma. Their mission is to work together with their diversity, lived experience, passion and compassion, to fuel warmth and wisdom among themselves and in their communities. They want to strengthen a mental health focus on wellness and life recovery through dialogue, education, systems change advocacy, and peer support. They currently offer training for Peer Specialist Certification, Leadership Academy, WRAP (Wellness Recovery Action Plan) Facilitation, Recovery Conversations for Providers, and more.

The Transformation Center works closely with the six Recovery Learning Communities (RLCs) across Massachusetts. RLCs offer training and support for peers working and volunteering to promote wellness and recovery in the local communities. These support programs focus on

- *Addictions Recovery: Resources for what is also known as "dual recovery," for people with combined addictions recovery and mental health recovery interests.*
- *WRAP: Support for people who have and wish to maintain a Wellness Recovery Action Plan and support for people who facilitate trainings for Wellness Recovery Action Planning. WRAP is a self-help tool that helps put people in the driver's seat, directing their own recovery through self-knowledge, self-determination and taking an active role in choices through advanced directives.*
- *Health and Wellness: Peer support for physical and spiritual health and wellness.*

The Transformation Center has taken a lead in trying to ensure that the values and ethics of WRAP are adhered to and supported in all settings and practices.

The vision of the Transformation Center is to become a center of excellence where people who use, provide, and fund services can find the information, education, and support needed to create excellence in services to all people diagnosed with a mental health condition in Massachusetts.

The Transformation Center
98 Magazine St
Roxbury, MA 02119
Telephone: (617) 442-4111
Toll-free: (877) 769-7693
TTY: (617) 442-9042
Email: info@transformation-center.org
Website: www.Transformation-center.org

Two Examples of Recovery Learning Communities (RLCs)

The Western Massachusetts Recovery Learning Community (RLC) supports individuals in finding their own paths to mental health recovery within the communities of their choice by offering trauma-sensitive peer supports and through the development of a regional peer network. The Western Mass RLC is entirely peer-run and is active in all four counties of western Massachusetts.

Currently the RLC consists of a central Resource Connection Center (RCC) in Holyoke, satellite centers in Greenfield and Pittsfield, workshops and trainings made available elsewhere in the region, advocacy support, and resource sharing.

Recovery Learning Community (RLC) for Western Massachusetts
Contact: Sera Davidow or Oryx Cohen
Address: 187 High Street, Suite #303, Holyoke, MA 01040
Telephone: (413) 539-5941; Toll-Free: (866) 641-2853

Fax: (413) 536-5466
Email: info@westernmassrlc.org
Website: www.westernmassrlc.org

The Metro Suburban RLC in Quincy, MA is a peer-run organization offering peer support and peer-run activities in a suburb close to Boston. It promotes trauma-informed peer support, advocacy, education and training opportunities for individuals who have lived experience with a mental health condition. As a community, it takes a proactive approach toward fighting stigma and developing a culture that supports recovery, resiliency and self-empowerment. It is a place to make friends, share recovery experiences, recognize and utilize talents and skills, and learn new skills.

Deborah Webb, Project Specialist
Activity Area B, 2nd Floor, 460 Quincy Ave., Quincy, MA 02169
Telephone: 617-472-3237 x305
Email: dwebb@metrosubrlc.org
Website: www.metrosubrlc.org

APPENDIX D
SAFE HOMES/THERAPEUTIC COMMUNITIES

The **American Residential Treatment Association** (ARTA) can help you make the best match between you and one of 30 member facilities in the USA offering residential care to adults with serious mental challenges, including schizophrenia, bipolar disorder, depression, personality disorders, and disorders combined with substance abuse. On their website, you will find general information on residential treatment. They also keep an updated Directory of Residential Facilities, with links to websites offering detailed program information.

http://www.ARTAusa.org

Some Examples:

CooperRiis Healing Community
101 Healing Farm Lane
Mill Spring, NC 28756
Phone: Toll free (800) 957-5155
Main number: (828) 894-5557
Fax: (828) 894-7111
http://www.cooperriis.org

Soteria-Alaska
401 E. Northern Lights Blvd., Suite 100
Anchorage, AK 99503

(907) 333-4343 • (907)360-6768
Email: Susan Musante/Project Manager: susan@soteria-alaska.com
E-mail: office@soteria-alaska.com
Website: http://www.soteria-alaska.com

Windhorse Integrative Mental Health (East)
211 North Street, Suite #1
Northampton, MA 01060
413-586-0207, ext. 333
info@windhorseimh.org

Windhorse Integrative Mental Health (West)
1411 Marsh Street Suite 103
San Luis Obispo, CA 93401
805-548-8931 x102

Soteria in Europe
Soteria Bern (Switzerland) http://www.soteria.ch

Soteria Zwiefalten (Germany)
http://www.zfp-web.de/K3/html/artikel.
php3?path=0:3:32:138&a_id=83

Toll-haus project (Germany) http://www.toll-haus.de/index.html

Soteria Frankfurt an der Oder (Germany) http://www.lunaticpride.
de/SOTERIA.HTM

Soteria Budapest (Hungary) www.soteria.hu

APPENDIX E
RESOURCES FOR REDUCING AND SAFELY GETTING OFF PSYCHIATRIC DRUGS

Harm Reduction: Coming Off of Psychiatric Drugs, is a free online book for those interested in learning more about psychiatric drugs, their side effects, and help in stopping: http://www.freedom-center.org/freedom-center-icarus-project-publish-coming-psychiatric-drugs-guide. The book's sponsors describe it: "The Icarus Project and Freedom Center's 40-page guide gathers the best information we've come across and the most valuable lessons we've learned about reducing and coming off psychiatric medication."

Safe Harbor (http://www.alternativementalhealth.com) includes links to find medical doctors (by zip code) who can assist with helping people safely get off of psychiatric drugs and to find medical personnel who will treat people without drugs.

Alternative to Meds Center (http://www.alternativetomedscenter.com) provides residential psychiatric medication withdrawal with medical and naturopathic oversight in Sedona, Arizona. Their purpose is to help a person regain their mental health and happiness. This is obtained by: stabilizing the neurochemistry using naturally occurring substances, removing heavy metals and other neurotoxins, and gradually replacing medications with natural alternatives. They combine orthomolecular medicine and customized heavy metal chelation therapies to address mental health.

Green Mental Health(http://greenmentalhealthcare.com)This holistic mental health care system reflects traditional environmental, humanitarian, and health-conscious values. Locations for residential withdrawal from psychiatric medications are in Costa Rica; Malibu, California; and New Mexico. The BioSanctuary medical director, Genita Petralli, is a recipient of the 2010 Human Rights Award. http://greenmentalhealthcare.com/ The website for the Malibu facility is http://biosanctuary.com/ malibu-facility.

The Road Back (http://www.theroadback.org) helps with tapering off all alcohol and other drugs and trains physicians how to help with tapering off patients who want to stop taking psychiatric drugs. It provides free counseling and sells a book by Jim Harper, *How to Get off Psychoactive Drugs Safely.*

Institute for Progressive Medicine (http://www.iprogressivemed. com) in Irvine, California was founded by Allan Sosin, MD, a board certified internist and nephrologist. It offers supervised withdrawal in a gradual process, making use of nutritional supplements to make withdrawal easier. Vitamins, minerals, and amino acids are given intravenously to minimize withdrawal symptoms. Sauna therapy enhances detoxification.

For Children: Non-Drug Treatment and Withdrawal from Drugs

The Block Center (http://www.blockcenter.com) is dedicated to finding and treating the underlying health problems in children and offering information on how children can safely get off of psychiatric drugs.

Drug Free Children (http://www.drugfreechildren.org) offers information related to "chemical restraints" on children.

The Doris J. Rapp Education Corporation (http://www.drrapp. com) offers information on environmental factors affecting health in children and adults.

APPENDIX F
PRINCIPLES THAT IDENTIFY ORTHOMOLECULAR MEDICINE: A UNIQUE MEDICAL SPECIALTY
by Richard Kunin, MD

In 1969 Linus Pauling coined the word "orthomolecular" to denote the use of naturally occurring substances, particularly nutrients, in maintaining health and treating disease. At that time, megadose niacin therapy for schizophrenia and dietary treatment of "hypoglycemia" were the major focus of the movement. Since then, orthomolecular psychiatry and medicine have emerged as a distinct and important specialty area in medical practice.

In the meantime, other medical movements have sprung up out of the public demand for hope in the face of a worsening epidemic of cancer, heart attacks and mental illness and in response to the outcry against adverse effects of modern medical treatments and invasive diagnostic and intensive care procedures. Alternative therapies have come forward to fill the vacuum left by modern medicine, which failed to provide effective treatments for the major epidemic diseases and in protest against medicine's overreliance on pharmacology, for the drug treatments seem to have fostered the epidemic of drug dependence, which is the major epidemic of our time.

The public majority was ready for a new medicine based on nontoxic, non-invasive, "natural" medicines to go with the re-discovered "natural foods."

Holistic medicine became a rallying point for the New Medicine by putting nutrition, exercise and meditation ahead of surgery, radiation and drugs. It was an answer to the adverse effects of Mega-Medicine, the "cut, burn, and poison" approach to "health." And, since holistic medicine did not focus on basic science data, it did not force a paradigm shift in the medical establishment.

Orthomolecular medicine, on the other hand, because it is identified with Linus Pauling, one of our greatest scientists, and because it rests on a vast body of research in the basic and clinical sciences, forces a major revision in medical thinking. Nutrition, which has been the stepchild of medicine and generally considered a dead issue in medicine, suddenly is at the crux of this new medical movement. No wonder then, that "orthomolecular" became a buzzword to the medical establishment, who saw it as only megavitamins and judged it as quackery.

By contrast, the word "Holistic" became the subject of numerous symposia and journal articles and has been welcomed by editors eager to promote the image of modern medicine as a progressive and responsive institution. But as it gained supporters, holistic medicine also gained additional theories and practices, some of dubious value, some downright unscientific. Even the most broad-minded and liberal-minded editor had to recoil from permitting such things as psychic healing and kinesiology within the pages of a refereed journal.

Soon the word "alternative," came to replace "holistic" in medical journals. Now the establishment could pick and choose individually between the various therapies that had gathered under the holistic umbrella: nutrition, biofeedback, chiropractic, acupuncture, herbalism, homeopathy, massage, hypnosis, iridology, kinesiology, astrology, psychic healing and other intuitive therapies, to name a few. The orthomolecular movement was faltered with identity confusion and, in fact, many of our own members seem to have chosen "holistic" as their preferred badge-word. This is good for the short run, I agree: it is attractive to patients and profitable while being noncontroversial and safer professionally as well. In the long run, however, I think "holistic medicine" has no future. It has already lost its identity, except as a clearinghouse for medical novelty. Most important, because it does not identify strongly with science, it has lost reliability.

Meantime, orthomolecular medicine retains scientific reason for being: its basic science foundations of nutrition, biochemistry and clinical nutrition have grown at a prodigious rate. Megavitamin niacin therapy, which was considered dangerous and controversial in treating schizophrenia, is now the standard of care in the hyperlipidemias. What began as megavitamin therapy now employs a broad database and a variety of therapies applicable to numerous medical and psychiatric conditions.

It is ironic that this positive growth of orthomolecular science and therapy has actually clouded the identity of the orthomolecular movement. On the one hand, we are confused with holistic medicine; on the other, we are seen as *only* the avante-garde of orthodox medicine. In hopes of defining our true identity, let me update the concept of orthomolecular medicine as *a new medical specialty*.

First of all, the orthomolecular database rests strongly on the following areas of scientific knowledge: nutrition, biochemistry, cell biology, physiology, general medicine, immunology, allergy, endocrinology, pharmacology, toxicology, gastroenterology, parasitology, nephrology, physical medicine and manipulation therapies, dentistry, veterinary science, food science, agriculture, and climatology.

The following nutrients and therapeutic modalities are used and fit the definition of orthomolecular: vitamins, minerals, amino acids, essential fatty acids, fiber, enzymes, antibodies, antigens, cell therapy, chelation therapy, dialysis, plasmapharesis, hydrotherapy, thermal therapy, phototherapy, electrotherapy (including electroconvulsive therapy), air ion therapy, light therapy, solar therapy, acupuncture, massage, exercise, Biofeedback, hypnotherapy and other psychotherapies.

All of the orthomolecular practice rests on a foundation of basic-science advances in biochemistry, biophysics, physiology, psychophysiology and ecology. We do not eschew drug therapy or pharmacology, but we do recognize their limitations and their potential for toxicity. Orthomolecular knowledge gives greater choice of benefits for our patients with less risk of adverse affects.

Aside from these areas of interest, there are by now some well-defined beliefs and principles that also distinguish orthomolecular practitioners from orthodox health practitioners...

Here is a list of 15 principles that identify the "spirit" of orthomolecular medicine:

- *Orthomolecules come first in medical diagnosis and treatment. Knowledge of the safe and effective use of nutrients, enzymes, hormones, antigens, antibodies and other naturally occurring molecules is essential to assure a reasonable standard of care in medical practice.*
- *Orthomolecules have a low risk of toxicity. Pharmacological drugs always carry a higher risk and are therefore second choice if there is an orthomolecular alternative treatment.*
- *Laboratory tests are not always accurate, and blood tests do not necessarily reflect nutrient levels within specific organs or tissues, particularly not within the nervous system. Therapeutic trial and dose titration is often the most practical test.*
- *Biochemical individuality is a central precept of orthomolecular medicine. Hence, the search for optimal nutrient doses is a practical issue. Megadoses (larger than normal doses of nutrients) are often effective, but this can be determined only by therapeutic trial. Dose titration is indicated in otherwise unresponsive cases.*
- *The Recommended Daily Allowance (RDA) of the United States Food and Drug Administration (FDA) are intended for normal, healthy people. By definition, sick patients are not normal or healthy and not likely to be adequately served by the RDA.*
- *Environmental pollution of air, water and food is common. Diagnostic search for toxic pollutants is justified, and a high "index of suspicion" is mandatory in every case.*
- *Optimal health is a lifetime challenge. Biochemical needs change, and our Orthomolecular prescriptions need to change based upon follow-up, repeated testing and therapeutic trials to permit fine-tuning of each prescription and to provide a degree of health never before possible.*

- *Nutrient-related disorders are always treatable, and deficiencies are usually curable. To ignore their existence is tantamount to malpractice.*
- *Don't let medical defeatism prevent a therapeutic trial. Hereditary and so-called "locatable" disorders are often responsive to orthomolecular treatment.*
- *When a treatment is known to be safe and likely effective, as is the case in much orthomolecular therapy, a therapeutic trial is mandated.*
- *Patient reports are usually reliable. The patient must listen to his or her body. The physician must listen to his patient.*
- *To deny the patient information and access to orthomolecular treatment is to deny the patient informed consent for any other treatment.*
- *Inform the patient about his or her condition; provide access to all technical information and reports; and respect the right of freedom of choice in medicine.*
- *Inspire the patient to realize that Health is not merely the absence of disease but rather the positive attainment of optimal function and wellbeing.*
- *Hope is therapeutic, and orthomolecular therapies always are valuable as a source of Hope. This is ethical so long as there is no misrepresentation or deception.*

To clarify the role of orthomolecular medicine in relation to medical orthodoxy. The essentials boil down to 7 cardinal rules:

- *Nutrition comes first in medical diagnosis and treatment.*
- *Drug treatment is used only for specific indications and always with an eye to the potential dangers and adverse effects.*
- *Environmental pollution and food adulteration are an inescapable fact of modern life and are a medical priority.*
- *Biochemical individuality is the norm in medical practice; therefore, stereotyped RDA values are unreliable nutrient guides.*
- *Blood tests do not necessarily reflect tissue levels of nutrients,*
- *Nutrient diagnosis is always defensible because nutrient-related disorders are usually treatment responsive or curable,*
- *Hope is an indispensable ally of the physician and an absolute right of the patient.*

Finally, let me repeat that our rallying point and badge-word must be "orthomolecular," a landmark concept that conveys the genius of Dr. Pauling, who saw the need to resurrect nutrition and put it first, not last, in our science of health and disease.

REFERENCES

Introduction

AAMC (1999). Medical school objectives report III. Washington, DC: AAMC.

American Psychiatric Association (2000). *The diagnostic and statistical manual of mental disorders.* Arlington, VA: APA.

Bragdon, E. (Ed.). (2012). *Spiritism and mental health.* London: Singing Dragon.

Henry, J. (2005). Parapsychology: Research on exceptional experiences. London: Routledge.

Lehmann, P., and Stastny, P. (Eds.). (2007). *Alternatives beyond psychiatry.* Germany: Peter Lehmann.

McTaggart, L. (2002). *The field: The quest for the secret force of the universe.* New York: HarperCollins.

Mosher, L. R., Fanzine, R., and Menn, A. Z. (1992). *Treatment at soteria house: A manual for the practice of interpersonal phenomenology.* Bethesda, MD: NIMH.

U.S. Department of Health and Human Services (1999). *Mental health: A report of the Surgeon General.* Washington, DC: DHHS.

Watters, E. (2010). *Crazy like us: The globalization of the American psyche.* New York: Free Press.

Whitaker, R. (2010). *Anatomy of an epidemic.* New York: Crown.

World Health Organization (1992). *Manual of international statistical classification of diseases, injuries and causes of death* (10th ed.). Geneva: WHO.

Chapter One

Berger, W., Mendlowicz, M. V., Marques-Portella, C., Kinrys, G., et al. (2009). Pharmacologic alternatives to antidepressants in posttraumatic stress disorder: A systematic review. *Prog Neuropsychopharmacol Biol Psychiatry, 33*(2), 169-80.

Birks, J., and Harvey, R. J. (2006). Donepezil for dementia due to Alzheimer's disease. *Cochrane Database Syst Rev. 1,* CD001190.

Bragdon, E. (2004). *Kardec's spiritism.* Woodstock, VT: Lightning Up Press, pp.60-63.

Bragdon, E. (Ed.). (2012). *Spiritism and mental health.* London: Singing Dragon.

Dixon, L. B., Dickerson, F., Bellack, A. S., Bennett, M., et al. (2010). Schizophrenia patient outcomes research team (PORT). *Schizophr Bull., 36*(1), 48-70.

Dubrui, S. A. (2004). "The Bipolar World" in The Icarus Project (Ed.) Navigating the space between brilliance and madness: A reader and roadmap of bipolar worlds." New York: Icarus Project.

Fountoulakis, K. N. (2008). The contemporary face of bipolar illness: Complex diagnostic and therapeutic challenges. *CNS Spectr. 13* (9), 763-74, and 777-79.

Fournier, J. C., DeRubeis, R. J., Hollon, S. D., Dimidjian, S., et al. (2010). Antidepressant drug effects and depression severity: A patient-level meta-analysis. *JAMA, 303*(1), 47-53.

Greenberg, J. (1989). *I never promised you a rose garden.* New York: Signet.

Hyman, S. (1996). Initiation and adaptation: A paradigm for understanding psychotropic drug action. *American Journal of Psychiatry, 15,* 151-61.

Katzman, M. A. (2009). Current considerations in the treatment of generalized anxiety disorder. *CNS Drugs, 23*(2), 103-20.

Kirsch, I. (2008). Challenging received wisdom: Antidepressants and the placebo effect. *McGill J Med., 11*(2), 219-22.

Lacasse, J., (2005). Serotonin and depression: A disconnect between the advertisements and the scientific literature. *PloS Medicine, 2,* 1211-16.

Lam, R. W., Kennedy, S. H., Grigoriadis, S., McIntyre R.S.; et al. (2009). Canadian Network for Mood and Anxiety Treatments (CANMAT): Clinical guidelines for the management of major depressive disorder in adults: III. Pharmacotherapy. *J Affect Disord., 117* Suppl 1, S26-43.

Mackler, D. (2008). *Take these broken wings* (documentary). www.iraresoul. com

National Institutes of Mental Health (2008). National survey on drug use and health. Bethesda, MD: NIMH.

Robinson, D. G., Woerner, M. G., McMeniman, M., Mendelowitz, A., Bilder, R. M. (2004). Symptomatic and functional recovery from a first episode of schizophrenia or schizoaffective disorder. *Am. J. Psychiatry, 161*(3), 473-79.

Shealy, N., and Church, D. (2008). *Soul medicine: Awakening your inner blueprint for abundant health and energy.* Santa Rosa, CA: Energy Psychology Press.

Shoenfelt, J. L., and Weston, C. G. (2007). Managing obsessive compulsive disorder: In children and adolescents. *Psychiatry (Edgemont), 4*(5), 47-53.

Tajima, K., Fernández, H., López-Ibor, J. L., Carrasco, J. L., et al. (2009). Schizophrenia treatment: Critical review on the drugs and mechanisms of action of antipsychotics. *Actas Esp. Psiquiatr., 37*(6), 330-42.

Thase, M. E. (2008). Do antidepressants really work? A clinicians' guide to evaluating the evidence. *Curr. Psychiatry Rep., 10*(6), 487-94.

Watters, E. (2010). *Crazy like us: The globalization of the American psyche.* New York: Free Press.

Whitaker, R. (2010). *Anatomy of an epidemic.* New York: Crown.

World Health Organization (2007). http://www.who.int/whosis/whostat2007/en/

Chapter Two

Bragdon, E. (2004). *Kardec's Spiritism.* Woodstock, VT: Lightning Up Press, pp. 60-63.

Center for Integrative Medicine at University of Arizona (2011). Definition of integrative medicine (IM). http://integrativemedicine.arizona.edu/about/definition.html

Watters, E. (2010). *Crazy like us: The globalization of the American psyche.* New York: Free Press.

Chapter Three

AME–The International Medical Spiritist Association can be contacted through their website: www.ameinternational.org

Azevedo, J.L. (1997). Spirit and matter: New horizons for medicine. Las Vegas, NV: New Falcon.

Bragdon, E. (2002). Spiritual alliances. Woodstock, VT: Lightening Up Press.

Bragdon, E. (2004). *Kardec's Spiritism: A home for healing and spiritual evolution.* Woodstock, VT: Lightening Up Press.

Bragdon, E. (June 2005). Spiritist Healing Centers in Brazil. In *Seminars in integrative medicine.* Elsevier Press.

Bragdon, E. (executive producer). (2006). *I do not heal, God is the one who heals* (30-minute documentary). www.createspace.com/214314.

Bragdon, E. (co-producer). (2008). *Spiritism: Bridging spirituality and health* (30-minute documentary). www.createspace.com/243118

Bragdon, E. (2011). South American Spiritism: Spiritist hospitals and healing centers in Brazil,. In M. Micozzi, *Fundamentals of complementary and integrative medicine* (4th ed.). St. Louis, MO: Saunders/Elsevier Press, pp.551-59.

Bragdon, E. (May 2011). Spiritist Psychiatric Hospitals in Brazil. *International Journal of Healing and Caring* (online journal).

Bragdon, E. (2012). Introduction. In E. Bragdon (Ed.), *Spiritism and Mental Health: Practices from Spiritist Centers and Spiritist Psychiatric Hospitals in Brazil.* Philadelphia: Singing Dragon.

Canadas, C.M. (2001). *A Eternal Busca da Cura.* San Paulo, Brasil: Boa Nova Editora.

de Souza, R. L. V., and e Paulo, J. R. (2012). The Spiritist hospital André Luiz. In E. Bragdon, (Ed.), *Spiritism and mental health practices from Spiritist centers and Spiritist Psychiatric Hospitals in Brazil.* Philadelphia: Singing Dragon.

Fuller, R. K., and Hiller-Sturmhöfel, S. (1999). Alcoholism treatment in the USA: An overview." *Alcohol Research and Health, 23*(2), 69-77.

Hageman, J., Peres, J., Moreira-Almeida, A., Caixeta, L., Wickramasekera, I., and Krippner, S. (2010). The neurobiology of trance and mediumship in Brazil. In S. Krippner and H. Friedman (Eds.), *Mysterious minds: The neurobiology of psychics, mediums and other extraordinary people.* Santa Barbara, CA: Praeger/ABC Clio, pp. 85-111.

Herve, I. (2006). *Reencarnacao: A Unica Explicacao [Reincarnation: The Only Explanation].* Porto Alegre, Brazil: Editora Age.

Herve, I., de Silva, S., Borges, R., Tejada, V., et al. (2003). *Apometria: A Conexao Entre a Ciencia e O Espiritismo [Apometry: A Connection Between Science and Spiritism]*. Porto Alegre, Brazil: Dacasa Editora/Livraria Palmarinca.

Instituto Brasileiro de Geografia e Estatistica (IBGE). 2000 Census. Sao Paulo, Brazil. www.ibge.gov.br

Kardec, A. (1986). *The mediums' book*. Brasilia, Brazil: Federação Esprita Brasileira (original work published 1861).

Kardec, A. (2004a). *Spiritism in its simplest expression*. Philadelphia: AKES, p. 190. (original work published 1859).

Kardec, A. (2004b). *Introduction to the Spiritist philosophy*. Philadelphia: AKES, pp.154-155 (original work published 1859).

Lake, J. (2012). Foreword. In E. Bragdon (Ed.), *Spiritism and mental health: Practices from Spiritist Centers and Spiritist Psychiatric Hospitals in Brazil*. Philadelphia: Singing Dragon.

Maisto, S., Clifford, P. R., and Tonigan, J. S. (2010). "Initial and long-term alcohol treatment success: 10-year study of the project MATCH, Albuquerque sample, clinical research branch." Center on Alcoholism, Substance Abuse, and Addictions (CASAA), University of New Mexico. http://casaa.unm.edu (accessed Feb 14, 2010)

Maisto, S. A., Clifford, P. R., Longabaugh, R., and Beattie, M. (2002). The relationship between abstinence for one year following pretreatment assessment and alcohol use and other functioning at two years in individuals presenting for alcohol treatment. *Journal of Studies on Alcohol, 63*, 397-403.

Moreira-Almeida, A., and Moreira, A. (2008). Inacio Ferreira: The institutionalization of the integration between medicine and paranormal phenomena. Presentation at the Convention of the Parapsychological Association and the Society for Psychical Research.

Moreira-Almeida, A. (2012). The Spiritist view of mental disorders. In E. Bragdon (Ed.), *Spiritism and mental health:Practices from Spiritist centers and Spiritist psychiatric hospitals in Brazil*. Philadelphia: Singing Dragon.

NIH (2001). The numbers count: Mental disorder in America. *NIH publication #01-4584*. Bethesda, MD: NIMH.

Rubik, B. (2012). The power of magnetized water. In E. Bragdon (Ed.), *Spiritism and mental health practices from Spiritist centers and Spiritist psychiatric hospitals in Brazil.* Philadelphia: Singing Dragon.

SAMHSA, Office of Applied Studies, National Household Survey on Drug Abuse, 2000 and 2001. http://www.oas.samhsa.gov/mhtx/ch6.htm (accessed Feb 14, 2011).

U.S. Dept of Health and Human Services. Press release. www.hhs.gov/news (accessed September 5, 2003).

U.S. Dept. of Health and Human Services of Applied Studies (2011). Results from the 2009 National survey on drug use and health: Volume I. Summary of national findings. Washington, DC: USDHHS.

United States Spiritist Council (USSC). Spiritist Centers in the USA. http://www.spiritist.us (accessed February 15, 2011).

Xavier F. (2000a). *Nosso Lar: A spiritual home.* Philadelphia: Allan Kardec Educational Society.

Xavier F. (2000b). *And life goes on.* Philadelphia: Allan Kardec Educational Society.

Chapter Five

Bach, E. (1996). *Heal thyself.* London: CW Daniel.

Kardec, A. (2004). *The Gospel according to Spiritism.* In *First Epistle of Peter.* Peter advises steadfastness and perseverance under persecution (1–2:10); to the practical duties of a holy life (2:11–3:13); and he refers to the example of Christ and other motives to patience and holiness (3:14–4:19).

Chapter Six

Dalgalarrondo, P. et al. (2004). Religião e uso de drogas por adolescentes. *Revista Brasileira de Psiquiatria, 26(2).*

Kardec, A. (2009a). Livro dos médiuns, Chapter VIII, item 131. Brasília: FEB.

Kardec, A. (2009b). A Gênese, capítulo XIV, items 32, 33, 45 and 46. Brasília: FEB.

Koenig, H. G. (2007). Religião, espiritualidade e transtornos psicóticos. *Revista Psiquiatria Clínica, 34 (1).*

Miller, W. R., and C'deBaca, J. (2001). *Quantum change: When epiphanies and sudden insights transform ordinary lives.* New York: Guilford Press.

Sanches, Z.V.; Oliveira, L.G..; Nappo, S. A.(2004). Fatores protetores de adolescentes contra o uso de drogas com enfase na religiosidade. *Ciencia & Saúde Coletiva, 9*(1), 43-55.

Xavier, F., and Luiz, A. (1959). Chapter 4, Indução Mental. In *Mecanismos da mediunidade,* Brasília: FEB. p. 47.

Chapter Seven

Dossey, L. (1997). *Prayer is good medicine.* New York: HarperCollins.

Gawande, A. (2008). *Better: A surgeon's notes on performance.* New York: Picadore Press.

Chapter Eight

Hochstatter, Z., and Cote, S. (2001). *Think about it* (documentary).

Chapter Nine

Carlgren, F. (2008). *Education towards freedom—Rudolf Steiner education: A survey of the work of Waldorf schools throughout the world.* Edinburgh, UK: Floris Books.

Mees, L. F. C. (1983). *Blessed by illness.* Herndon, VA: Steiner Books.

Steiner, R. (1995). *Anthroposophy in everyday life.* London, UK: Rudolf Steiner Press.

Chapter Ten

APA (2000). *The diagnostic and statistical manual* (DSM-IV-R). Arlington, VA: American Psychiatric Association.

Casey, S. (December 2010). Leap of faith. in *O: The Oprah Magazine.*

Estação da Luz (Light Station). (2011). *The mothers of Chico Xavier* (Brazilian film).

Fenwick, P., and Fenwick, E. (2008). *The art of dying.* New York: Continuum.

Guggenheim, B., and Guggenheim, J. (1996). *Hello from Heaven.* New York: Bantam.

James, W. (1988). *William James: Writings 1902-1910.* New York: Library of America.

Jung, C. G. (1976). *The Portable Jung.* New York: Penguin.

Chapter Eleven

Aebi, E., Ciompi, L., and Hansen, H. (1993). *Soteria im Gespräch. Ueber eine alternative.* Bonn, Switzerland: Schizophreniebehandlung Psychiatrie-Verlag.

Anthony, W. (2001). *The recovery vision: New paradigm, new questions, new answers. Mental health: Stop exclusion, dare to care, world health day 2001.* Boston University Center for Psychiatric Rehabilitation. http://www.bu.edu/cpr/webcast/recoveryvision.html

Ciompi, L. (1997). Die emotionalen Grundlagen des Denkens: Entwurf einer fraktalen Affektlogik. Göttingen, Germany: Vandenhoeck & Ruprecht.

Ciompi, L., Dauwalder, H. P., Maier, Ch., Aebi, W., Trütsch, K., Kupper, Z., and Rutishauser, Ch. (1992a). The pilot project "Soteria Berne": Clinical experiences and results. *Brit. J. Psychiat. 161,* 145-53.

Ciompi, L., Dauwalder, H. P., Aebi, E., Trütsch, K., and Kupper, Z. (1992b). A new approach to acute schizophrenia. Further results of the pilot-project Soteria Berne. In A. Werbart and J. Cullberg (Eds.), *Psychotherapy of schizophrenia: Facilitating and obstructive factors* (pp. 95-109). Oslo, Norway: Scandinavian University Press.

Ciompi, L., Maier, Ch., Dauwalder, H. P., and Aebi, E. (1993). An integrative biological-psychosocial evolutionary model of schizophrenia and its therapeutic consequences: First results of the pilot project "Soteria Berne." In G. Benedetti and P. M. Furlan (Eds.), *Psychotherapy of schizophrenia* (pp. 319-333). Seattle, WA: Hogrefe & Huber.

Ciompi, L., and Hoffmann, H. (2004). Soteria Berne: An innovative milieu therapeutic approach to acute schizophrenia based on the concept of affect-logic. *World Psychiatry, 3,* 140-46.

Community Mental Health Services Federal Block Grant, FY2006-2007 State Plan (2006). http://www.hss.state.ak.us/dbh/federalblock.htm.

Feldmar, A. (2001). "Minute particulars" from "In a nutshell," a *Mental Patients' Newsletter.* http://www.andrewfeldmar.ca/works

Harding, C. (1996). *Some things we've learned about vocational rehabilitation of the seriously and persistently mentally ill.* Abstracted from presentation at Boston University Research Colloquium, Brookline, MA.

Harding, C. (2001). *The Recovery vision: New paradigm, new questions, new answers. Mental health: Stop exclusion, dare to care, World Health Day 2001.* Boston University

Center for Psychiatric Rehabilitation. http://www.bu.edu/cpr/webcast/recoveryvision.html

Heinreich, J. (Nov.19, 2005). Lisbeth and Don Cooper. *Tyron Daily Bulletin.*

Mackler, D. (2011). *Healing homes* (documentary). www.iraresoul.com

Mosher, L. R. (1999). *Soteria and other alternatives to acute psychiatric hospitalization: A personal and professional review. The Journal of Nervous and Mental Disease, 187,*142-149.

Mosher, L., and Burti, L. (1994). *Community mental health: A practical guide.* New York: W.W. Norton.

Mosher, L., Hendrix, V., and Fort, D. (2004). *Soteria: Through madness to deliverance.* Bloomington, IN: Xlibris.

President's New Freedom Commission on Mental Health Final Report (2003). Achieving the promise: Transforming mental health care in America, 2003. http://www.mentalhealthcommission.gov/reports/FinalReport/FullReport-06.htm

Siebert, A. (1999). Brain Disease Hypothesis for Schizophrenia Disconfirmed by All Evidence. *Journal of Ethical Human Sciences and Services, 1*(2), 179-89. http://www.antipsychiatry.org/siebert.htm

Whitaker, R. (2002). *Mad in America: Bad science, bad medicine, and the enduring mistreatment of the mentally ill.* Cambridge, MA: Perseus.

Whitaker, R. (2010). *Anatomy of an epidemic.* New York: Crown.

Chapter Twelve

Angell, M. (June 23, 2011) "The epidemic of mental illness: Why?" *The New York Review of Books.*

Angell, M. (June 29, 2011). The illusions of psychiatry. *The New York Review of Books.*

Breggin, P. (2008). *Medication madness.* New York: St. Martin's Press.

Carey, B. (June 23, 2011). Expert on mental illness reveals her own fight (interview with Marsha Linehan). *The New York Times.*

Chamberlin, J. (2004). Preface. In P. Lehmann (Ed.), *Coming off psychiatric drugs.* Germany: Peter Lehmann.

Goldberg, C. (June 8, 2007). Mental patients find understanding in therapy led by peers. *The Boston Globe.*

Hall, W. (Ed). (2007). *Harm reduction guide to coming off psychiatric drugs.* New York: Icarus Project & Freedom Center.

Lehmann, P. (Ed.). (2004). *Coming Off Psychiatric Drugs.* Germany: Peter Lehmann.

Mackler, D. (2011). *Open Dialogue* (documentary). www.iraresoul.com

Seikkula, J., Aaltonen, J., Alakare, B., Haarakangas, K., Keranen, J., and Lehtinen, K. (2006). Five-year experience of first-episode nonaffective psychosis in open-dialogue approach: Treatment principles, follow-up outcomes, and two case studies. *Psychotherapy Research, 16*(2), 214/228.

Whitaker, R. (2010). *Anatomy of an epidemic.* New York: Crown.

Chapter Thirteen

Chaudhary, R. R. (2009). *Renewal of the center: Posttraumatic repair through the STAR process* (unpublished master's thesis). Pacifica Graduate Institute, Santa Barbara, CA.

Grof, S., and Grof, C. (Eds.). (1989). *Spiritual emergency: When personal transformation becomes a crisis.* Los Angeles: Tarcher.

Leifner, L. M., and Adame, A. L. (2010). *Mainstream alternative treatments of emotional distress. PsycCRTIQUES, 52*(32). (Retrieved from PsycINFO June 28, 2011.)

Leifner, L.M., and Philips, S. N. (2003). The immovable object versus the irresistible force: Problems and opportunities for humanistic psychology. *Journal of Humanistic Psychology, 43,* 156-173.

New Freedom Commission on Mental Health (2003). "Achieving the promise: Transforming mental health care in America, 2003." http://www.mentalhealthcommission.gov/reports/FinalReport/FullReport-06.htm

STAR Foundation (Producer). (2005). *The psychology of birth* (DVD). Available from http://www.starfound.org

Chapter Fourteen

Findeisen, B. (2010). *Lasting impressions.* Manuscript in preparation.

Findeisen, B. (1993). Rescripting destructive birth patterns. In W. B. Lucas (Ed.), *Regression Therapy: A Handbook for Professionals, Vol. II* (pp. 64-73). Crest Park, CA: Deep Forest Press.

CONTRIBUTING AUTHORS' CONTACT INFO

Chapter Five:

Sylene Almeida, MD (Pediatrics/Emergency Medicine) is a clinician in Brasilia, Brazil. She is also a homeopath, Jin Shin Jitsu practitioner, and developer of "Flowers of the Wind," flower essences from the Serrado that help those with psychiatric issues as well as physical problems. She lives near Brasilia, Brazil.
Website: http://www.floresdovento.com.

Chapter Six:

Francis Mourão, psychiatrist and homeopath, education specialist, technical director of the Bom Retiro Spiritist Psychiatric Hospital; francis@hospitalbomretiro.com.br
Ivete Contieri Ferraz, psychiatrist, MA in psychopharmacology and addictions, technical manager of Bom Retiro Spiritist Psychiatric Hospital; ivetecf@hotmail.com
Elke Pilar Nemer Pinheiro, addiction specialist, MA in health sciences, psychologist at inpatient integral unit for dependencies at Bom Retiro Spiritist Psychiatric Hospital; enemer@terra.com.br
Janaina Graziela Anzolini Bunese, psychologist at inpatient integral unit for dependencies at the Bom Retiro Spiritist Psychiatric Hospital; specialization in cognitive behavioral therapy; janagblin@gmail.com

Bom Retiro Spiritist Psychiatric Hospital, Department of the Spiritist Federation of Parana, located on Rua Nilo Peçanha, 1552, Bom Retiro, a district in the city of Curitiba, Parana, Brazil; www.hospitalbomretiro. com.br

Chapter Seven:
Linda Haltinner, DC, is the Founder and Medical Director of Sojourns, a non-profit, multidisciplinary, integrated, holistic clinic offering general family healthcare, biological medicine, wellness support, and health education programs in Southern Vermont. Its client-centered, integrated wellness-based approach, combined with its commitments to education, community outreach and economic accessibility help define the clinic as an innovator in the healthcare delivery system.
Telephone: 802.722.4023
Fax: 802.722.4137
Email: client_services@sojourns.org
Website: http://www.sojourns.org

Chapter Eight:
Sergei Slavoutski (PhD candidate)
Email: Sergei@insightfulhealings.com
Phone: 925-858-6644

Chapter Nine:
Jessica Randall (Acupuncturist, Meditation Teacher)
The River
3510 1st Ave. NW
Seattle, WA 98107
Telephone: (206) 782-7572
Email: jr_acupuncture@yahoo.com

Brad Weeks, MD (Orthomolecular Psychiatrist)
P.O. Box 740
6456 S. Central Ave.

Clinton, WA 98236 (on Whidbey Island)
Telephone: 360-341-2303
Email: admin@weeksmd.com
Website: http://www.weeksmd.com

Chapter Thirteen:

Barbara Findeisen, MFT, is President of the Association for Pre- and Perinatal Psychology and Health (APPPAH), and was a founding member of the International Association for Regression Research and Therapies (IARRT). She is a graduate of Stanford University, and has been in private practice since 1976. Ms. Findeisen is the producer of two documentary films, "Journey to Be Born" and "The Psychology of Birth." She created and is Clinical Director of the STAR workshop, a profoundly transformative 10-day retreat designed to accelerate self-healing and personal growth.

Kenyon Ranch, HC 65 Box 278, Tumacacori, AZ 85640
Telephone: 520-398-8073
Email: kenyon.ranch@earthlink.net
Website: http://www.kenyonranch.com

Appendix F:

Richard A. Kunin, MD (Orthomolecular Psychiatrist)
2698 Pacific Ave, San Francisco, CA 94115
Telephone: (415) 346-2500

INDEX

addiction. *See* drug abuse and addiction

Advocates, Inc., 160–61

Agnews' State Hospital, 183

Alaskan Supreme Court, 133–34

alcoholism, 42–43, 76. *See also* cases:
    Eddie; drug abuse and addiction

Almeida, Selene, 25, 61–62, 223

Alternative to Meds Center, 203

American Psychological Health Services
    (APHS), 187

American Residential Treatment
    Association (ARTA), 137–38

André Luiz Spiritist Psychiatric Hospital,
    47

Angell, Marcia, 154

anthroposophical medicine, 115

anxiety. *See* cases: Eddie

Armstrong, Anne, 121–22

attachments. *See* spirit attachments

attention-deficit/hyperactivity disorder
    (ADHD), 8, 9, 63

Azevedo, J. L., 42

Bach, Edward, 64

Bach flower remedies. *See* flower
    remedies

balance, 175

Bassett, Tracey, 160

being with, 182

stages of, 183–86

Benor, Daniel, 12–13

Bezerra Menezes Spiritist Center, 81

bioenergy, 105

Bioenergy Therapy, 104–5

bipolar disorder, 3, 6, 21, 76, 194

case material, 6–7 (*see also* cases:
    Gerry; cases: Sylvia)

"Bipolar World, The" (DuBrul), 3, 6–7

blessed water, 46

Block Center, 204

Bom Retiro Spiritist Psychiatric Hospital,
    71, 224

Bom Retiro "Spiritual Care Society," 74

Brazilian perspective. *See* Spiritism;
    Spiritist treatments

Breggin, Peter, 155–56, 158, 187

Bunese, Janaina Graziela Anzolini, 223

Casa de Dom Inácio de Loyola (House
    of St. Ignatius of Loyola), 33–34,
    53–59, 84, 118–19

case histories, 34–37

Current room, 54–55, 118

psychic surgeries, 35–36, 55

cases

Arturo, 69–70

Chuck, 183, 185, 186

Eddie, 34–38, 176

Gerry, xvi–xvii, 24, 108–11, 176,
    177

Hermann, 63–64

Lydia, 94–95

Nan, 93–94

Sergei, 101–4

Sylvia, 3–5, 176

Teresa, 62–63

Casey, Susan, 118

Center for the Study of Empathic
    Therapy, Education & Living,
    187–88

chakras, clearing the, 100–101

Chamberlin, Judi, 157–58

children, 204

Ciompi, Luc, 134

clairvoyants, xxv, 21, 47. *See also*
    mediums

clubhouses. *See* safe homes/safe
    houses

cognitive restructuring, 102, 103

Cooper, Don, 138–42, 144

Emma Bragdon, PhD, *is the Director of the Foundation for Energy Therapies (www.SpiritualAlliances.com). She is also the author/editor of five books and co-producer of two documentary films on themes related to spiritual healing and optimal wellness. Since 2001 she has been exploring the resources of Brazil's Spiritualist traditions, particularly the use of mediums in helping people with serious mental illness to recover. She is a consultant for those incorporating spirituality into integrative healthcare.*

Dr. Bragdon makes her home in Vermont, USA and Brazil.

Email: EBragdon@aol.com

Website: http://www.EmmaBragdon.com

Made in the USA
Charleston, SC
07 March 2012